4/13

20

LIVING IN
MOROCCO

PHILIPPE SAHAROFF and SABINE BOUVET

Flammarion

CONTENTS

Moroccan buildings are often set in breathtaking sites. Sidi Abderrahman's tomb, immaculately white on a rock island, appears from the Corniche of Casablanca. Visitors can walk at low tide, or take a boat at high tide (page 1). Sidi Osni, a private palace in Tangier, offers a spectacular view of the mosque dome and the Strait of Gibraltar (pages 2–3). The exquisite Amanjena Hotel in Marrakech was built around a former irrigation pond (pages 4–5). The Kasbahs and mud fortresses in the Dadès gorges are in harmony with the surrounding landscape (right).

A VISION OF PARADISE

A visitor gazes through a Moorish window over a golden-hued city at dusk. This is a timeless, mythical place, an imaginary Orient that clouds the mind, that simmers still under the heat of a sun that lingers on the horizon. The refreshingly cool sound of the fountains glides through the hot air like a snake through dry grass. Sparkling with shade and light, a garden planted with roses, jasmine, and datura fills the air with subtle fragrances. Suddenly, a deafening squawking from the cypress wakes our visitor from his daydream. He claps his hand sharply and silence returns to the old city—the medina—of Marrakech. A waiter in loose trousers and braided waistcoat walks into this immutable paradise, carrying a hand-crafted tray and brushing past the delicate flowers that blend into the colorful tiles lining the pathways.

In Morocco, time seems to stand still; the passing years have had little impact on the activities of everyday life. Everything here seems to have been preserved intact, which is why people from the painter Henri Matisse to the playwright Tennessee Williams—as well as many tourists—have enjoyed the country over the past century. It is precisely this exoticism, this timeless luxury—which enters people's minds as they read a travel diary or remember a scene from a film—that lures thousands of travelers here every year.

Nature, as we know, is both bountiful and diverse in Morocco, but this is not the only feature that draws so many people to this country, the most hospitable in the Maghreb. Morocco seems to have invented the very concept of elegant living. The sites, architecture, cuisine, craftsmen, and ultimate refinement in each detail of everyday life—along with the profusion of colors and fragrances—form a harmonious whole, bidding you to savor each pleasure.

Morocco is a feast for the mind and body, a concoction of emotions and impressions that rarely come together so successfully. The core of this attraction is the home, which seems to embody a sense of well-being. While the Moroccan home resembles an austere rampart from the outside, its entrance leads to an arched patio or garden carefully designed to foster hospitality, festivities, and meditation. Let's take a look. Push open the low door and stoop down to enter. Your eyes, accustomed to

The main courtyard of a *riad* contains an interior garden, often planted with aromatic trees and fragrant plants that perfume the entire house. Crystal-clear water murmurs from the courtyard fountain in the Palais Salam Hotel in Taroudant, home to a pasha in the nineteenth century (above). This house in the Palmeraie of Marrakech (right) was designed by Elie Mouyal.

darkness, discover a silent, colorful space centered around a pool that reflects the peaceful blue of the sky. Multicolored *zelliges* (tiles) cover the floor, adorn the fountain, and climb halfway up the stuccoed walls and the columns of carved wood. There is no distinction between the sky and the earth; your spirit relaxes and wanders freely among the vibrating colors.

Color is everywhere, imbuing everything. Morocco is, above all, a land of color, both in shadow and in light. Its nourishing color, rising from the pink, ocher, and brown of the earth, is reflected upward into the sky. Color is indeed omnipresent—found, for example, in the *riads*, which are considered in Muslim belief to be the earthly reflection of paradise. One of the most beautiful is at *La Gazelle d'Or* (The Golden Gazelle) in Taroudant, which takes its name from its Andalusian-style garden in the center of the luxury hotel. Moroccans are passionate about plants, and gardens have strongly influenced all the decorative arts in this country. The garden is the heart of a Moroccan home and profuse vegetation is the inspiration for the central motif found on the carpets in each and every room. The garden influence appears in the colorful arabesques that decorate the ceiling beams, in the ceramics, fabrics, and marquetry designs, and in manuscripts with Kufic calligraphy—not to mention in the succulent and refined Moroccan cuisine, appreciated by food-enthusiasts around the world.

Souks are an endless source of exciting discoveries and are irresistible attractions. Usually located near a mosque in the center of the medina, souks are organized into sections devoted to specific crafts. Its intricate network of narrow streets is sometimes covered with *mamounis,* which filter a dappled light down to the alleys below. The most spectacular and beautiful colors are those in spice shops, dyers' vats, and tanneries.

And finally, the desert, which lies just beyond the snow-covered Atlas Mountains, is surrounded by fortified villages constructed of packed mud, known as *pisé.* Are these mirages? You'll see when you wake up in the chilly early light and smell the scents of amber and mint. The dirt track to the next oasis may be a very long one.

José Alvarez

LANDSCAPES

Travelers to Morocco can find plenty of stunning vistas: the ocean beyond the ramparts of Essaouira (preceding pages), or as viewed from the former British consulate (facing page), or the immensity of the desert, as here among the Tinfou sand dunes (right). With an abundance of wide open spaces, Morocco leaves the visitor with a feeling of infinity and eternity—a tangible sensation that can even be felt within the four walls of a luxurious home. Indeed, everything in traditional Moroccan architecture and decor creates an ideal condition for retreat. The desert offers another type of refuge; those who travel through it embark on a unique inner voyage as well.

BETWEEN THE DESERT AND THE SEA

Morocco's diverse landscape offers a multitude of different experiences. The views alter with each mile as you travel through the country, passing from sheer cliffs plunging into the Mediterranean to the unspoiled Atlantic coastline; from arid plains to fertile valleys; from desert regions to steep mountains. At first glance, the country displays the physical contradiction between the conflicting sides of nature: gentle and rough, beautiful and austere, generous and poor, seductive and indomitable. Morocco extends over infinitely large spaces: it borders the Mediterranean Sea to the north and the Atlantic Ocean to the west, while the eastern and southern boundaries stretch to the burning desert sands. Inland, nature has formed the immense mountain chains known as the Atlas range, whose peaks slice diagonally across the country. The highest peaks in the Maghreb (northwest Africa), these purple-hued mountains reach over 13,100 feet (4000 meters), their summits capped with snow in the winter. The lush green oases that nestle at their base, between the arid rocky plains leading to the golden dunes of the Sahara, are thick with date palms. These valleys explode in a matchless display of finery for several weeks of the year, with fleecy white blossoms on the almond trees and fragrant wild roses. Man is an inseparable element in this grandiose setting, even in the most hostile places. Throughout the centuries, people have chosen inhospitable places to build impregnable Kasbahs. These citadels of ocher earth walls blend in with the rugged beauty of the southern landscapes. The all-powerful Moroccan nature is simply breathtaking; it will make your heart beat faster; you'll stare in astonishment and experience the pure happiness of being immersed in a spectacular environment. Morocco makes you come alive.

These routes are designed like a series of vivid and breathtaking paintings, reflecting the powerful beauty of the landscapes that lie between the cities. We will travel from the Rif mountain range in the north to the Mediterranean Sea, from the Atlantic dotted with blue and white cities to the lush greenery of the southern oases, through a land of ocher earth and snow-capped summits. From here, we'll reach the hot desert and leave our footprints in the orange-colored sand of the Sahara dunes. Finally, the imperial cities will lead us into the labyrinth of the medinas, as we search for the magnificence of the sultans and the grandeur of Islam.

THE RIF AND CHEFCHAOUEN

The Rif and the surrounding area, situated in the north of the country, are green year-round, which is very unusual in Morocco (left). The most beautiful velvety colors appear in the spring; at this time (and starting as early as January), the fertile valleys are carpeted with thousands of wildflowers. These form a natural Pointillist canvas of bright colors, as herds of animals graze peacefully about. A shepherd, wrapped up in his *djellaba* (facing page, top), offers a timeless image. Crops, like these terraced olive trees (facing page, middle), create graphic patterns in the landscape. Fruit, almond, walnut, and olive trees, along with other fruits and vegetables, thrive in the fertile valleys of the Rif and on the plains of the Middle Atlas Mountains (facing page, bottom).

For many travelers, the Rif—a rebellious and secretive region apart—is often their first view of Morocco. Unlike any other place in the country, nature has given the Rif high barriers, which have helped forge the strong, fiercely guarded Berber identity. This immense mountain range, a sort of impregnable citadel, cuts across the entire northern region and defines the Rif's borders. Entrenched berhind its natural defenses, the Rif is hard to reach and is rarely visited by tourists.

The Rif is also a fertile land. A single color dominates the countryside: green. It may be the velvety, mossy, and tender green of the cannabis plants (the leading crop in the region), or the deep green of pine and cedar forests. Wherever you are, the color carpets every landscape, from the sharply pointed peaks to the gentle valleys. It is an unusual color in Morocco, another reminder that the Rif is in a different world, a miracle in this country, where one-third of the land is covered by desert. Protected and cut off from the rest of the country by a natural barrier, the people of the Rif have developed a critical and independent nature. They remain attached to their traditions and have been strongly influenced by their unique geographical situation.

Traveling through this region is like scaling a mountain. On the Mediterranean side, thick with cork-oak and maquis, the Rif has precipitous cliffs that plunge straight into the sea. Below is a series of sometimes inaccessible beaches, tempting coves, and deep, natural creeks. Each one seems to proffer a piece of unexplored paradise. On the mountain side, between Ketama and Chefchaouen, the road winds from peaks and summits up to the pinnacle of Djebel Tidirhine, at 8032 feet (2448 meters). The road leads through high altitudes, with spectacularly steep precipices. In the midst of the lush greenery are steep slopes, terraces planted with crops, and whites houses nestling in the high valleys. The Rif villages and white-washed houses have nothing in common with the other regions of Morocco. Clinging to the sides of the mountain, they inevitably remind the traveler of the *pueblos blancos*—whites villages—of Andalusia. Like the Andalusian villages, they do not have an actual medina; the

The color blue is what remains most strongly in the memory of visitors to Chefchaouen. Blue is omnipresent, on doors, walls, staircases, and archways, its brilliance matched only by the sparkle of the white-washed buildings. Also memorable are the children's smiles and the echo of their laughter in the narrow streets. The traditional *fouta*, a striped piece of fabric that women wear around their waists, adds a note of color (facing page, top).

entire town is contained within the walls. Indeed, as you walk through the narrow streets, you feel more as though you're in an Andalusian village than in the Rif. The kids here will call to you in Spanish: *"Hola amigo! Qué tal?"* It's no coincidence that this feels like the Iberian peninsula. When the Muslims fled Grenada, many of them moved to Chefchaouen, bringing with them the specific Moorish style of architecture. The fabulous blue that covers the walls of many homes was brought here by the many Jewish families that also arrived in great numbers from Spain. They painted their houses this color to ward off the mosquitoes and, it is said, to distinguish their homes from the traditional green of Islamic houses.

If there is one town to see in the Rif, it's Chefchaouen, an unforgettable place. After passing through the endlessly green landscapes of the Rif, Chefchaouen, some 1970 feet (600 meters) above sea level, is a sudden immersion into blue. The houses are all partially covered with this unique blue wash, the lovely shade sparkling in the thin mountain sunshine and splashing light through the narrow streets. The villagers repaint their houses regularly, and it's common to see a bucket of this famous mixture plonked down in an alleyway. The blue wash seems to have been flung from a gigantic pail of paint over the whole village from top to bottom, covering the walls of houses as it dripped down and forming puddles the color of glacial lakes at the base of staircases.

Chefchaouen seems to touch the pure mountain sky and the two summits—Tissouka (6726 feet/2050 meters) and Meggou (5302 feet/1616 meters) that form the Djebel ech Chefchaouen (The Horns). The air is crisp and cool. It is delightful to wander aimlessly through the tiny winding streets paved with small stones. Mischievous children poke their heads out from passageways to wish you well with wide smiles. Women stand together at the thresholds of their homes, with a *fouta* (a brightly colored length of striped fabric) wrapped around their waists. The people of Chefchaouen have clear intense faces, with eyes the colors of the walls, as if, by gazing at so much blue, their eyes

have picked up the reflected color. Walking through the village is a rare pleasure. You may sometimes step into an entirely blue-washed passageway that makes you feel as though you've dipped into a calm, smooth sea in the morning, reflecting back the blue of the sky. You'll find yourself bathed in light, inundated with blue. A few more steps, and you'll pass through a dark archway, carrying with you a sensation of refreshing calm.

The mountain is close by. It protects Chefchaouen. It faces the village, verdant, steep-sided, with its abandoned mosque. This was constructed on the mountain by the Spanish just before the Rif War, but it was boycotted by the villagers. White spots of color are visible between the olive trees: these are goats, grazing near the tombs. From the terrace of the Parador Hotel, which was once a luxury establishment, you have front-row seats from which you can admire this peaceful valley. If you'd rather enjoy the local scene, stop at the tiny terrace on the small Aladdin café/restaurant. It sits slightly back from the street and offers a clear view of the landscape and the Place Makhzen, which has several handicraft shops. The shaded Place Uta El-Hammam is a good place to stop and enjoy a break at one of the café terraces. It's near the entrance to the large mosque, which has a surprising fifteenth-century octagonal minaret, and the ocher walls of the Kasbah, which enclose Andalusian gardens from the same period. The white mass of the village gradually starts to stand out against the mountainside as you cross the small bridge over the Ras el-Mar river and its public wash-house in the shade of several fig trees. After a short hike, this mass transforms into an interlocking series of white cubes topped with tiles, or terrace rooftops with a few minarets. In earlier times, Chefchaouen was a holy city, forbidden to Christians. Charles de Foucauld was the first Christian to set foot there in 1883, by pretending to be Jewish. He wrote, "It's all life, wealth and freshness. Water appears from springs everywhere … cascading over the ferns, the bay laurels, the fig trees and the vines. I have never before seen such a cheerful countryside, or air so filled with prosperity, nor such a generous soil…"

SEASIDE TOWNS:
FROM TANGIER TO ESSAOUIRA

From the unique blue of Chefchaouen, we travel alongside the blue of the sea for nearly 2200 miles (3500 km) on the Moroccan coast, including some 1500 miles (2500 km) from Tangier to the border of Mauritania. The landscape south of Tangier consists of greenish-gray waves breaking over deserted beaches that stretch as far as the eye can see. Morocco's wild and imposing Atlantic coastline is completely unspoiled. With relatively few buildings, it is a realm of wind and sand dunes. A few white-washed villages dot the coast. Many of them have historic links with Portugal, recognizable by the ramparts overlooking the sea. They provide a wealth of interesting places to stop along this route.

TANGIER

Let's start with Tangier. According to ancient Greek and Roman legends, this was the site of paradise, where the Hesperides watched over a garden of golden apples. Today, the best way to reach Tangier is by boat from the Spanish ports of Tarifa or Algesiras, or from Sète (France) or Genoa (Italy). Once there, you'll discover a city built entirely around the sea, climbing up the hillsides like an amphitheater and facing a magnificent bay. The small medina holds pride of place on the northeast, forming a contrast with the dense and anarchic jumble of buildings with rough-cast walls in various shades of white, beige, and gray. The modern city sprawls out along the length of the bay. The sky is often cloudy, covered with fog and mist. Yet it changes constantly: the *chergui* (the east wind) and the *gharbi* (the west wind) that sweep across the countryside are said to drive people mad.

Tangier stands midway between the Atlantic Ocean and the Mediterranean, between Europe and Africa. An indefinable city, situated on the far northern edge of the country, it is isolated, something that it has in common with the Rif region, due primarily to its history and geography. Tangier faces the Strait of Gibraltar. Separated from Spain by a mere 10 miles (15 km), it is a link between the two continents

Arriving by boat, visitors discover first the Bay of Tangier opening on to the sea, then spot the small medina, which is on a hill to the northeast. The medina clings to a cliffside, just above the fishing harbor. Europe seems a long way behind as you reach this first—or last—city of Africa, and set out to discover just what has inspired so many writers for the last hundred years (facing page and bottom right). You have now passed to the other side of the Strait of Gibraltar and can see Europe and the Spanish coast some 10 miles (15 km) in the distance (top right). Here, another world entirely spreads before you. It's hard to say if Tangier is really in Morocco. Yet it is an introduction, and an essential first step into this land.

Women walking through the Place du Petit Socco (above). In the nineteenth century, this quarter was the center of the city, the heart of all business transactions and, filled with cafés and hotels, a popular meeting place. Offices and legations moved here, blending in with the restaurants, casinos, and dance halls. The nightlife in this small sector was booming, with parties non-stop. This is where the myth of Tangier—smugglers, gunfire, and street fights—began.

and forms a crossroads at which multiple influences converge. The multifaceted city of Tangier is both a seafaring port open to the sea and nearby Europe, and a gateway to Africa.

Light is the key to this setting. The city no longer offers the same fever-pitch of entertainment as during its glory days, but for those who choose to live in Tangiers, one thing has remained the same: the light, an indestructible natural element untouched by passing time or fleeting fashion. Henri Matisse came to Tangier for the light, even though he remained closeted up in his hotel, La Villa de France, for weeks, waiting for the rain to stop so that he could paint. A long list of famous people have come here for inspiration or revelation, diversion or a peaceful life. The author Paul Bowles, who moved to Tangier in 1948 and remained there until his death in 1999, is inextricably linked to the city. Truman Capote, William Burroughs, Jean Genet, Samuel Beckett, Tennessee Williams, Paul Morand, Pier Paolo Pasolini, and Roland Barthes, among others, spent many productive days in Tangier. Writers were not the only people to have been bewitched. Barbara Hutton and Malcolm Forbes came here to indulge their extravagant lifestyles in the total freedom offered by this world of dilettantes.

In 1923, a Franco-Anglo-Spanish decree declared Tangier an international free port, and a myth was born. Placed under the authority of an international commission, the city radiated an enchanting, fiery charm, helped by the way it was portrayed in film and literature. Consecrated by this romantic reputation, Tangier played host to a cosmopolitan lifestyle peopled with diplomats, adventurers, dandies, artists, spies, and smugglers. Tangier left its mark on the world's imagination as a society devoted to pleasure. But times change. In 1956, the zone became incorporated into the newly independent Moroccan government and the wealth moved abroad. Tangier's days of glory were over.

The city may have lost the luster of its golden age, but it has kept its appeal. The Vielle Montagne is without doubt the place that best reflects this light-hearted *joie de vivre*. A trip up the steep hill, whose hairpin bends lead to a peaceful summit, far from the bustle of the medina, will lead you to a

multitude of lovely sleepy villas, dotted around the wild countryside and surrounded by elegant gardens. The sea glistens below, at the base of the cliffs. You can't get any closer to the gentle life of Tangier than this.

The Fuentès café and restaurant, where international correspondents and intellectuals met up during the city's heyday, is in a slightly disheveled state. On the adjoining Place de Petit Socco, the former administrative buildings recall how the city played host to foreign legations. And this rendezvous with history is a good starting point for a stroll through the steep narrow streets of the medina. Continue downhill, past the Grand Mosque, which has been successively a Roman temple, a mosque, a Portuguese church, and once again a mosque. You'll then pass in front of the Borj El-Jadjaoui and the canons

bought from the English on Gibraltar, and on to the harbor and the slightly tattered charm of the Hotel Continental, one of the oldest hotels in Tangier, where Edgar Degas once stayed. This may be a good time to settle down on a café terrace, in the shade of the palm trees, and watch the ferries shuttling back and forth. The famous Kasbah door painted by Henri Matisse is nearby. Another door, carved into the wall, leads out of the medina to the edge of the windswept cliff onto a promontory overlooking the sea. The view of the Strait is spectacular. On a clear day, Spain is easy to see.

If you're looking for a fine view, by all means stop by the legendary Café Hafa. Clinging to the hillside, with white-washed terraces dug straight out of the cliffs, the Café Hafa has stood guard over the Strait of Gibraltar since 1921. This is a great place to while away the hours, watching the Spanish coast and the hypnotizing horizon as you try to measure the distance separating Europe from Africa. Regular clients are stretched out on mats smoking kif. In an earlier day, William Burroughs, Paul Bowles, Truman Capote, and Jean Genet spent much of their time here. The rickety chairs and tables, which look as if they have been recycled from a school, seem to be hanging in mid-air. A chalk mark is the only clue to the existence of this well-known place. People come here to drink a coffee or mint tea, play backgammon or embrace, their gazes lost in the distant horizon.

The sleepy Marshan quarter, characterized by large buildings with elegant facades and carefully tended gardens, lies just behind the path that runs along the coast.

The sea is never out of sight as you leave Tangier. The road runs along the Atlantic coast toward Cap Spartel. The landscape is fairly gentle, and the air is fragrant with the scent of the eucalyptus and umbrella pines that line the road. The best time to travel this route is at sunset. The cape is still midway between two different worlds. Here, 1033 feet (315 meters) above the waves, at the extreme northwestern point of the African continent, you can watch the waters of the Mediterranean Sea mingle with those of the Atlantic Ocean. The ocean climate has left its mark on the countryside: the abundant rainfall keeps the lush cape flourishing with irises, cistus, broom, and heather. An ocher-colored lighthouse rises from among a dense grove of palm trees. It was constructed atop the headland in 1865 at the request of foreign diplomats.

An immense beach stretches just past the Hotel Mirage, built on a stunning site. The mist floating above the foam of the grayish-green waves smudges the distinction between the coastline and the sky. This is a lovely introduction to Morocco's bracing and windy Atlantic coast, which is swept by breaking waves. This natural, unspoilt beauty continues along the entire length of the country toward the south. Along the way you'll find a number of picturesque small ports, remnants of the region's former link with Lusitania, an ancient region corresponding broadly to modern Portugal.

ASILAH

Asilah, 30 miles (45 km) south of Tangier, is a small, peaceful port girdled by ramparts. The spectacular white-washed walls gleam in contrast to the deep blue of the Atlantic. It is a restful, neat little town, and a popular vacation spot. The green- or blue-shuttered houses on the seafront stand within walls lapped by the waves. The wrought-iron gates recall the town's link with Spain, and the fifteenth-century ramparts, with three doors, are reminders of its Portuguese history. Bab el-Bahr, the Gate to the Sea, leads to a beach strewn with

Strollers meander to this balcony overlooking the Atlantic Ocean for a view of Asilah, a small white town built within ramparts that give directly on to the water. In the foreground is a cemetery with tombs decorated with mosaics. These cover the ground at the base of the cupola of a marabout (left). Explore inside the city walls along the fifteenth-century Portuguese ramparts (top right). The square Portuguese tower (bottom right) gives a clue to Asilah's past. It was an observation post; from the top, guards could watch the coast. Visitors can also admire the naive frescoes (above, far right) that have decorated the walls of the calm medina streets since the 1970s—when the music festival began.

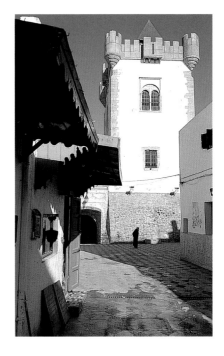

fishing boats. Asilah is a charming place to stroll through, as you search for traces of its diverse past. Before becoming a popular seaside resort, it had a tumultuous history of multiple conquests. Carthaginians, Romans, Normans, Arabs, Portuguese, Spanish, Sa'adis, Turks, and Austrians all set their sights on and invaded the lovely town. Today, the only real activity you'll find in Asilah is on Thursday, the day of the souk. In the morning, farmers spread out their crops in large baskets.

The bastion, or fortified position, overlooking the rocks, is the best place from which to watch the sunset. The promontory offers the ideal vantage point at dusk, as the old town and coastline seem to disappear into the sea. A tiny cemetery below is laid out within the ramparts, and contains several dozen tombs covered with enameled ceramic inlaid in the white earth. From a distance, it looks like a terrace covered with vertical strips of mosaic. This interesting site is another reason to walk to the bastion.

CASABLANCA

If you want to get an idea of how Casablanca first appeared to the Portuguese and, later on, to the Spanish conquistadores, approach the city via the Corniche. Sidi Abderrahman's marabout, or tomb, a tiny white village perched on a rock, rises out of the sea just over one mile (two kilometers) from the city. You can reach it by boat at high tide or walk across at low tide. This holy site is off-limits to non-Muslims.

In the sixteenth century, the Portuguese fortified a small white house and named it Casa Branca. When the Spanish arrived in the seventeenth century, they saw only a few white houses sheltered behind the half-ruined walls; they called the place Casablanca. Since then, the small town has become the country's largest city and a showcase of Moroccan architecture from the period of the Protectorate (1912–56).

Casablanca may be the most European of Morocco's cities. Indeed, it was entirely conceived and designed by colonial powers. The French general Louis Lyautey (1854–1934) was the driving force behind this new city in the early 1920s. As you walk through the downtown area, you'll see a number of straight avenues, elegant buildings, public gardens, and large squares, including the Place Mohammed-V (formerly named the Place des Nations-Unies and now the heart of the new city), as well as imposing administrative buildings. The buildings running along the length of the Boulevard Mohammed-V illustrate the architectural daring of the time, something like an avant-garde manifesto. European architects—including Henri Prost and Joseph Marrast—outdid one another in creative projects, making Casablanca their own personal architectural playground. Art Nouveau and Art Deco styles are combined with more austere Western lines and a Moroccan graphic vocabulary: geometric faience on building facades, *zelliges* and marble in lobbies, cubic forms and covered porticoes; all contribute to a colonial Moorish style.

With the gigantic Hassan-II Mosque, inaugurated in 1993, the king has perpetuated the Moroccan architectural tradition, confirming Casablanca's role as an experimental showcase. It is the largest mosque in the world after Mecca, and is constructed partially over the Atlantic as if it were floating, the implication being that only the ocean can stop the progression of the Islamic faith. It is situated at the edge of the city and is constantly at the mercy of the elements. The minaret rises over 650 feet (200 meters) skyward. It is a must-see. Open to non-Muslims, the architectural and decorative elements are grandiose in scale: columns of pink granite soar to the roof, which can slide back to leave the central prayer room open to the sky. From the outside, the beautiful proportions are gigantic yet harmonious. This unforgettable silhouette is now an inseparable element of the Casablancan cityscape.

The imposing Grande Poste building in Casablanca is a lovely example of the colonial Moorish style of architecture that flourished during the Protectorate (1912–56). This style also influenced the design of other administrative buildings such as the courthouse, the police station, and even the state bank. The *zellige* tiles on the facades were reinterpreted to comply with the tenets of the Art Deco style of the period. The growth of Casablanca followed a concerted urban planning program (facing page). Hassan II (reigned 1961–99) perpetuated this architectural program and the tradition in which sovereigns continue to build. The marble mosaics and colorful *zelliges,* sculpted plaster and monumental painted wooden doors of the Conference Center illustrate the fine quality of Moroccan craftsmanship (left).

The Hassan-II Mosque,
inaugurated in 1993, is
a symbol of Islamic
grandeur. It perpetuates
the architectural tradition
and innovative spirit
that characterizes
Casablanca. It is an
excursion into a world of
wealth and monumental
size. The proportions are
gigantic, comparable
to the Yamoussoukro
Cathedral in the Ivory
Coast. The columns are
made of pink granite;
the walls are lined in
marble, onyx, and
travertine; and the glass
chandeliers come from
Murano, Italy. The roof
above the prayer room
slides open (above
right). The Habbous
area includes the new
medina, designed by the
French in the 1930s
in a traditional style,
with archways (right).
The area illustrates the
colonial ideology that
aimed to reconcile
local architecture
with modern building
requirements. It's a
good place to discover
local handicrafts,
and see the Pasha's
Palace (far right).

FROM CASABLANCA TO OUALIDIA

The coastal road leads from Casablanca to El-Jadida. The Portuguese, used to building high-walled towns, constructed this fortified port. El-Jadida is a jewel of sixteenth-century military architecture, with charming streets paved in stone. One of the highlights for visitors to the town is the Portuguese cistern, a fascinating and beautiful structure. Based on the Roman model, it was used to collect and store water. Streaks of light pierce the darkness like sunbeams from the sky, illuminating the stagnant water of the pool, which in turn reflect the twenty-five arches of this subterranean room. Orson Welles, struck by the spectacular beauty of the place, used this mysterious backdrop for several scenes in his 1951 film version of *Othello*. It is hard to imagine a more magical or dramatic setting.

Before reaching Essaouira, you can make a short trip to Oualidia to see its magnificent beach. It consists of a half-moon lagoon bordered by two dunes, with a rocky island in the middle. The site is so perfect it looks as if it was designed by some invisible power. After a swim in the calm water, stop for a meal of shellfish or lobster; particularly good are the famous Oualidia oysters. Ornithologists will also be happy here: flamingoes, gulls, godwits, stilts, and terns are abundant.

ESSAOUIRA

It's hard to leave Essaouira once you've experienced its incomparable charm. An ever-present breeze keeps the air cool in summer and mild throughout the rest of the year. Another asset is the long sandy beach that stretches out past the harbor. The ruins of a castle emerge from the waves at the end of the bay. It's even more magical in the early morning, when the fog creeps off the sea and lingers around the crenellations, and the half-buried stones look like some kind of unearthly apparition.

Essaouira was once an important crossroads between Timbuktu and Europe. Several different groups of people lived here: Jews, Arab and Berber tribes, along with the brotherhood of Gnaouas, descendants of slaves from sub-Saharan Africa. The Gnaouas are said to have healing powers, particularly the gift of exorcism. But today, they are

The fortified city of El-Jadida is a good example of military architecture. It was designed by the Portuguese, who maintained a strong presence along the coast. The rampart walk hugs the coastline from the Anges bastion to the Saint Sébastien bastion, and then turns inland as far as the Saint Antoine bastion (above). Today, the port's primary activity is fishing (left).

best known throughout Morocco for their frenetic rhythmic dancing and songs. You may see them around the town, dancing to the beat of their drums.

The city's architectural heritage is unique. In 1764, Mohammed III (reigned 1757–90) hired Théodore Cornut, a disciple of the French military engineer the Marquis de Vauban, to design Es Saouira, which literally means "the well-designed." Earlier, the Portuguese had named the port Mogador. The French architect constructed the ramparts of the *sqala* (bastion) facing the sea, which gives French visitors a feeling of déjà vu, as it is similar to walled towns such as Saint-Malo and Belle-Ile in France. Walking through the town, you'll be struck by the white walls and bright blue doorways, which look like those in the Cycladic islands of Greece. Théodore Cornut's work is visible throughout the medina in the layout of the network of gridded streets. This is a unique example of a planned city from an earlier period in Morocco's history.

In the 1960s, Essaouira became a magnet for hippies from all around the world, who were eagerly following in the footsteps of American guitarist and singer, Jimi Hendrix. He lived in the small village of Diabat, a symbol of counterculture at the edge of the city, beyond the *oued* (river). The site was the inspiration for Hendrix's song, "Castle Made of Sand." In the late 1980s, Essaouria was "rediscovered" by surfers and wind-surfers, and it soon became a favorite destination. People come to Essaouria to experience a natural environment that is pure and powerful and to live simply in harmony with the elements.

Life is easy here and, naturally, it's easy to get used to it. You could quite happily spend most of your time in the same area, the Place Moulay-Hassan, starting with breakfast at the pastry shop, Chez Driss, and strolling from café to café. You'll probably want to make a stop at Jack's bookstore, a strategic center of local life, to find a house for rent or take a look at the international papers. If you want to pursue your literary bent, climb up the hill to the terrace of Taros, the literary café located in a square in a 200-year-old house. Alain Kerrien, a Frenchman from Brittany, fell under the spell of this house and called it Taros, a name used by sailors to describe a favorable

The Portuguese cistern at El-Jadida is a fascinating sight (top left). It was initially built as an armory and was later used to collect and store water. The light filtering through the twenty-five arches of the vast room creates a beautiful cinematographic effect. The American actor and director Orson Welles filmed several scenes for his 1951 version of *Othello* here. The cistern had been forgotten about until the early twentieth century, when it was rediscovered by a grocer who wanted to enlarge his shop. Excavation work unearthed the cistern, which seems to have been abandoned since the Portuguese era. In a medina, the doors are often the only decorative element on the outside of a house. Here, the doors of Azzemour, a small fortified town 8 miles (12 km) from El-Jadida, display a kaleidoscope of colors (facing page).

A flight of gulls and fortified walls glimpsed through an ancient archway; white walls faded by sea mist and illuminated by evening light (top left); women, engrossed in conversation, wearing the traditional cotton or wool fabric known as the *haik* (bottom left): all these are symbols of the unique atmosphere of Essaouira, which has attracted successive waves of travelers. During the 1960s and 1970s, hippies came for the easy lifestyle and unspoiled natural environment. Essaouira was later "rediscovered" by surfers and wind-surfers, in search of waves, wind, and pristine nature. The peaceful atmosphere of this seaside town and its climate continue to charm travelers today. The Porte de la Marine (right) leads to a small fishing port, which dates to the founding of the town by Mohammed III (reigned 1757–90).

wind from the sea. He has retained the old *zelliges* and cement tiles, and their bright yellow color adds a Moorish touch to the already cheerful surroundings.

Next, think about exploring the *sqala*. Craftsmen have set up shops in the former ammunition warehouse at the base of the fortifications. They fashion objects from thuja wood; these are a specialty of the town. Another common sight is a woman draped in a *haik,* who may emerge from an alley then disappear in a scent of mystery. Such an image is typical of Essaouira, and the favorite subject of painter Michel Vu, who has been living here since the 1970s. For him these garbed women evoke memories of times past. This city is a great source of inspiration and creativity, and is home to many art galleries, including one run by the Dane Frédéric Damgaard, who exhibits poetic and Surrealist works by local painters.

Don't miss a walk through the bustling port when the fishermen are returning with their catches. Walk among the nets, and amid the huge hulls being repaired at the docks. You might succumb to the tempting aroma of grilled sardines, and stop for a friendly meal at one of the tables set up outside.

TOWARD THE SOUTH

Before leaving our magnificent Atlantic journey, two other charming places, off the beaten track, are worthy of note. Aglou, 10 miles (15 km) from Tiznit, has a gleaming white and blue marabout on the sea, standing out boldly against the breaking waves in the background. A few fishermen are the only humans present in this otherwise deserted spot. A cliff rises from the water's edge; below is a small natural harbor. The fishermen live in dwellings carved out of the rock face.

Finally, 6 miles (10 km) before Sidi Ifni is Legezra, an even more remote place. To reach it, you have to follow a small unmarked path that leads to the beach below. It is worth the effort: four arches have been eroded out of the red rock by the rising and falling tides, creating a site of extraordinary beauty. Walk along the beach opposite a small rocky island where fishermen set up for the day. You can get a real sense of the power of the sea by exploring under the stone arches.

A view of the beach stretching along the bay. The brilliant white town of Essaouira appears like a mirage floating above the ocean waves (above). Take a walk along the *sqala* to see the waves crashing against the base of the fortifications, the port in the background, and the entire Bay of Essaouira as far as the distant dunes of Cap Sim (right). Or take a walk along the ramparts beneath the towering date palms (far right).

THE SOUTH: INTO THE ATLAS MOUNTAINS

The Telouet Kasbah has been abandoned, and the cracked terraces are now home to families of storks. The Glaoui family lived here and entertained sumptuously. The strategic position of the Kasbah commands respect to this day. Surrounded by small villages on the hillside, it overlooks an *oued*. The finely crafted windows in the reception room look out over the countryside (above left). The minaret of a small village stands out against the bare mountainside on the Tizi-n-Tichka road (above right).

T he Atlas is an immense range of mountains running diagonally across the country, northeast to southwest. They stretch from the arid foothills of the Anti Atlas Mountains to the edge of the immense Sahara desert and to the highest peaks of the High Atlas Mountains, which are often snow-capped in the winter months.

Leaving the Atlantic coast, you will travel inland toward Tafraoute and the Ammeln Valley, in the heart of the Anti Atlas Mountains. The air here is hot and dry. An *oued* creates a thick strip of greenery deep within the immense red rock walls. This is the Ammeln Valley, deep in a canyon. The best way to discover the site is on foot, by walking along the irrigation channels that link the twenty-seven villages clinging to the sides of Djebel Lekst 7740 feet (2359 meters) high. The red rough-cast houses are hard to distinguish from the mountainside itself. Almond trees, date palms, and olive trees grow along the narrow strip of fertile land at the edge of the *oued*. The region offers a multitude of possibilities for excursions: you could decide to travel straight to Tafraoute, if you like, if only to watch the sunset within the impressive amphitheater of red granite mountains. Just a few miles away is an interesting example of land art. In 1985, Jean Vérame, a Belgian land artist, covered several enormous boulders with blue and red paint. The lunar landscape of chaotic rocks from which emerge a few gently colored rounded blocks is a strange sight. Over time, the paint has started to chip off, but the overall effect is still spectacular.

The next destination offers an unusual panorama: goats perched atop trees as if suspended in the air. This is the route leading back down from the higher altitudes of Tafraoute via the Agadir road, before crossing the Souss Valley to Taroudant. Argan trees grow everywhere in this arid land. Goats love the fruit of this tree and climb up its thorny branches to reach it. The argan tree produces an oil which is extracted from the kernels inside the nut. It is the last species of tree that grows in this southern region before the Sahara starts. It does not suffer during droughts and lives to be well over 100 years old. This majestic survivor from the Tertiary Period is unknown outside of

The winding Tizi-n-Test road, which climbs to the summit at 6864 feet (2092 meters) tackles the first foothills of the Atlas Mountains. Each turn in this dizzying climb offers magnificent views of beautiful narrow valleys and deep gorges. Fortified villages appear to the side of this tortuous road, perched atop seemingly inaccessible summits. The buildings made of *pisé,* and the strategic location, have withstood many enemies, a hostile climate, and time itself. In this stark countryside, this isolated construction takes on an almost supernatural dimension. The Tizi-n-Test road is probably one of Morocco's most beautiful, as it passes through forests of juniper, cedar, and pine trees before reaching the summit. From here, you can gaze out over the Souss Valley (left).

A magical moment: seeing Oukaimeden (10,739 feet/3273 meters) in the snow. In the winter, it is not uncommon for these red villages to receive a dusting of snow. This enchanting vision will remain in the minds of all those lucky enough to have seen it. The road leads up from the green Ourika Valley to this red sandstone mountain covered by a white mantle. This is when the Moroccan landscape looks like something out of a fairy tale (left). The route continues to Tin Mal, where the mosque stands out in sharp contrast against the rocky background. It was built in 1156, when the commander of the Almohads decided to construct it. Sultans used this fortress as a place to hide the treasures of their empires, which extended as far as Andalusia. Tin Mal is the holy city of the Almohads (right).

this region; it grows only in the southern area of Morocco, the center of argan oil production. Women are generally in charge of this activity and, according to local custom, visitors are offered amlou, a mixture of almonds, honey, and argan oil.

The traditionally wealthy area offers the visitor a rare attraction: the famous ocher ramparts of Taroudant, the pride of the city that is sometimes called "the little Marrakech." The walls date from the early eighteenth century. The first thing to do after arriving in town is to tour the ramparts. The 4-mile- (7-km)-long ramparts are divided into a series of crenellated walls, with bastions and five doors. The long, earth-colored wall has become the symbol of the city.

Taroudant is a colorful town, where the women wear indigo blue veils. The labyrinth of the souks is always lively, and you'll return with memorable images —or laden down with packages of beautiful, handmade objects. Local craftsmen fashion sculptures from limestone, known as the "marble of Taroudant," which is common in the area. If money is no object, then indulge yourself at the luxurious and legendary La Gazelle d'Or hotel, which has bungalows dotted around a magnificent garden. Another good reason to spend a night in Taroudant, this hotel is frequented by a mainly foreign clientele seeking a discreet and peaceful hideaway.

Looking out from the city, the peaks of the High Atlas Mountains rise over the ramparts. You can follow any of several different routes around the mountain range to get a good idea of the diverse landscapes. Starting from Taroudant, the windy Tizi-n-Test road heading toward Marrakech leads to the Tizi-n-Test summit, which rises to a height of 6864 feet (2092 meters). A dizzying view stretches out over the Souss Valley and the summits of the Atlas Mountains. The route continues to Tin Mal, the birthplace of the Almohads, a Berber dynasty that reigned from the twelfth to the thirteenth century and extended as far as Spain.

Tin Mal seems to appear from the middle of nowhere, in the midst of this remote countryside. The minaret of the mosque (constructed in 1156 and contemporaneous with the Koutoubia Mosque in Marrakech) rises high into the sky. It is surrounded by a few houses and the vestiges of the ramparts

The Telouet Palace has been abandoned since the Glaoui and his family were exiled from the region in the late 1950s. The former splendor is now just a distant memory (left). However, the Ait Benhaddou *ksar*, or fortified village, has been classified a UNESCO World Heritage Site, and the *pisé* structure stands almost intact. Filmmakers fall in love with this setting and many have helped to restore and conserve this site, which has appeared in numerous films. The door in the foreground, for example, is not original, but was made by a set decorator and left behind once the 1985 film, *Jewel of the Nile,* was shot. UNESCO may have these added elements removed. Perched on top of a rocky promontory, the best preserved fortified village in Morocco has now been almost totally abandoned by the local population, which lives in the village below (right).

of the once-glorious fortress. You can climb to the top, as this mosque (and the Hassan-II Mosque in Casablanca), are the only ones where non-Muslims are allowed to enter.

Oukaimeden (10,739 feet/3273 meters) is at its best covered with snow—which also gives you the opportunity to ski on the African continent. There are not many runs, but it's a unique experience. The road starts to climb above the Ourika Valley, which was created by a river that sometimes rages through this lush countryside. You'll then take a series of sharp turns leading to craggy gorges, with villages constructed of *pisé* or stone clinging to the red sandstone mountain. Finally, the road leads to a strikingly different landscape—a snow-covered plateau surrounded by white-capped peaks. In the summer, the high-altitude meadows of Oukaimeden have a wonderfully cool climate, making this a perfect destination for hikers looking for rock paintings. Petroglyphs representing animals, weapons, and human figures are carved into large slabs of pink sandstone.

This route offers another facet of the High Atlas Mountains that cannot be seen from the Tizi-n-Tichka road, which leads from Marrakech to Ouarzazate via the Tizi-n-Tichka summit (7415 feet/2260 meters). The rocks on the bare mountainside are shaped into giant folds. As you climb, the vegetation peters out and the landscape becomes a vision of austere rock. This is the highest road in the country, and is the same route once taken by all the caravans heading to and from Mali. Constructed in the nineteenth century, the Kasbah of Telouet was home to the Glaoui, Morocco's last great feudal lord, who supported the French during the Protectorate (1912–56) in opposition to the future king. On his death in 1956 at Telouet, his property was confiscated and his family sent into exile. The Kasbah has been uninhabited since and the cracked stone terraces are home to storks. It is a moving sight, offering a stark constrast between the rough architecture outside and the splendid decorative elements still visible in two of the rooms.

You'll reach a magnificent *ksar* before Ouarzazate. Ait Benhaddou is Morocco's most beautiful and best-preserved fortified village. Indeed, its architecture is so sumptuous that it

The Tizi-n-Tichka road is a never-ending string of breathtaking views. If you are lucky enough to travel through here on a beautiful winter's day, with pure light and clear skies, you will see how spectacularly these small villages in the middle of nowhere stand out, isolated and in stark contrast to their surroundings. The snow-capped peaks of the Atlas Mountains create a sublime backdrop to a lost village (right).

has been used as a setting for a number of memorable films: *Lawrence of Arabia*, *Sodom and Gomorrah*, and *Jesus of Nazareth*. Classified as a UNESCO World Heritage Site, the village is still intact, despite (or perhaps because of) restorations. During the rainy season, you have to cross the waters of the *oued* to reach it. Most of the time, however, the riverbed is dry. Constructed on top of a promontory and against the hillside, Ait Benhaddou has successfully withstood the passage of time. It has a solid wall, reinforced with crenellated towers that are now used as storehouses. The only entrance into the village is via a single heavy door leading to the houses that are packed tightly together; in times of conflict, they provided shelter from invaders. The view from the rampart walk is over a palm grove amid a desert of stones. The Atlas Mountains stand tall in the distance. The best view of the impregnable *ksar*, however, is from outside, at sunset, when the evening light illuminates this earthen village.

From its starting point in Ouarzazate, the "Road of the Thousand Kasbahs" is, along with Taourirt, a typical example of *pisé* architecture. Classified a historical monument, the restored facades are remarkably well crafted. Herringbone patterns, diamonds, triangles, arches, and other repetitive designs create geometric motifs in the *pisé*, or are arranged in open stonework patterns of unbaked brick, decorating the outside of the buildings. Inside, you can visit the Glaoui's apartments, which still have the original painted stucco decoration. This was the largest of the residences belonging to the pasha of Marrakech. Taourirt is a Berber village that predates Ouarzazate; the Glaoui Kasbah was built sometime later. The small medina with tiny, winding streets, hidden behind the facades of the Kasbah, is still inhabited (left).

OUARZAZATE, GATEWAY TO THE OASES

Ouarzazate is the starting point for trips to the Dadès and Drâa valleys, routes dotted with palm groves and splendid Kasbahs that go on for dozens of miles. Here is a model of harmony between nature and mankind, a colorful land under a burning sun. Visitors to Ouarzazate are struck by the violent and never-ending contrast between the insolent green of the oasis and the vibrant red of the landscape and the buildings. The *pisé* is the same color as the earth from which it is made, and can range from brown to ocher, pink, garnet, or purple-violet, depending on its provenance. The second impression visitors receive is the emotional shock of looking on a civilization that has lasted for so many centuries and still offers unchanging visions of everyday life.

The "Road of the Thousand Kasbahs" starts in Ouarzazate. The Kasbah Taourirt, the former Glaoui home in the city, is the first example. Classified a historical monument, it has been restored with great care. A Kasbah is always designed according to the same principles: a square, fortified house made of *pisé*, consisting of an enclosure flanked by four corner towers. The walls are as thick as a fortress's. There are relatively few openings and these slope slightly toward the interior, amplifying the effect of the pyramidal perspective and massive appearance. The upper sections of the outside walls are sometimes decorated with geometric patterns—herringbone, diamonds, triangles, arches, and other repetitive motifs—that are incised or carved into the *pisé* or arranged in open stonework patterns of unbaked bricks.

Designed originally as military citadels, Kasbahs were adopted by feudal chiefs as dwellings. Traditionally, animals were stabled in the bottom floor, the fodder was kept on the next floor up, with the living areas and the kitchen located on the upper levels. Some Kasbahs were as luxurious as palaces, with a multitude of sumptuously decorated rooms. Most often, however, the rooms were furnished sparsely, with just a few chests, benches, and carpets. These buildings, scattered throughout the entire Dadès Valley, appear extremely impressive and imposing.

The Msemrir Kasbah in the Dadès gorges is a typical walled fortress. With its central enclosure flanked by four towers, it gives the impression of being impregnable. It is further strengthened by having very few openings in the wall. This citadel stands tall against the dramatic folded rock formations of the mountain (left).

The Amerhidil Kasbah, which is pictured on the fifty-dirham bill, appears behind date palms surrounding an oasis. The interior of the Kasbah is decorated with painted plaster, as in this peacock tail motif (above).

The palm groves of Tinherir and Todra are like gardens of Eden. Here, as in every oasis, you'll feel as though time is standing still. Every season hosts a different activity: October is the date harvest, the almond trees are in flower in April, and in May the ephemeral roses bloom. The lives of the villagers are rooted in tradition. The date palms stand as columns of freshness and greenery, and are considered to be sources of life. They provide shelter for the orchards and small plots of wheat, alfalfa, vegetables, and henna. Rainfall is scarce in these regions. The Todra River provides a parsimonious distribution of water to these valleys. The river has been redirected into irrigation channels, but the balance is a fragile one, and the oases are threatened by drought (facing page and right).

The road leads from the Amerhidil Kasbah in Sloura to the Bou Tahar *ksar* in the Valley of the Roses before reaching the Dadès gorges, where the land starts to become mountainous. You'll leave the fertile valleys and palm trees behind as the route plunges into the spectacular chaos of the purplish rocks. The Ait Arbi and Tamnalt Kasbahs appear one after another. A precipitously deep canyon marks the end of this climb.

You now have several options. You can climb up the path to the edge of the Eastern Atlas and discover a desert that was once known as "Little Tiber" by the French. Starkly beautiful, it is now called Imilchil. The climate in this austere region is brutal, and the environment hostile, yet Imilchil is the ideal starting point for many hikes through the region. Another option is to hike the trail leading to the Todra gorges. The route is rugged and dotted with rounded hillsides, precipices, and canyons that look like a setting from a wild West movie.

Visitors to this isolated region may come across a solitary shepherd leading his herd to high mountain pastures, a lone figure in an immense desert. A trip through this desolate land can give one a sense of the absolute in nature. Then suddenly a crack appears in the land ahead. This is the entrance to the Todra gorges, marked by steep-sided walls of lofty beauty that rise to over 980 feet (300 meters). Continue along the Todra riverbed on foot in the cool of the morning before the sun penetrates into the gorges.

As you go back down to Tinerhir, you'll discover a Kasbah perched high atop a rocky promontory overlooking a paradisiacal palm grove. The Glaoui transformed this eagle's nest into one of their fiefs. From here, take one of the paths through the palm grove and in the evening stroll along the irrigation channels, enjoying the fading sunlight in the palm trees, olive trees, and fields of yellow and green fields. This labyrinth is in one of Morocco's largest oases.

The road heading south from Ouarzazate leads to the Drâa Valley, where some fifty Kasbahs and *ksours* are dotted among the green patches of palm groves and *pisé* buildings.

The first clump of palm trees appears at Agdz, over which rises the Djebel Kissane, which follows the Drâa River for some 25 miles (40 km). The most fertile part of the valley starts here and continues on to Zagora. If you want an authentic look at life in this peaceful valley, turn off the road. Follow the sand track on the opposite side of the *oued*, crossing over at the village of Tansikt, which has a *ksar* in the middle of two palm groves. You'll be rewarded with an impressive view of the Djebel Sarho.

Mankind's place in the universe is never so clear as in the desert. Here, in Merzouga, eastern Morocco, is no exception. Some travelers climb these immense stretches of sand in search of peace. Others come to nourish themselves with the wisdom of the Sahara. All arrive seeking to glimpse infinity, if only by sleeping beneath the open sky, under a million stars.

THE LURE OF THE DESERT

After following the Drâa River as far as Zagora, and continuing a bit farther south, you will catch sight of the first sand dunes, which appear around Tamegroute. This small town is well known for its *zaouia,* a religious center housing the shrine of the brotherhood's patron saint. The building also contains an impressive library with 4000 manuscripts. The influence of the *zaouia* extends beyond the Drâa Valley as far as the Dadès Valley, the Souss Valley, and the Anti Atlas Mountains. Tamegroute is also well known for its ceramics. A pottery workshop, founded within the religious sanctuary in the sixteenth century, is still functioning: craftsmen here continue to practice their art, producing pieces of great simplicity which they adorn with a characteristic green glaze.

The small dunes of Tinfou are just a few miles away and, just behind them, the Sahara Desert begins. Once you have reached the end of the Drâa road, you are at the southernmost point of Morocco.

On the other side, beyond the Dadès Valley and east of Tinerhir, are the sculpted dunes of Merzouga. The orange color of the sand as it gleams golden at sunset may be one of the most unforgettable images of your trip. Arrive at dawn, when the dunes are still plunged in darkness, so that you can watch the light flood over them. In the foreground, a few camels can also be seen, gathering around a well. If this first view of the desert makes you want to see more, a guide can arrange to take you on a longer trip. You'll spend the night in a nomad's tent and wake up to a vision of astonishing beauty.

The Sahara is a world unto itself, one of sand and stone, where the heat can be unbearable and the sky wraps both men and objects in a heavy glare. The palette of the desert's color is limited; nothing really catches the eye except the tender green young shoots that spring up when the temperature drops—a sign that not even the desert can triumph over nature's renewal and rebirth. To travel in the Sahara is to make an almost spiritual journey in search of striking revelations, whether a simple, bare truth, or a reflection of the surrounding landscapes.

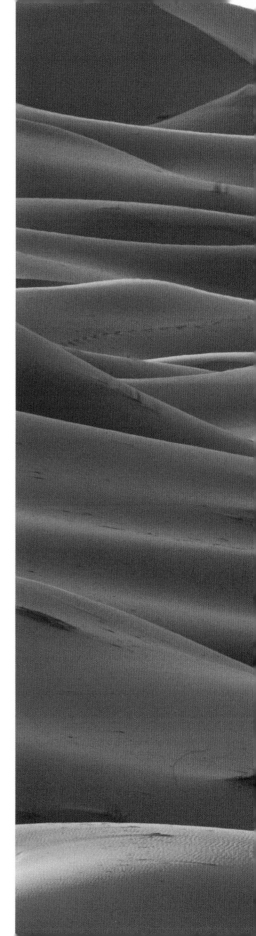

THE IMPERIAL CITIES

The imperial cities display all the magnificence of Moroccan royalty. The royal palace of Marrakech, for example, exhibits its treasures in the various apartments; these are adorned with the entire palette of the traditional decorative arts. The star-shaped ceiling in the throne room is entirely decorated with *zouaks*. This palace underwent extensive renovation work during the reign of Hassan II, under the direction of French architect André Paccard (facing page). The palace mosque has an equally spectacular all-wood decor; the door is a lovely composition of *moucharabieh*. But all these masterpieces are reserved to the king and his entourage. The royal palaces are not open to the public and are safely protected behind the high walls. Here, though, is a rare view (right).

Rabat, Meknes, Fez, and Marrakech are all major centers of Moroccan royalty. The cities, each surrounded by imposing ramparts, are graced with palaces that now house the current royal family and that once belonged to their ancestors. The ramparts, made of *pisé*, include square towers that are used as barracks, granaries, arsenals, water cisterns, and even, in the Meknes Palace, as stables. Despite the relative fragility of the building material, the walls radiate a sense of unrivaled strength.

Inside these walls is the medina. Today these medinas form the historic center of each of the cities, a bustling hive of activity, with souks in each district. Homes are built around the four major landmarks that govern daily life: the mosque, which is the central pillar of life and houses the *medersa* (Koranic school with instruction for both children and adults); the fountain; the *hamman* (steamroom and baths); and the public oven. The bread oven is also often used to heat the steam for the nearby hamman.

Although the medina appears to turn its back on the outside world, it is, in fact, an amazingly vibrant place that incorporates a multitude of influences from near and far. As you walk down a narrow street, you may hear a group of schoolchildren in a Koranic school chanting religious psalms or, farther along, hear the latest raï or techno-fusion song from a scratchy transistor radio. If you're caught in the dense flow of people, be careful to make way if you hear a motorcyclist or mule driver shouting "*Balek! Balek!*" as he tries to get through the crowd. The windowless facades of both the modest and sumptuous homes in this network of small, constantly busy streets reveal no clues as to what lies inside.

RABAT, THE CAPITAL

Rabat clearly displays its royal heritage: the immense palace, constructed in the early twentieth century, seems to occupy a major section of the city. Yet there is another monument that best symbolizes Rabat. This is the Hassan Tower, the minaret atop the Hassan Mosque. When it was begun, the tower was

The mausoleum of Mohammed V in Rabat reflects the grandeur and glory of Moroccan royalty. It is situated at the base of the Hassan Tower, unfinished since the Almohad dynasty (1130–1269). This is a highly symbolic site: on his return from exile in 1956, Mohammed V led the first Friday prayers there since Morocco's independence. The mausoleum is a classical structure that showcases Moroccan craftsmanship. The roof is topped with green tiles, the color of Islam. Two sets of stairs lead to the building. These columns are all that remain of the original mosque that was built alongside the Hassan Tower, which was designed as the mosque's minaret (left and facing page, top). They are linked to the mausoleum by flagstones. Viewed from Salé, the Oudaias Kasbah stands out like a white village by the sea (facing page, bottom).

intended to be the largest in the Muslim world. The Almohad dynasty (which also constructed the Koutoubia Mosque in Marrakech) began the structure in the twelfth century. Although the mosque has remained unfinished since that time, the minaret personifies the grandeur of the Moroccan kingdom and the golden age of Hispano-Maghreb art. The minaret's slender, finely-crafted silhouette overlooks the estuary of the Bou Regreg River, which separates Rabat from nearby Salé. The pure architectural lines of this tower bear an unmistakable resemblance to those of the Giralda in Seville (Spain) and the Koutoubia Mosque in Marrakech. By comparing the Hassan Tower with these other two, it becoms clear that the tower in Rabat was originally intended to be twice its current height. When Mohammed V returned from exile in 1956, he led the first Friday prayers here after the independence of Morocco. After his death, his mausoleum was built next to the Hassan Tower. These sites are magnificent symbols of Morocco.

Rabat's charm, however, lies inside the walls of the Oudaias Kasbah, a city within the city. This lovely spot, bordered by the wall, overlooks the sea. Constructed on a promontory overlooking the estuary and the Atlantic Ocean, this area has a village feel to it that is quite different from the elegant avenues and wide boulevards that criss-cross the rest of the Moroccan capital. The Oudaias Kasbah is a place apart, with its own rhythm. Take some time to enjoy the relaxed pace at the terrace of the picturesque Café Maure, the most charming locale in Rabat and the city's most popular meeting place. The open-air café is on a small square by the sea and is arranged in a large semicircle, like an amphitheater, with small mosaic walls covered with mats serving as seats.

Before leaving Rabat, be sure to visit another legendary site, the Chellah Necropolis. The gardens contain the tombs of many saints and mystics, including marabouts, who are still venerated today. You can also discover vestiges of funerary steles from the Merenids period. The Merenids, a Berber dynasty, usurped the Almohads and reigned from the thirteenth to the fifteenth century.

Religious sites in Meknes are havens of tranquility. The only presence at the Bou Inania Medersa is a cat perched on the *moucharabiehs* (top left and right). The decor of the fourteenth-century Koranic school is exquisite. Built according to the traditional *medersa* layout, it includes a central courtyard with a fountain, surrounded on three sides by galleries. The prayer room is on the fourth side. The *mirhab* (prayer niche indicating the direction of Mecca) is set in an arch decorated with stucco. The decoration combines *zelliges*, plaster, and wood carving. The mausoleum of Moulay Ismail, the king of Meknes (reigned 1672–1727), is more austere. This is one of the *zellige*-decorated courtyards (bottom left). Volubilis is another historic site situated in the midst of natural beauty (facing page).

MEKNES, THE CITY OF OLIVE TREES

The road leaves Rabat heading inland and east toward Meknes at the base of the Middle Atlas Mountains. Since time immemorial, Meknes and the surrounding region have been famed for their olive trees. Indeed, Mednessa ez Zeitoun, or "Meknes of the olive trees," is the name of the tribe that founded the town. The covered market, a prelude to the souks, is a must-see for anyone interested in local specialties.

From this pulsing world of noise and scents, you move into the absolute silence of the Bou Inania Medersa. The fourteenth-century Koranic school lies behind the enormous panels adorned with chased bronze and openwork designs. Everything here is conducive to contemplation: the pool with clear water in the central courtyard; the prayer room decorated with glazed tiling, plaster, and carved wood; and the tiny monastic cells on the upper floor that once housed students. From the rooftop, the city looks to be bristling with green minarets, including the minaret of the nearby Grand Mosque. Green glazed tiles are omnipresent on the roofs of the palaces and religious buildings in Meknes and Fez. This is the sacred green color of Islam, the Prophet's favorite color, and said to be the color of paradise as promised in the Koran.

The other aspect of Meknes that is of interest is the ancient imperial city, designed by Moulay Ismail, king of Meknes, and built opposite the medina. The size of its ramparts, which are 15 miles (25 km) in circumference, offers a glimpse into the grandiose plans conceived by him. Indeed, Meknes has been called the Versailles of Morocco. Moulay Ismail (reigned 1672–1727) was a contemporary of Louis XIV's (reigned 1643–1715), and established diplomatic relations with the French king. Like Louis XIV, he constructed majestic monuments to his own glory. The Bab al-Mansur gate at the city entrance is a model of elegant design. Covered with finely crafted, interlaced lines set against a background of green tile, this is the most beautiful gate in Meknes and, according to some, in all of Morocco. The palace constructed by Moulay Ismail was meant to be a pure extravagance: it consisted of no less than twenty separate pavilions guarded by 1200 black eunuchs and surrounded by three concentric

sets of walls. All that remains of this complex today are the granaries and arched silos. People still come to pay tribute to the sultan's mausoleum, a magnificent site consisting of a series of courtyards with bright yellow walls and a central fountain.

As you leave Meknes for Fez, take a short detour into Antiquity with a trip to Volubilis. These Roman ruins overlook a plain, with olive trees as far as the eyes can see. Strolling through Volubilis, the former capital of an ancient Roman province, you'll feel as if you're walking through the forum in Rome. Nothing in the immediate surroundings reveals that you are actually in the third millennium. The landscape seems to have remained unchanged since the time when Juba II, king of Mauritania (25 BC–AD 23), decided to build one of his capitals here. The ruins, some of which are almost completely intact, give a good idea of just how large the town was.

FEZ, ILLUSTRIOUS CITY OF ISLAM

The best way to first see Fez, located some 40 miles (60 km) east of Meknes, is to contemplate the city from above, by climbing the hill of the Merenid Necropolis. The ruins of the tombs from this dynasty emerge in the foreground, highlighted by the setting sun. From this vantage point the medina looks to be a compact labyrinth of houses, souks, *medersas*, mosques, and narrow streets. It is immense and, from this distance, seemingly silent. Yet the moment you set foot in this maze of winding alleys, you'll be drawn into the stream of busy passersby and the effervescence of countless different sights and sounds. Let yourself be carried by the uninterrupted flow of pedestrians, stopping whenever something piques your curiosity. Fez, a noble city of scholars and an imperial city classified as an UNESCO World Heritage Site, has great treasures, the legacy of its illustrious past. The city provided refuge to the Muslims and Jews who had been expelled from Spain, and so became the caretaker of Hispano-Moorish traditions. Its topography has remained virtually unchanged since the twelfth century.

The Mellah, the medieval Jewish quarter set up in the Kasbah of the Syrian archers in the early thirteenth century, leads the visitor through a network of incredibly narrow alleyways. The sun never penetrates here, and sometimes there's not even room for two people to pass each other. In the gloom you can make out a number of beautiful doors; the right doorjamb often still carries the remnants of a mezuzah, a small wooden box containing a parchment with a biblical passage. Today, the quarter is inhabited almost exclusively by Muslim families, but there are other traces of the Jewish presence, which lasted seven centuries, in the shadow of the nearby royal palace. Unlike Muslim houses, Jewish homes had windows and balconies facing the street.

As you wander haphazardly through the streets of the old city, Fez el-Bali, you'll come across splendid Koranic schools, although many are in dire need of restoration. The fourteenth-century *medersas* of Bou Inania, Attarin, Cherratin,

Fez is a city best seen from above. The ruins of the Merenid Necropolis are dramatically beautiful at dusk and offer an ideal vantage point from which to survey its layout. These tombs are situated on a hill overlooking the medina. The ramparts below are the oldest section of the city. The nearest bastion (above left) dates from the twelfth century. In the city itself, the medina appears under the green cover of its rooftiles. The Kairaouiyine Mosque, the city's Grand Mosque, stands out from the other buildings (below left). The huge structure can hold up to 20,000 worshipers. It is called the Kairaouiyine Mosque after the quarter in which it stands, which was in turn named after the refugees who arrived in the ninth century from Kairouan, Tunisia. It is also the site of a prestigious university (facing page).

Worshipers must perform their ablutions before entering the Kairaouiyine Mosque. Prayer is one of the five pillars of the Islamic faith. This religious duty requires that adherents undergo a preliminary purification of the body. Here, a worshiper performs the ritual at a fountain (left), a scene that can be observed from the rooftop of the Attarin Medersa, which overlooks the neighboring mosque.

and Sahrij are gateways into a fascinating spiritual world. These centers, which dispensed teaching in the Islamic faith to students who arrived from far and wide, are telling evidence of the former intellectual and religious importance of Fez. It is not hard to see why the soul is drawn into a contemplative state in the midst of such havens of peace. A central pool, filled with calm green water, reflects the decor, a tangle of cursive writing and intertwined designs in stucco, wood, and stone—a refined medium and calm environment that are conducive to prayer.

The vantage point from the terrace of the Attarin Medersa offers a view into the nearby courtyard of the Kairaouiyine Mosque. Fez's Grand Mosque was one of the first intellectual centers in the Maghreb. The most celebrated scholars of Islam came here to teach. It also has one of the most famous libraries in the Arabic world. The Grand Mosque contributed greatly to the reputation of Fez as a pious, scholarly city.

As you leave the mosque, the tumult of the souk soon overtakes you. Don't try to find any specific destination; let yourself be guided by the scents, sounds, colors, and materials. The tanners' quarter will probably leave you with the most striking impression. Created in the Middle Ages near the *oued* (water is essential to the tanning process), the craftsmen lived in a world permeated with the strong smells of dyes and animal skins. For the tourist with a sensitive sense of smell, a sprig of mint held to the nose may help. Climb up the terraces to get an overall look at the tanneries: below is the amazing sight of a multitude of copper basins crowded against each other. The tanners are sometimes standing hip-deep in the dye bath.

Next stop is the Palais Jamai, one of Morocco's most beautiful hotels. Housed in the former residence of the Vizir Jamai, the hotel was built onto the ramparts in the nineteenth century. It is surrounded by Andalusian gardens and offers an incomparable view of the medina.

Zelliges are an ubiquitous part of Fez's decorative landscape. The *zaouia* (tomb) of Moulay Idriss, a venerated saint, is behind a wall along a street lined with *zelliges*. Worshipers fill up the tiny streets near the sanctuary; the air feels imbued with mysticism. Vendors sell incense, candles, and other religious objects. Ex-votoes and offerings can be set in a small opening in the wall (left). The Bab Boujeloud Gate is one of the entrances to the city. The sumptuous En-Najjarine Fountain, which is inside the medina near the Place En-Najjarine, is also covered in glazed ceramic tiles. Many of the inscriptions above these structures remind their readers of the words of the Koran, which states that the gift of water is the first act of generosity. (opposite right).

MARRAKECH, GATEWAY TO THE SOUTH

In winter, it is not unusual to see the outline of the Koutoubia Minaret, the 230-foot (70-meter)-high tower that has stood over Marrakech for eight centuries, etched sharply against the background of the snow-capped Atlas Mountains. The sultry summer heat and ubiquitous red of the city inevitably raises comparisons with the nearby Kasbahs in the southern region. Marrakech, after which the country itself is named, is a hub of cultural exchanges and trade. It was a major city on the caravan route and an obligatory stop for merchants arriving from distant lands. It is also a holy city, with the mausoleums of seven venerated saints; these are all important pilgrimage sites.

Today, the city attracts numerous foreigners, drawn here by the colorful lifestyle and pleasant climate; a good number of them have opted to settle here. These wealthy travelers purchase *riads* and *dars* that are in need of restoration, and relish the languid Moroccan lifestyle. Some live quiet lives in and among the Moroccans, while other property owners have converted their homes to provide bed-and-breakfast accommodation.

For a first overview of the city, take a walk around the ramparts. Some 12 miles (19 km) long with nine monumental doors and two hundred bastions placed at regular intervals, these red stone ramparts seem impenetrable. For many people, the first direct contact with the city is at the Place Djemaa el-Fna. This immense, bustling square, just opposite the entrance to the souks, is the heart and soul of the city. Jugglers, tumblers, acrobats, snake charmers, orange juice vendors, fortune-tellers, and talisman vendors add to the picturesque ambience. Weaving through the crowd, water-sellers in characteristic cone-shaped hats are recognizable by their red outfits and the tin drinking cups hanging around their necks. Find a table in the midst of this noisy hubbub, snack on a grilled brochette, harira (lentil soup), or boiled snails, and settle down to watch the ongoing show. Djemaa el-Fna is certainly a tourist attraction, but this doesn't diminish its authenticity. In earlier times, public squares were stages for many traditional scenes. Djemaa el-Fna sets the tone

for a day in Marrakech and attracts both tourists and locals. The square leads to the entrance to the souk, the largest and most diverse in the country. There is a seemingly infinite variety of objects for sale—a ceramic drum, a tagine dish, a small Berber hat, a lampshade made of hide and decorated with henna, a braid of palm leaves, baskets, and much more.

After this hectic experience, you may want to enjoy the peaceful ambience of a Moroccan garden. The Menara is a good option. This small, perfectly proportioned pavilion is topped with a roof of green tiles; the structure is reflected in the immense pond of water surrounded by a grove of olive trees. Constructed in 1866, this elegant structure was reserved for viziers and sultans; legend has it that it was a favorite place for romantic encounters. The pool and water system was created in the twelfth century. It provided water for the entire city as well as for the fields. Another refreshing place was built during this same period: the Agdal Garden, which also has an extensive system of channels built to irrigate the orchards and olive trees.

The Majorelle Garden was designed by the French painter Louis Majorelle in the mid-twentieth century. It is more intimate than the other gardens. Visitors are struck by the contrast between the lush greenery and the bright blue—the painter's trademark color—that adorns the buildings. The garden is now owned by Yves Saint Laurent and Pierre Bergé.

Ever since the Almohad dynasty, which reached its golden age in the twelfth and thirteenth centuries, the different rulers of Marrakech have opted to live outside the city center, choosing to construct palaces in the midst of lush vegetation. The Bahia Palace, for example, is a marvelous example, featuring a Moorish garden filled with cypress, banana, orange, and jasmine trees. This palace was built for a royal favorite and consists of a series of courtyards and patios, each one with trees and flowers. The overall effect is one of refreshing calm. Each room of the lavishly-decorated apartments contains the best that Moroccan craftsmanship has to offer: the palace is a small jewel.

The pink, red, and ocher ramparts and walls of Marrakech presage the warm colors of the south, the earth tones of the Kasbahs. The Mechouar, in front of the royal palace, is the official parade ground, where members of religious orders, civilians, and the military congregate every year to swear allegiance to the king (facing page, top). The ring of ramparts around Marrakech consists of *pisé* fortifications and towers used as granaries, barracks, arsenals, and even water cisterns. Despite the fragility of the material, the walls seem extraordinarily strong. The bright white walls of the small marabout constrast with the adjoining Koutoubia Mosque (facing page, bottom). To really get a feel for Marrakech, head for teeming Place Djemaa el-Fna, to experience the local atmosphere (left).

Another treasure awaits the visitor to this area of palaces: the el-Badi, also known as "The Incomparable." The name alone gives an idea of the sublime beauty of the palace, which was pillaged by Moulay Ismail, the king of Meknes. The onyx, precious marble, stucco ceilings, and gold-leaf decoration are now only impressive ruins, but the central pond, surrounded by four corner pools, and the beds of orange trees give some idea of the former beauty of the gardens. Today, the palm grove created in the eleventh century is a sought-after oasis of paradise, far from the tumult of the city—indeed it is so sought-after that it may be threatened by real-estate developers. A small, winding road leads through the palm trees. Along the way are a number of *pisé* walls, which conceal sumptuous homes. A network of paths almost as complicated as those in the medina lead farther into these 32,000 acres (13,000 hectares), where you can sense the first stirrings of the desert.

Marrakech is a city of
many pleasures,
but it also has an
ambience that is
conducive to rest and
meditation. Today, some
places, like Le Comptoir
Paris-Marrakech, have
recreated the
enchantment of the
Moroccan lifestyle.
The floor of the
bar/restaurant's patio
is strewn with pillows,
creating an irresistible
decor (facing page).
The Menara pavilion
is in an idyllic setting
around a large pond,
against a backdrop
provided by the
snow-capped peaks of
the Atlas Mountains
(left). The Dar Si-Said
Museum, with its
beautiful gazebo,
showcases an
excellent collection of
Moroccan art (right and
top right). Dar Tiskiwi,
a private home and
museum created
by crafts collector
Bernt Flint, is a
magnificent example
of urban refinement
(bottom right).

The Ben Youssef
Medersa is one of
the most interesting
monuments in
Marrakech. This
theological school
was founded by a
Merenid sultan in the
fourteenth century.
It was entirely
reconstructed one
century later by a
Sa'adian sultan, who
turned it into the largest
such school in North
Africa. The decor is
lavish, with *zellige*-
covered walls and
stucco plasterwork
(bottom left). The
decorated Sa'adian
tombs contain the
sepulchers of the
Sa'adian sultans.
Their successor,
Moulay Ismail,
regularly destroyed the
monuments of his
predecessors and walled
in the tombs. They were
rediscovered in 1917
(bottom far left). In a
completely different
style, the Almoravid
dome of Al Bu'diyine
overlooks the ablutions
fountain (top).

The Bahia Palace is
another private home,
along with the Dar Si
Said, which stands in
the district of Marrakech
where many palaces
were built. It was
constructed by a grand
vizier to the sultan.
It took so long to build
that it gave rise to
a proverb—"the Bahia
is finally finished"—an
expression used to
describe the completion
of a complex project left
undone for a long time.
It was the son of the
grand vizier who
eventually finished the
palace. Meanwhile, the
scope of the project
expanded with each
passing year. The
"Palace of the Favorite"
incorporated the best of
Moroccan decorative
traditions. The result is
spectacular: a courtyard
paved with marble and
zelliges, a banquet
hall, arched gallery,
a series of apartments,
and multicolored
zouaks, with delicately
painted woodwork
(left and right).

SOUKS

The famous hand of Fatima is said to protect whomever wears it. This emblem is always included in the outfit worn by a water-carrier, a familiar figure in the souks (preceding pages). The hand motif is also frequently used on silver jewelry and is the most valued amulet; the open palm is beleived to attract good fortune and to ward off the evil eye. In the souks, a multitude of small shops crowd side by side along the alleyways, displaying their wares to passers-by. Overhead trellises and canvas awnings provide much-needed shade, as in this view of the Marrakech souk (right). Snugly-fitting *babouches*—flat slippers—are the pride of Tafraoute (facing page).

A FEAST FOR THE SENSES

In the heart of the medina is a magical world that is full of extraordinary sights, sounds, smells, and sensations—the souks. Enter this mysterious labyrinth of market stalls, and you'll be greeted by gleaming pyramids of olives and dried fruits, and multicolored displays of spices. At the dyers' souk, freshly dyed textiles in dazzling colors are stretched out on reed stalks like colored sails in the wind. Farther into the maze you will see showers of sparks, a sure sign that you're approaching the blacksmiths' souk. The dull thud of woodworking will take you to the place where the joiners and cabinet-makers ply their trade; while the sound of hammering means that the metalworkers must be busy. If you follow a certain high-pitched noise, you will eventually come across the craftsmen who are cutting out *zelliges*. As you make your way through the maze, you'll pass a magnificent array of earthenware in a wide range of colors, and if you can bear the stench from the tanneries, you might venture inside to touch the beautifully soft skins.

These small businesses allow Moroccan culture to express itself in all its richness, diversity, and creativity. A visit to the souks is the best way of experiencing local life and of getting the feel for the medina. It can be an extraordinary experience to lose your way in the twilight world of alleyways and passages with their multitude of tiny stores and workshops. Join in the hustle and bustle, and you'll be carried along by the flow of local people going about their business: moreover, you'll discover a wealth of age-old skills and traditions.

The souks abound in crafts and foodstuffs, and are organized according to a traditional layout that is often centuries old. Each guild is assigned to a specific district, to which it gives its name, and each district is like a world of its own. The vendors who deal in precious goods—silversmiths, moneychangers, booksellers—usually have pride of place near the Great Mosque, where mass prayers are performed on Friday (the Booksellers' Mosque in Marrakech is so-called because of the manuscript vendors who used to gather there in the Middle Ages). The stalls nearest the mosque sell candles, incense, and other liturgical objects, which contribute to the extraordinarily mystical atmosphere that fills the narrow alleyways leading to the sanctuary.

To the left of Place el-Hedim in Meknes, behind the arcades where the potters display their wares, lies the covered market. It stands at the entrance to the medina, and is the ideal place to go shopping. It's one of the most beautiful and animated markets in the country. Here you will find all the ingredients you need to try your hand at Moroccan cooking; you can buy not only dried fruits and herbs, nuts and olives, but also hens and sheep, and even multicolored birds. It's an unforgettably picturesque scene, full of exotic sights, sounds, and smells. Shopping there is a way of experiencing local life (right). In Marrakech, this "Berber pharmacy" stocks all kinds of amulets and remedies in order to help heal the body and spirit. Herbal medicine and superstition go hand in hand in Morocco (facing page).

As you move farther away from this spiritual center, the items you find being offered for sale become more commonplace. You will pass, for example, stalls selling perfumes, spices, leather goods, cabinetwork, and clothing, before finally coming to foodstuffs, which are sold at the entrance to the souks. Crafts that are either noisy (metalwork) or smelly (tanning, pottery) are generally kept apart from the rest of the products on display.

Souks are not the sole prerogative of towns. Country villages also hold their own weekly markets, often in a large square by the roadside. Tradesmen come from all around to sell their wares. Sometimes they put up tents in which they set out their goods; sometimes they simply display them on the ground in the open air. On market days, it's practically impossible to drive a car through the village: traffic moves at a snail's pace. It's a good opportunity to observe the villagers, the country people from the surrounding area, and the tradesmen who flock to these great gatherings, which are always teeming with life and fascinating to observe. Such occasions always provide unforgettable scenes that you can store away in your memory, like watching the shepherd and his sole sheep making their way through the jostling crowd like a couple holding hands: the master walks tall and straight in his *djellaba*, while the sheep leaps and gambols, doing its best to keep up.

The vendors always encourage tourists to feast their eyes, but it would be a shame to stop at that: why not taste the delights of bargaining, too? This practice is an age-old custom and an integral part of the Moroccan way of life. If you're interested in a particular item, name your price. The ritual can then begin. You'll soon get the hang of it: you sit on a pouffe or a rug in the store, sipping your mint tea amid a pile of jumbled objects, and the discussion gets under way. There's no hurry, you have all the time in the world. Refusing to bargain would disappoint the vendor because it would deprive him of one of his greatest pleasures—but don't offend him by bargaining if you're not genuinely interested.

Now let's explore the market in more detail.

MARKET FLAVORS

The stalls that sell foodstuffs in Moroccan souks are always irresistibly appealing. Sellers do their utmost to create the most brightly colored and attractive displays possible. Depending on the vendor's means and ambitions, they range from the modest (just a few bright red peppers spread out on a piece of cloth on the ground) to the extravagant (stores with elaborately constructed pyramids of olives). Whatever the size of their stalls, vendors always use color to its best advantage. A typical feature of the souks is a shining mountain of oranges; sometimes you can hardly see the vendor sitting right in the middle of this dazzling sea of glistening fruit. Moroccan oranges are famous worldwide for their slightly acidic flavor, and there are always plenty of peddlers more than willing to sell you a glass of freshly squeezed juice.

The vendors who sell dried fruits and condiments rival each other in ingenuity to construct extraordinary pyramids of olives, preserved lemons, and pickled onions, which will have your mouth watering as you imagine them served with salads or tagines. There are heaps of black olives, green ones, sour ones, and purple ones with a touch of red. Sometimes they are preserved in a flavorsome marinade of herbs or red peppers and piled up in jars, forming what looks like an enticingly delicious decorative panel. Then there are the serried ranks of dried figs and dates—and in the land of the date palm, the latter are divine. Date-lovers will find that these fruit come in an infinite variety: elongated, round, brown, caramel-colored, hard or soft, but whatever they look like, they are always succulent and irresistible. They are also sold at the roadside straight after harvesting, either in mounds piled up on the ground or in pristine condition, still hanging on branches cut straight from the tree. Dates are also delicious stuffed with almond paste: these tasty sweetmeats are best when nibbled and accompanied with a glass of mint tea. These and other such delicacies will tempt you from little wheeled trolleys on the corners of the market lanes: ask the vendor to cut you a piece from a slab of almond paste in the

Olives are one of the riches that Morocco has in common with all Mediterranean countries. Among the many varieties produced by the country's olive groves, the most surprising is the *dahbia*, which has an aroma reminiscent of red berries. Meknes, in the heart of the olive-growing region, is renowned for its market, a veritable olive souk (facing page). Spices and secret mixtures, dried fennel, marinated olives, preserved lemons, and peppers; all are essential ingredients in Moroccan cuisine, and are used to flavor, season, sweeten, or add spice to traditional dishes (above). The mixture called *ras el-hanout* is made of about twenty spices, and is mainly used in tagines.

most unlikely pistachio-green or candy-pink. If you have a sweet tooth, you've come to the right place.

There are other pyramids, too, of a very different style from the first: follow the heady smell of spices to find small conical mounds of colored powder, smoothed down by the grocer's expert hand. Elsewhere, you'll see these precious foodstuffs spilling out of hessian bags, like fine sand brought back from the desert, or a painter's pigments ranging over a gradation of earth colors. In the spice souk, the palette ranges from the beige-pale gray of ginger to the flame red of pepper via the gold of saffron: these flavors are all essential in Moroccan cooking. Spices are used to color and flavor all dishes, be they sweet or savory, and Moroccan cooks are expert in their use. Each spice is intended for a particular meat, fish, vegetable, or pastry dish. *Kammoun*, or cumin, adds its distinctive flavor to kebabs of grilled meat or to eggs, and Moroccans use it much as we use salt and pepper. The mild, almost sweet flavor of cinnamon is used to season pastilla, semolina, and orange salads. It can also be sprinkled on a dish to add an attractive finishing touch. Saffron was once used as a dye, and Berber women still use it as a cosmetic. Last but not least, there is a precious mixture generally used in tagines, called *ras el-hanout*. Each spice merchant prepares it according to his own special recipe, using twenty or so spices, which include cardamom, cinnamon, turmeric, cloves, curry, ginger, iris, rosebuds, nutmeg, pepper, capsicum, and gum arabic. Spices are supposed to have healing powers, too, with either stimulant or soothing effects.

Many Moroccans use the health remedies prepared by herbalists. In the Middle Ages, the science of medicinal plants became the object of scholarly treatises; nowadays, such knowledge is passed on orally. These traditional healers often have young apprentices whom they train over a long period of time.

Apothecaries have a profusion of plants at their disposal, and many of them concoct elixirs to heal all manner of ailments, from rheumatism to evil spirits. The herbalists tend to keep the recipes of their homemade remedies a closely

The vendor often has to squeeze himself into a tight space in order to fit among the mountains of merchandise on display in his little store. Once installed, he reigns like a king over the profusion of dried fruits (right): figs, dates, pistachios, almonds, and more, happy to give his customers expert advice on the flavor of each. Moroccans eat a lot of dried fruits, which are often presented to guests as a sign of welcome. Dates are served with *harira* soup during Ramadan. Olives, glistening in their marinade, attract the expert eye of housewives, who know exactly what sort they need to buy for the dish they have in mind (top right). Moroccan-style tea is drunk with a lot of sugar, and fresh mint is an essential ingredient. Moroccans drink several cups a day, so plenty of fresh mint is needed (bottom right).

guarded secret. Among the classics, there is *sanouge*, or nigella seeds, which are prescribed for colds and sinusitis. The same plant can also be used to treat chest congestion or backache. Ambergris is said to have painkilling properties. Walnut bark is cut into little sticks, which are chewed by the locals to clean their teeth and gums; they are a natural substitute for toothbrushes and toothpaste, and are used all throughout the African continent.

Various natural colorants such as kohl are used as cosmetics. Kohl is a fine powder made from native stibnite (which used to be known as antimony). It is black, and women use it as eye make-up. Herbalists also sell henna, the powder made from dried leaves, which is supposed to have protective powers; the Prophet called it "the plant of paradise," and it is much appreciated by Moroccans for its tonic, antiseptic, and colorant properties. It is widely used by Moroccan women, who apply it to their hair to obtain golden or reddish highlights. Henna is also used by women to decorate their hands and heels with intricate drawings. These fine networks of arabesques, crosses, dots, and foliage create temporary tattoos which are nowadays purely decorative but were once used to indicate a person's ethnic origins.

Marrakech has always been the center for the herb trade, and you can find up to 143 species of dried plants in its souks. These are supplied by the varied flora of the surrounding regions. Marrakech is also, therefore, the home of herbal medicine, which is supplemented with talismans—objects inbued with magical powers—or aphrodisiacs, according to a whole range of beliefs.

If you're fond of fresh herbs, you're sure to find something to suit your taste in the souks. So many different flavorings are available here that sometimes you can hardly see the vendor behind his thick hedge of aromatic greenery. Herbs, like spices, are essential ingredients in Moroccan cuisine. The merchants in their tiny, crowded stores mostly sell thick bouquets of fragrant mint, which Moroccans use in huge quantities for the tea they drink several times a day. There are a dozen or so species of mint, which people buy in armfuls every day, thereby ensuring that it's always fresh. The delicate flavors of

Morocco is a sun-drenched country: it is no wonder that its fruit and vegetables taste so good. Tomatoes are deliciously sweet and tasty. Watermelons and melons are juicy and refreshing. Attractive red arbutus berries are a rare commodity, sold in small quantities (facing page, bottom left). The best bananas come from the Taghazoute region, where they grow on plantations along the Atlantic Ocean. Vegetables—turnips, carrots, beans, squash, zucchini, eggplant, and so on— are served with couscous or tagines. All these form a lovely palette of colors and flavors, and are skillfully arranged by the vendors (facing page). Herbalists take advantage of the wide variety of Moroccan flora to make herbal remedies from dried plants (right).

Women sometimes come to market to sell their home-produced argan oil (right), or their homegrown fruit and vegetables (far right). The water-carrier is a familiar figure in the market; he is festooned with metal cups and wears the lucky hands of Fatima (below).

thyme, marjoram, absinthe, and anise are sometimes added to mint tea. Coriander, used in the cuisine of countries around the world from India to Spain, Portugal to Greece, is a favorite here, and is often used in salads. When crushed its tiny seeds give off a beautiful aromatic flavor, and its distinctive taste is a typical feature of many Moroccan dishes. Parsley, sage, and rosemary complete the range.

The oil-bearing seeds produced by the argan timber tree are the source of the rare commodity, argan oil. It's best to buy argan oil in the region where it's produced, which is in the Souss Valley in the south of the country. However, argan oil is traditionally homemade for personal use rather than shop-bought. A significant amount of time—and fruit—goes into its production: it takes twelve hours and 100 kilos of nuts to obtain a single liter of oil. It is usually women who produce the oil; much patience is needed as it's an extremely slow process with many delicate stages.

First the nuts have to be picked, dried, and cracked open. Next the kernels have to be extracted, then sorted, roasted, and ground by millstone until a thick paste is obtained. Water is then added to this paste, and the mixture is kneaded in a shallow dish until the oil suddenly emerges from it as if by magic. When personal production exceeds what the family expects to use, the women will take the surplus and sell it at the market. Beware of merchants in the

Another stallholder offers irresistibly tempting, honey-drenched Moroccan pastries, arranged in shining mountains. Try *chebakias, m'hannchas,* and *baklavas* for their delicious combination of honey and almonds. This subtle mixture is encased in phyllo pastry, which is then worked into a wide variety of shapes. The best time to enjoy these treats is when you're relaxing on a Moroccan divan amid a pile of cushions, with a glass of mint tea in your other hand; they will taste even more exquisite than usual.

market selling diluted oil, however. Pure argan oil has a very distinctive, beautiful amber color and tastes slightly of roasted hazelnuts. It is a treasured ingredient in traditional cooking. Moroccan women also consider the oil to be an elixir of youth, and count it among their ancestral beauty secrets: they apply it to their skin and hair, while mothers rub it into newborn babies' skin.

Bread is the staple of the Moroccan diet. It can be bought from the grocer, who stores it in small cabinets with glass doors, but is usually homemade. Women prepare the dough at home, kneading it to the proper consistency, then they take it to the local oven to be baked. In the morning it's common to see young girls or women walking elegantly along, carrying a bread board on their head or shoulders on which little balls of dough are carefully covered with a cloth, ready for baking. Later in the day, you may see them on their way back home again, carrying piles of crispy golden loaves sprinkled with sesame seeds, still steaming hot from the oven. One of the most familiar scenes in Moroccan daily life is seeing the baker swiftly and expertly sliding a batch of bread into the oven with his long wooden oven peel.

Finally, if you are fond of sweets, you're bound to be tempted by the piles of pastries shining with honey. These delicious sweetmeats are always displayed beautifully. There are many different traditional Moroccan recipes, but they are generally made of phyllo pastry stuffed with almonds, walnuts, or dates in a delicious combination of crisp and melting textures. To make *chebakia* for instance, the pastry is fried and twisted, then sprinkled with sesame seeds. You'll also enjoy *baklava*, gazelle horns dusted with icing sugar, lady fingers, macaroons, honey and almond *briouats*—each one more delicious than the last. You'll soon learn to recognize your personal favorite by its shape: elongated, triangular, twisted, or half-moon. Whatever your tastes, a visit to a Moroccan market is bound to whet your appetite: you'll be invited to sample a pastry here, a fig or an olive there, and your sense of smell will be pleasantly stirred by the wonderful variety of spices.

WEAVERS AND DYERS

Another eye-catching sight is an indigo, saffron, or purple sky of freshly dyed skeins stretched out to dry on reed stalks: this is the dyers' souk. If you come back the next day, you'll walk underneath a string of colored veils that flutter in the gentlest breath of air. The process of manufacturing textiles begins here, in these huge, black, steaming vats in which the craftsmen stir wool or cotton skeins. If you venture behind the scenes you'll see them at work.

Nowadays, the dyers tend to make less and less use of natural pigments, including the famous indigo, which used to come off and dye the skin when it mingled with the dyers' sweat (which is why they were called "blue men"). Once used to dye the long turbans and robes of the Tuaregs, this natural pigment is no longer in favor. Today, indigo is costly to cultivate, and chemical colorants are widely used instead. Red, however, is still derived from a bath of madder, with alum as a fixing agent. Crushed apple-tree bark makes this popular color even more vivid.

The weaving workshops produce cotton and wool pieces, or more luxurious sabra and silk. The Rif area is renowned for its *foutas* or *mendils*: these are typical pieces of cotton or wool (depending on the season), which have bright, predominantly red and white stripes. Women tie them around their waists: when you see a woman walking along the road with this stiff piece of fabric knotted round her waist and a wide straw hat on her head, you can be sure you're in Rif country.

In Essaouira, women prefer the *haik*, a large piece of raw cotton or wool in which they drape themselves from head to foot. The sight of these draped figures walking in the wind in front of the ramparts or along the beach is a very familiar sight in Essaouira.

Apart from these weavings, which are characteristic of a certain region, the burnoose or *selham* is worn by men all over the country, especially on feast or prayer days. A simple, full cape featuring a large hood, made of wool or

When you stroll through the alleyways of the Marrakech medina and the sky suddenly turns rainbow-colored, you will know that you have arrived at the dyers' souk. The skeins of wool you will see stretched out over your head create a world of their own, which is divided into color-coded regions. The skeins will be used to weave rugs and blankets, but for the moment they are drying in the hot sun (facing page). In another Marrakech alleyway, incredibly light, transparent cotton veils, which have come straight out of their vats of boiling dye, flutter from long bamboo stalks (left). These will later be sold to be worn wound around the head, or as scarves, providing protection against the wind and sun.

When the skeins of wool come out of the huge stone vats containing the bath of hot dye, they are hoisted up above the labyrinth of the dyers' souk. Later, they will be used to weave rugs. Natural pigments such as indigo are no longer in favor; it was this purple dye, which mingled with their sweat, that gave the dyers their nickname of "blue men." Nowadays, chemical colorants are more common; but with its range of colors, a visit to the dyers' souk is still like walking through a rainbow (right).

raw felt. The *selham* was first worn by the Berbers and bears a curious resemblance to the woolen cloak worn by Roman legionaries. It probably dates from before the Arab conquest. Young men wear the famous tarboosh, a cylindrical, flat-topped hat in dark-red felt with a black tassel, almost emblematic of Morocco.

If you fancy wearing a traditional garment yourself, try the *gandoura* (a sleeveless cotton tunic), or the *djellaba*, the ultimate cotton or wool outer garment with a hood and wide sleeves. The *djellaba* is unisex, but the caftan is women's wear. This long, often light robe, which buttons down the front, can be a very refined outfit when adorned with beautiful trimmings, or when it is made of precious fabrics such as cashmere or silk.

Apart from these strictly traditional items, the weavers create striped blankets in an infinite variety of colors. You can use these thick, supple weavings as bedspreads, throws, thick tablecloths, or drapes. It is well worthwhile stepping inside the workshops where the craftsmen are busy at their looms, to watch their skillful, quick-fingered work. The shopkeeper will gladly explain everything about the different kinds of yarns they use, the design that has been chosen, and the particular loom selected to achieve a pattern; the pieces you buy will have all the more value when you return home with them.

The city of Fez in the north of the country is rich in history and craftsmanship, but particularly prides itself on its brocade. Its richly brocaded silk, gold, or silver pieces are traditionally used as drapes between rooms, where they shimmer in the light, adding a beautifully decorative touch. Fez is renowned for its silk; in the souks there is a covered market with a whole row of small stalls, filled from top to bottom with bobbins of silk thread arranged according to color. The merchant sits behind his little counter at the foot of this multicolored mountain, and climbs his ladder to fetch the particular shade the customer requires. Another Fez specialty is its famous embroidery—the extraordinarily delicate and refined work is always created by the women. Tablecloths or cushion covers are adorned with these elaborate two-tone designs.

Some European designers who admire this work are keen to ensure that it survives as a top-quality art form. Thanks to this outside interest, Moroccan design has been given a whole new lease of life. In Marrakech, for example, French designer Brigitte Perkins has devoted all her energy in recent years to pursuing her passion for Moroccan weaving. She creates pieces that are remarkable both for the work that goes into them and for the quality of the materials used. This former fashion designer has set up her own hand-weaving workshop with traditional looms. It is supervised by a specialized team of *maalems* (master weavers) who are helping her rediscover traditional skills. She now creates custom-made weavings in extraordinarily beautiful shiny cotton and sabra, in Egyptian cotton, in cotton and silk, or in a linen and sabra mixture.

Of all Moroccan handicrafts, embroidery is the most delicate. It took consummate skill to embroider this antique caftan (left), and it was done using a technique that is reserved for precious fabrics and garments. Such embroidery is done by women in Morocco. Embroidery with gold thread on a Fantasia saddle is a man's job (below, left), whereas rug-making is carried out by women, though it is the men who take the rugs to market to sell (below, right).

She also uses sabra to embroider cotton in the traditional Fez style. Each piece she creates is unique. To see Brigitte Perkins unfolding her superb designs, one after the other, is to enjoy an exquisite, shimmering display of subtle harmonies of color and fabric.

Valérie Barkowski is an interior designer who assisted Quentin Wilbaux in the restoration of several riad houses in the Marrakech-Medina project. Her work is in a more contemporary vein than Brigitte Perkins's; she specializes in pure cotton bed linen that is wonderfully light and cool. Among her creations are simple white sheets sprinkled with fine Moroccan embroidery, and pillowcases with colored tassels. Her own brand, "Mia Zia," includes a line of finely striped, multicolored merino knitwear, her personal trademark. These light-hearted designs express the joy she feels at working in this country.

BERBER AND ARAB CARPETS

No trip to Morocco is complete without a visit to a carpet store. Before entering, you'll see samples of the rug collection hanging on the walls of the alleyway outside. In the dark interior the rugs are piled up by the dozens, and you'll begin to get the measure of the huge range of styles. It would be impossible to describe all the different styles here, but a few indications will help you recognize some of them. First of all, there are two major categories: the rural, tribal Berber carpet, which dates back to antiquity, and the urban, Arab carpet, whose origins date from some time around the eighteenth century.

A typical tour of Morocco provides a good overview of regional variations: you'll see carpets sold at the roadside by men who come down from the Atlas Mountains with the work produced by the women in their village. Each region has its own traditions in terms of wool, plant colors, and designs, and these are handed down from one generation to the next. The geometric designs of Berber tattoos are often reproduced on simple, rural carpets. The little town of Chichaoua, situated between Marrakech and Essaouira, produces carpets which feature geometric designs along with stylized figures of people and animals (dromedaries, scorpions, and snakes, for example). These carpets feature blue, yellow, black, green, or white ornamentation on a red background. The Zemmour weavers of the Middle Atlas Mountains create a similar background on their knotted, deep pile rugs (the design shows on the short-pile side as well).

The number of knots is a measure of quality in a carpet: the more there are per square inch, the greater its value. Carpets from the eastern Middle Atlas have a white background, decorated with brown or orange motifs, with metal sequins sometimes sewn into the carpet. The widest range of Berber carpets from the Middle Atlas can be found in the souk at Khemisset. Using a fine wool that is particularly silky and bright, the Ouaouzguite women in the High Atlas weave thin pieces whose colors tend toward warm reds and browns, with geometric designs arranged in wide bands.

This carpet-seller is displaying his wares in a lovely old mansion in Fez (far left). Each customer is entitled to a "private view." Here, the finest specimens are unrolled on the marble and *zellige* floor to be shown to their best advantage. There are carpets in every room—even upstairs, where they are draped over the balustrade of the patio. It's like an Aladdin's cave, in which people sit on benches to admire the display. As it is in a wealthy Fez home, the carpets are "urban" or Arab, inspired by Persian or Tunisian models. They are decorative and sophisticated, whereas the Berber rugs (bottom left) are more utilitarian and can serve as blankets or mattresses. The design of the rugs varies from one region to another; rugs like these are displayed outside the stores (top left).

Beautiful lamps are
made of goat- or
sheepskin decorated
with henna, like
this one (above),
made by Foued in
Essaouira, and adorned
with stylized ethnic
motifs. The fine
leather lets the light
shine through. As far
as *babouche* slippers
are concerned,
suppleness is what
matters most (right).

LEATHERWORK

Morocco has long been renowned for its pre-eminence in the craft of leatherwork. As early as the sixteenth century, leather goods were being shipped back to Europe from Morocco, giving rise to the word "maroquin," which means morocco leather.

All leatherwork begins with the tanning process. The most commonly used hides are those of sheep, although camel hides are sometimes used. The skins are first immersed in a series of large vats that are packed tightly side by side. They are kept in a tanning solution for several days before being moved into a bath of strongly colored dye. Finally, they are stretched out to dry on the souk rooftops or in the vicinity of the town, where they create a glorious kaleidoscope of colors.

Little, then, has changed significantly in the manu-facturing process since the first shiploads of leather were sent to Europe centuries ago. The fine, supple skins continue to be admired today. Depending on their nature and their quality, they are used to make all manner of decorative everyday objects. You can buy a simple pouffe, or a more decorative one with golden motifs; a bag like the one that the Berbers wear slung across the shoulder, a purse, or a beautiful transparent lantern, embellished with henna motifs, which allows a lovely soft light to filter through.

Tafraoute is the best place to buy the traditional *babouche* slippers favored by Moroccans. They are color-coded (beige or yellow for men, red or other bright colors for women). Some luxury slippers are finely embroidered with gold, and can be very expensive. These luxury products often have heels, and can be recognized by their pointed toes. The gold thread motifs are reminiscent of delicate, intricate metalwork.

In Fez, leatherwork is done right in the middle of the medina. Ever since the Middle Ages, the tanneries have been situated near the Fez River that runs through the town and supplies the water necessary for treating the skins. The tanners' district, or Chouara, is one of the most spectacular parts of the imperial city. If you climb up to the terraces above the vats, you'll get a good overall view of the craftsmen at work, using their age-old techniques. You'll see the groups of stone vats; each one contains a bath of strongly colored dye in which the craftsmen are sometimes immersed up to their thighs. Tanning consists of transforming the uncured skin into durable leather (above and right).

COPPER AND SILVER

Let's leave the brightly embroidered *babouches* for the bright showers of sparks that come from the blacksmiths' souk. The craftsmen are black with soot as they work the metal under their blow-torches, creating delicate wrought-iron gates or simple locks and keys. Whatever their specialty, they demonstrate their skill and creativity, transforming an ordinary sheet of metal into a finely worked and elegant object. There are goldsmiths and silversmiths, and metalworkers who use iron, brass, bronze, and nickel silver (a common alloy of nickel, copper, and zinc that can be hammered until it is very fine).

Tin is used to make simple, lightweight lanterns, wall lamps and lamps with openwork designs. Some are shaped like large stars, and shed a bright light over a wide area when hung from the ceiling. Copper is also used creatively: beaten or smooth, burnished or unpolished, it makes lovely washbasins; sometimes it is chiseled with Islamic motifs and fashioned into beautiful trays or perfume burners.

Bronze—an alloy of copper and tin—is used to create traditional-style tumblers and marvelous chiseled, damascened trays. Damascene is the art of decorating by inlaying or encrusting. In Fez, certain craftsmen excel at this, creating the most exquisite designs. There are entire dynasties of craftsmen who are masters in the art of inlaying precious metals. They produce such extraordinary works with embossed, chiseled, and silver-inlaid designs that they can sometimes boast royal commissions (like the distinguished craftsman Abderraham Benlamlih).

The silversmiths use the same motifs (interlacing, arabesques, palmettes, and inscriptions) in their jewelry designs. In Tiznit, jewelers use silver to make traditional Berber-style necklaces, bracelets, rings, earrings, ankle bracelets, and fibulas. Jewelry is often embellished with amber, coral, or semi-precious stones. The ubiquitous, open-palmed hand of Fatima is said to protect its wearer by warding off the evil eye. Gold is considered the ideal finery for a wealthy bride, be it chiseled, filigreed, open-worked, or studded with enamel or precious stones. The city of Fez, with its history of wealth and refinement, is the best place to buy gold. Essaouira comes next: a century ago, certain Fez craftsmen took their skill and expertise to the city then called Mogador, and developed their own style.

Whatever you may ultimately decide to purchase—whether tribal jewelry, a perfume-burner, a tea-tray, or a lantern to brighten your evenings—it is sure to impart a touch of the spirit of Morocco to your home.

The silversmiths
and metalworkers
have a wide range
of techniques and
materials at their
disposal to produce
anything from
fine jewelry to
monumental works.
Silver is a favorite
for jewelry. These
pendants contain
amber, while small
niello-silver coins
tinkle on tiaras
(facing page, first two
photographs from left).
Metalwork is also
used for decoration,
like this detail from
a panel in the
Kairaouiyine Mosque
in Fez. The craftsmen
hammer sheets of metal
to make center lights for
mosques, or bronze
doorknockers.
In Fez, the finely
chiseled copper
doors of the Royal
Palace illustrate
the skill of the Fez
master craftsmen
(facing page, four
photographs on the
right). The dyers' souk
in Marrakech abounds
in copper trays and
lanterns (right).

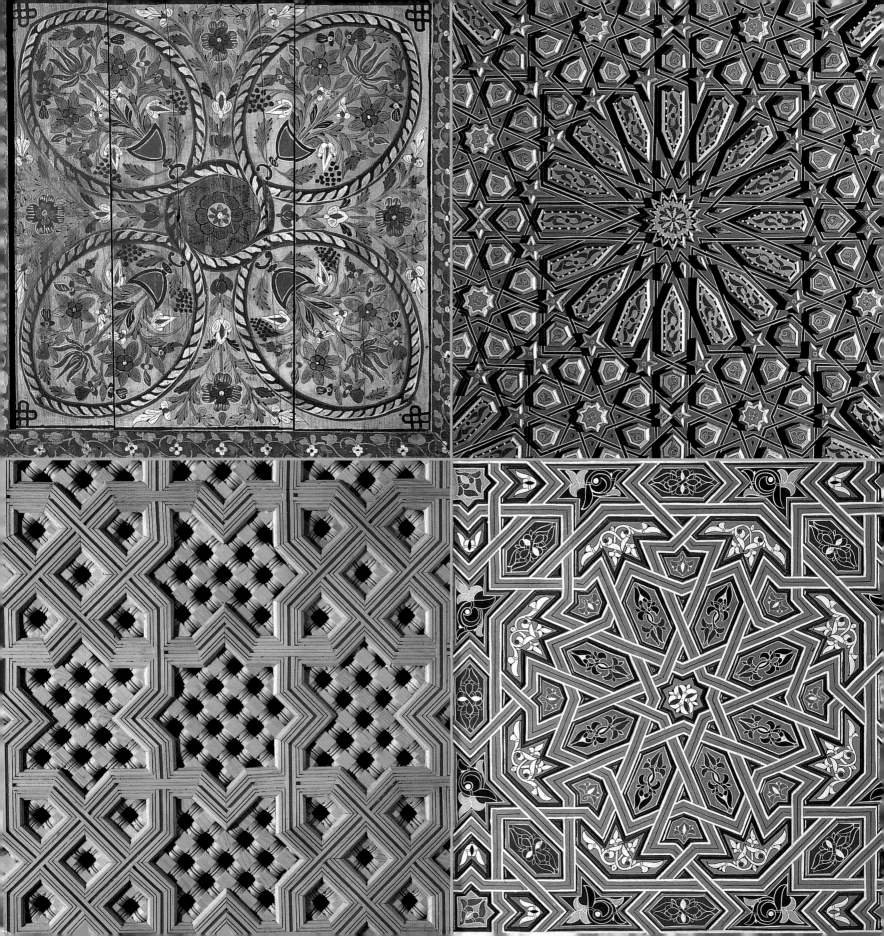

WOOD CARVING AND MARQUETRY

Whether wood is painted with floral motifs (facing page, top left), carved and painted (facing page, top and bottom right) or made into *moucharabiehs* (facing page, bottom left), it is an inevitable component of the decor of any Moroccan mansion. Cedarwood, which has warm tones and acquires a patina with age, is the most popular, and the designs are usually geometric. Carved or molded wood is used for doors. When painted, it makes magnificent ceilings, indoor shutters, window frames, or furniture. Beautiful chests are made of wood inlaid with bone, ivory, or mother-of-pearl. For *zouaks,* each craftsman uses his own brushes, which he makes himself using a small piece of cedarwood and some donkey's tail hair (right).

The strong scent of wooden objects will forevermore remind you of a walk through a Moroccan souk or a visit to a lovely home. The two main types of wood used in Morocco are cedar and thuja; the former is associated with Fez, the latter with Essaouira. In the Fez medina, the heady fragrance of cedarwood greets you at the entrance to the workshops. This peppery scent spreads like a perfume through fine Moroccan homes, in which the furniture is made principally of cedarwood. In the souks, cabinetmakers, carpenters, and joiners are grouped in the same alleyway. It's a veritable hive, in which you can see the craftsmen at work, handing down their skill from generation to generation. They work with cedarwood from the Middle Atlas Mountains, making beautiful tables, wardrobes, shelves, and chests, which they decorate with geometric designs. Most spectacular of all, however, are the sculpted Dutch doors: these are massive, heavy, sometimes 20 feet (6 meters) high and intricately carved with rosettes, stars, curves, and crescents. They are always to be found in mansions and palaces, where they separate rooms and patios. They have two hinges, and open out onto side walls, but as they are heavy to push open, they always contain a small, single door, through which you may pass by ducking your head down and stepping over the frame. Cedarwood comes in lovely, warm tones and acquires a patina with age.

In the workshops, you will also be able to watch the craftsmen at their lathes, making the famous *moucharabiehs* that are characteristic features in Moroccan interiors. These are placed at the windows of houses to filter the light, isolate the rooms from the outside world and enable women to see without being seen. They are also used as balustrades around patios. Working with cedarwood is closely linked to traditional building processes; woodwork is at its most architectural in the design of ceilings, which may be either painted, decorated with moldings, or both.

The unique and heady fragrance of thuja instantly evokes Essaouira, where the cabinetmakers' workshops nestle in the ramparts, whipped by the waves. Atlantic humidity would seem to be the beauty secret of this burnished wood, which can rarely withstand the dry interiors of Western homes. Craftsmen prefer to work with the root, which they use to make all kinds of wonderful boxes, tables, trays, frames, chests, pencil boxes, and backgammon sets. These craftsmen are veritable masters of marquetry, adding lemon-tree wood, ebony, mother-of-pearl, or bone to their designs. When waxed, polished, and varnished, the result is often a true work of art.

POTTERY AND CERAMICS

E arthenware awaits us next. As is the case for carpets, there are two main categories of pottery. One group is comprised of the rural and utilitarian, the other is made up of the urban and ornamental. Even the most rudimentary pottery is decorative, however, with its beautiful material and harmonious forms. In Berber areas, pottery is often reduced to its simplest expression, and the objects that are produced there will not have changed very much at all since the earliest times: plates, jugs, and butter dishes are all left in their natural, warm, earthen color.

The potter's wheel is regarded as the preserve of male potters; in the Rif area in the north, women potters work instead by hand, as they have always done, to produce beautifully pure shapes, which they decorate with simple, black-outlined motifs.

Down in the south of the country, at the gateway to the Sahara, there is a little village called Tamegroute, which has been famous since the sixteenth century for the lovely green enamel of its ceramics. The village potters get their clay from the underground galleries of the nearby Drâa Valley, and use it to create a wide range of approximately fifty, beautifully simple forms. The range includes ornamental tiles (*karmoud*), which are produced in great quantities, wedding dishes for presenting dried fruit and oil lamps (*kandil*), and soup bowls (*zlefa*), which are specially made for Ramadan. Sometimes an individual potter may add decorative incisions that have been inspired by Berber motifs.

This characteristic green enamel comes from the Fez tradition, and every item is of a slightly different, many-hued green. The ten potters' workshops that exist today have inherited the spirit of Nassirya, who was influential in the foundation of Tamegroute in the sixteenth century. The ambition of the brotherhood there was to raise the small village to the rank of a medina worthy of that of Fez. Like the larger city, Tamegroute is an important spiritual center, thanks to its famous *zaouia,* a religious center that also dates from the sixteenth century.

Moroccan pottery is usually made by men. They knead the clay and work it on the wheel, sometimes correcting the shape with a fingertip. It is a craft that requires great dexterity. The potter's workshop is often nothing more than a small, low-ceilinged, open room (facing page, top right). Charlotte Barkowski is one of the few women producing pottery commercially in Morocco; in her vast Akkal workshop in Marrakech, each potter has a specific task. Their work is recognizable for its lovely enamel, and for the forms that are inspired by tradition but made beautifully simple (facing page, top and bottom left). As for traditional pottery, that is decorated with a painted pattern (facing page, center right), as in Safi and Fez, where the color blue dominates (right).

Fez is renowned for the bright green enamel tiles that adorn the roofs of its palaces and mosques, but is especially famous for the blue of its ceramics. This imperial city began to develop its own subtle sense and technique of enamel decoration through contact with the Arabs of the East and, more especially, with Andalusian masters in the ninth century. Fez pottery resulted from the dynamic fusion between the Muslims of the East and West; it synthesized the trends of both Cordoba and Kairouan. From the eleventh century on, its cobalt blue made the imperial city famous. Over the centuries, it went from a pale blue-gray to an almost violet azure-blue, before finally finding the right tone in the nineteenth century: an intensely bright and pure blue, which is also said to have been inspired by the blue of Chinese porcelain. It is covered in stylized, ornamental motifs—often stars, rosettes, arabesques, geometric designs, and plant foliage arranged in radiating symmetry.

The reputation for high-quality Moroccan ceramics originated in Fez, where this art form is in a class of its own. The pieces feature a characteristic, classical elegance in the lines, and a unique decoration that is either blue or composed of yellow or green motifs with bluish outlines. The great Fez mansions always display choice pieces of this earthenware, which is ornamental rather than utilitarian, and is considered to be a sign of wealth.

After Fez, the Atlantic city of Safi is undoubtedly the second most important center for ceramics production. Each potter has his own trademark style, which he keeps a closely guarded secret. Serghini, whose family have been master ceramists for seven generations, is the best-known craftsman in the region: he perpetuates the traditional forms and brightly colored (often predominantly blue and yellow) decorations, sometimes adding other, more unusual motifs such as fish, stars, and suns.

Ahmed Laghissi is less well known than the other craftsmen, but he has a distinctively personal style that incorporates unusual designs such as fine foliage and

arabesques. He uses deep, strong colors to express his individual approach. Each piece is unique and makes its own contribution to the revival of the art of earthenware. Keep an eye out for this artist, whose work is always an interesting blend of past and present.

In Essaouira, Aïcha Hemmou—a woman for once!—adds Berber motifs to simple monochrome crockery, which ranges from coffee services to goblets, spice jars, and more. Her designs are always delightfully fresh and innovative. Finally, Charlotte Barkowski heads the Akkal workshop in Marrakech, where she designs a range of refined crockery with simple colors and forms. She adds a contemporary touch to great classics like the tagine. The earthenware is unleaded, of course, in accordance with modern safety standards. This young designer is a favorite with restaurants and guest houses in Marrakech, which order custom-designed services in their own colors—as do certain prestigious Parisian interior design stores. She has managed to breathe new life into Moroccan design, and has made an important contribution to the current trend toward purity and simplicity.

ZELLIGES

Back to basics, with a key element in traditional Moroccan decor: *zelliges*, or wall tiles, which follow on naturally from the work of potters. These tiles are small pieces of glazed terracotta, arranged in regular geometric designs with infinite variations.

The craftsman's skills play a part in both the stages of the process: firstly, when he cuts pieces of ceramic into diamond-shapes, stars, squares, or when he decorates the tile with Kufic, or more flowing cursive script; and secondly, when he assembles the tiles. Once assembled, they are cemented together with mortar to produce decorative panels. Thousands of *zelliges* are used to decorate the floors, walls, fountains, and columns of mansions, palaces and religious buildings; their motifs recur in a variety of combinations. The result is always different, but always forms a breathtakingly beautiful mosaic. The craftsman must have a keen sense of color and composition, and a very sure hand: his technique and precision enable him to create veritable symphonies of color.

A perfectly balanced and harmonious mosaic is the fruit of long, hard labor. The inspiring beauty of these intricate panels makes it easy to overlook the hours of work that went into making them. *Zelliges* are an integral part of architectural ornamentation in Morocco. They are a decorative art in their own right, part of the traditional harmony between chiseled cedar and carved stone or plaster.

To mount panels of *zelliges,* the craftsmen coat the backs of the pieces with a layer of cement about one inch thick. Once this is dry, they can move the panel and attach it to a wall. The *maalems* (master craftsmen) use an engraver, ruler, and compasses for this highly detailed work (below). The decor consists of geometric motifs, repeated over and over to cover the entire surface. Of the many possible compositions, the sixteen-pointed star is a recurrent theme. Each form of *zellige* (that is, every small piece of enameled terracotta) corresponds to a color. They are placed together according to strict rules, creating colorful tableaux that then adorn the interiors of beautiful buildings, as here at the Royal Palace in Casablanca (right).

Zelliges are everywhere in Morocco; they are an integral part of everyday life. In Casablanca, this fountain at the little market on Avenue Mohammed-V keeps the market vegetables cool (above).

The decorative arts
reach their apotheosis
with the creation of
gebs, or carved plaster.
Every square inch
is intricately chiseled
with a delicacy that is
reminiscent of lacework.
The fresh plaster is
carved on the
spot by the craftsmen,
using chisels (right).
Certain motifs in
mosques or palaces
can be as
much as 5 inches
(12 cm) deep. The
muqarnas—reliefs of
honeycombed plaster—
are extraordinary
(above).

CARVED PLASTER AND STONE

Another fundamental element of Moroccan decor—which shows the *zelliges* to best advantage—is *gebs,* or carved plaster, an Arab-Andalusian legacy. This extremely delicate work is done by masters in the art form, and it traditionally covers the walls and ceilings of mansions and palaces, in accordance with the tendency in Islamic art to cover an entire surface.

First, the plaster is applied to the walls and ceiliings in fine coats. After smoothing it, the craftsman defines the specific areas on which he wants to stencil the different figures and calligraphies. Interlacing or words from the Koran may also be chiseled onto walls and ceilings. The stencil is held against the stucco, and dabbed using a little bag that is filled with black powder; the dark areas are then carefully chiseled out. Several motifs are superimposed one over another, and various depths are used, depending on the intricacy of the design and the fluidity of the pattern.

Certain designs incorporate the powdery whiteness of the plaster, others might be colored in blue or in red. In Marrakech, there is a preference for using color in *gebs*. This work requires great patience and precision on the part of the craftsman, who sometimes has to balance precariously several feet above the ground on makeshift scaffolding while producing delicate designs.

This art form reaches its zenith with *muqarnas*, which are deep reliefs of honeycombed plaster. Suspended from domes or on capitals, they look like carved bees' nests.

The *maalems* exercise their exceptional carving skills on stone too, with a similarly decorative style. Marble provides a smooth, shining surface for calligraphy and interlacing; light and shade interplay on the delicate friezes made by the craftsmen. Any error with the chisel on this hard, resistant material is impossible to correct.

The souks vibrate to the rhythm of daily life. The age-old rituals you see performed there will not be easily forgotten and whatever you take home will not only remind you of the extraordinary experience of a trip to Morocco, it will also make you want to return.

Carving lace-like designs requires similar skills whether working with stone or plaster, and the craftsmen continually try to outdo one another in their displays of dexterity. They use traditional motifs such as interlacing and palmettes, and mix these with purely geometric designs to produce a decor that covers the whole surface. The relief catches the light, adding density to the design and intensifying its delicacy (above left). The stone that comes from Salé is rather thick and porous, which makes the carving of it all the more admirable (above, center). Carved plaster is used to embellish not only arches and ceilings, but walls as well (above, right).

96

The terrace of the Villa
Oasis in Marrakech,
home of Yves Saint
Laurent and Pierre
Bergé, displays a
harmony of blues and
greens—the colors of
the famous haute-
couture designer, and of
the Majorelle Garden
(preceding pages).
The garden was planted
by Jacques Majorelle,
the villa's first owner.
Located in the Palmeraie
and surrounded by
luxuriant vegetation in
dazzling colors (facing
page), this house was
designed by Elie Mouyal
to compliment the
garden, with a
long canal linking the
main house to the
guesthouse. The plants
give this property its
color and spirit; indeed,
the goal was to make
the house an integral
part of the landscape
(right).

ORIENTAL REFINEMENT

Exploring Moroccan interiors is a voyage into the secret world of *riads* and *dars*. This is a world reserved for a select few: from the outside these homes reveal nothing of the refinement and lavish comfort within. Long windowless walls surround the homes, which are hidden along the narrow streets of the medinas. A heavy wooden door is the only exterior sign of a dwelling. If it were possible to see through these walls and wander about at leisure, you'd find that the reality is often even more extraordinary than you could have imagined. Some of these places are breathtakingly beautiful. We were fortunate enough to walk through some of the doorways and go beyond the staggered entrance that protects the residents from inquisitive eyes. Inside, we discovered the delightfully cool courtyards and gardens that seem to be worlds away from the bustling souks. We enjoyed the serenity of these self-contained worlds, which seem to exist within a bubble, or even in paradise. Indeed, the *riad* is a symbol of Eden. In Arabic, this word means "garden," and, by extension, refers to a house with a garden. The main courtyard of a *riad* leads to a lush garden filled with orange trees, fragrant flowers, and aromatic shrubs. One or more fountains provide the constant murmuring of running water. As for the *dar* (which means "home" in Arabic), it is designed according to the same concept, but is smaller and usually has only a small patio. The current popularity of these traditional homes has led to some confusion, and the term *riad* is often used improperly to describe what is in fact simply a *dar*.

Some of these old homes are like small palaces, which have been transformed into family homes that perpetuate the opulence of days gone by, while others have been converted into sleek, decidedly contemporary spaces. More recent homes outside of the medina, but still in the city, also cultivate the exuberant ambiance of exotic North Africa and the eternal image of the Orient. Finally, many of the homes with immense gardens, far from the medina, are reinterpreted versions of Muslim architecture; some of these are still built using the age-old *pisé* techniques. Others are simple, charming places to live.

Let this be an invitation to visit homes that we are rarely able to see. The owners were happy to tell their stories. For some, these houses were inheritances. For others, dream homes. All, however, share an enthusiasm for living *à l'Orientale*.

In keeping with Elie
Mouyal's "back to the
earth" philosophy, this
dining room has a rustic
air, with a *bejmat* floor.
On the table and
sideboard are retro
dishes designed in the
1920s. Light floods in
through the glass doors
(above).

ELIE MOUYAL
TRADITIONAL EARTHEN ARCHITECTURE

Elie Mouyal has succeeded in achieving a goal he set when still a young architect: to convince city people to use unbaked clay and earth as a building material. Long before Elie Mouyal became known for his style, unbaked earth was the most common material for homes in the Moroccan countryside. In just twenty years, he has revitalized this technique and convinced his wealthy urban clients to go along with his ideas. For his first projects, he managed to earn the trust of his patrons and clients, who allowed him to use their land to test his concepts. He soon discovered the limitations of the traditional methods and experimented to develop his own techniques. After working with several different types of unbaked earth and clay techniques he came up with "an improved and decidedly modern tradition."

Elie Mouyal returns to historical sources to explain his process and offers his own version of unbaked earth and clay construction through the ages: first was the *dob*, made of a molded earth brick and dried straw, set in the sun to dry. This ancient mud and straw technique originated in Egypt and Mesopotamia. *Pisé*, a more complex brick made in Morocco, came next. Enormous bricks, weighing one and a half tons each, were made using wooden forms. This technique was called "*adobe*;" once dry, the bricks were assembled. This is how the Kasbahs were built. Then, in the fifteenth century, an improved technique for making *pisé* appeared in Morocco. This involved using lime. "I arrived twenty years after United Nations' engineers had completed their project on Moroccan architecture. I returned to their work and improved on some of the areas of research that had been unsuccessful, and also drew on traditional methods."

In a sense, Elie Mouyal worked as a research student when he returned to his country after finishing his architectural degree in Paris. In France, he found a mentor for his work in a professor and theoretician who emphasized the link between all buildings and the environment and history. "He was extremely critical of the modern movement and of urbanism."

The natural and rough simplicity of brick is showcased in this room, with alternating walls of brick and tall windows. Light caresses the soft earth (top right). On the outside, the sun shines warmly on the bricks, bringing out their color. Elie Mouyal's architecture fits naturally into the environment. The multiple terraces around the house are also living areas. This design offers several possibilities for living outdoors or in the shelter of the house: under the pergola in the garden, or upstairs under the awning (facing page). The inside and outside blend together seamlessly. The house is open to the garden, which becomes an extension of the house itself, with a dining room set up outside (bottom right).

Elie Mouyal adopted this ideological foundation as his own and reinterpreted it in his own architectural language. Early on, the media showed an interest in his quest to promote earthen architecture and his own designs. "I am grateful for the earth techniques for producing my architecture. They also provide my work with a modern legitimacy: the form of a room is dictated by its function and by the material used. It is a way of remaining coherent with the material. You cannot contrive designs when working with the earth." For Elie Mouyal, nothing is more handsome than a handmade, kiln-fired brick—it's the real thing, authentic. He promotes the sensual, tactile, and visual attraction that is so characteristic of handmade materials.

He believes that even decoration is a logical result of this concept of building. There's no need to add anything more. "All the decorative elements of the house depend on the masonry. I aim to perpetuate the global tradition of masonry that was shared by Egypt, Iraq, Persia, Byzantium, the Roman Empire, and the Romanesque era in the Middle Ages."

Elie Mouyal broke away from the Moroccan tradition that calls for flat wooden ceilings and introduced the idea of arches, domes, and vaults in majestic spaces. He stresses that ceilings have always been the most important elements in a building. "In a church or a mosque, the eye is drawn to the ceiling. In the past, however, the floor had become more important. It was often covered with precious marble or marquetry wood flooring." Elie Mouyal has reversed this trend: his floors are neutral, "the better to place carpets on," and the eye is drawn irresistibly upward—"high enough to get a perspective"—and to contemplate the arches at leisure.

His idea, therefore, was to create an alternative to the monumental style of Moroccan architecture, which is an extension of the official architectural style adopted almost unanimously by the Moroccan upper classes. In opposition to "this more or less commercial academic style," he proposes a modern approach without, however, totally eliminating decorative elements, provided that the ornamentation is included in the architecture. He considers brick to be a perfect decorative material, providing brilliance, porosity, a matt effect, and reflectivity. Brick alone is enough to create a decor.

This building in the heart of the Palmeraie is another illustration of Elie Mouyal's grandiose vision. With this house, the architect was able to indulge his preference for vast proportions, as can be seen in the imposing facade, complete with arches (top left). It also illustrates his belief that interior decoration is a natural result of the structure. This opening in the kitchen (bottom left) has exposed brickwork, which creates a pleasing, decorative effect. This living room (right) incorporates traditional Moroccan elements. The wall seat rests on a brick base. *Tadelakt* covers the walls. The *moucharabieh* filter the light and preserve the room's intimacy. The bricks in the European-style living room rise up toward the ceiling in pillars and majestic vaults (far right, top). The bathroom has a dome-shaped ceiling (far right, bottom).

Elie Mouyal's clients are passionate about his style. A Parisian gallery owner is the proprietor of one of Mouyal's first projects in the Marrakech Palmeraie area. She trusted him completely, and stood by his side from his promising early years through to his spectacular present-day success. Her story started when she attended a party in the Palmeraie, given by a friend who was celebrating the recent purchase of a piece of land; during the festivities, she discovered a small earthen house that was being used as temporary lodgings while the construction work was underway. "A jewel," she says, and she instantly fell in love. "I wanted a house built of earth. So when I bought my land, I searched everywhere for this architect. Nobody else would do." They met and talked for three straight hours. Elie Mouyal scribbled ideas during the entire meeting "and for better or for worse, he didn't want to change anything, not a single line!"

When you walk onto the property, you're greeted by clusters of flowers, followed by a large, tree-filled garden. There's no sign of the house at first; then, finally, it appears in a halo of shrubs in bloom. The first impression therefore comes from the garden, the key element of the property, around which the house was designed. Indeed, everything began with the hundred-year-old olive trees, which neither the architect nor the owner would have dreamed of removing. These noble trees, with trunks twisted by age, form a central axis that is echoed by the house. They frame a small canal, aligned with the main entrance. The guesthouse faces the entrance at the opposite end of the canal. The greenery and the water are intimately linked in this harmonious fusion. Even the pool is unusual: disproportionately large, it creates an immense pool of water, as if nature herself had created this enchanting element in the middle of the garden. This symmetrical pool is as long as the house. Elie Mouyal did not only create a house; he designed the landscape and integrated it into his overall concept. The original rocky desert has been transformed into an oasis of vegetation. A carpet of bright green grass stretches beyond the pool to the olive trees. The owner of the house loves plants, and would happily let the climbing plants overgrow her home if she didn't so admire Elie Mouyal's work.

Elie Mouyal loves generous volumes, as can be seen in the design for this imposing pavilion alongside the swimming pool. This design is an Elie Mouyal trademark: he likes to position buildings in the axis of a canal, or integrate a pool with the decor of a garden and home (facing page). This villa, constructed for a Moroccan general, has traditional elements that have been somewhat reinterpreted: the windows with half-closed interior shutters were inspired by the *moucharabiehs*. They filter through a soft light and let those inside see without being seen. Elie Mouyal uses wood and bricks, which frame each window. This Moroccan living room is a model of intimacy (top right). The brick masonry facade is an important element of the decor. Used for the lintel of one of the buildings, it creates a frieze-like motif (bottom right).

Sheltered by the thick brick walls, the interior remains cool and fresh; the small windows prevent the heat from entering the house, while letting in a small amount of light. Indeed, it is often dark inside, a characteristic feature of all of Elie Mouyal's houses. As soon as you step over the threshold you can see the cross-shaped floor plan, worthy of a Byzantine basilica. To the right is the dining and living room; to the left, the bedrooms; and straight on, a living room/library. The rooms are arranged around a central courtyard topped by a dome. Domes are a common motif in the architect's visual vocabulary, and appear like a leitmotif throughout most of his designs. For a Moroccan general, he designed a house with a dome that functioned as a well of light that illuminates the entire kitchen. Elie Mouyal employed a judicious use of windows to let natural light into the house in varying degrees. He also designed an exterior kitchen for the main house, sheltered under an overhanging projecting roof, yet totally open. He also used this technique in another country home, known as "the farm" as it sits in the middle of the countryside. The light enters straight into the room. The bathroom in the farm receives an abundant amount of light; it floods through a dome placed over the bathtub. Elie Mouyal once again used this same concept for an elegant modern villa in the heart of the Palmeraie, but in this case the dome is not transparent; the sun comes through side windows placed under arches surrounding the bathtub. A splendid succession of light-colored brick vaults in the living room reflects the luminosity of the room.

The owners are all in agreement: they love the feeling of living under these domes and in such large spaces. Indeed, they are always willing to display their homes and talk about how wonderful they are to live in. The mathematical and rational architect has his own explanation for this phenomenon: "They live within an intangible source of harmony without understanding where it comes from. In fact, it is entirely due to the geometry, the interplay of masses, the thickness of the walls, and the different shapes of the roofs."

Plants are essential components in this home, which belongs to a Parisian gallery owner. The house was designed to be in harmony with the landscape (facing page, top left). The palette of earthen architecture creates an ideal setting to showcase artwork and contemporary furniture. The tables and chairs in the dining room were designed by a Moroccan cabinetmaker (facing page, top right). The living room boasts a painting by Hélène Lothe (who exhibits at L'Éclat de Verre gallery). It reflects the colors of the walls (facing page, bottom). The guesthouse at the end of the canal sits peacefully in the midst of the garden. The bathroom, lined with *tadelakt,* leads to a bathtub surrounded by *zelliges,* placed under a domed roof (left).

This arched entrance is
a perfect illustration of
the voluptuous
dimensions that
Tunisian-born Charles
Boccara loves to
create in large homes.
The room sits beneath
an immense dome
(right) that rises in a
continuous line from the
walls. The glass tiles set
into the dome allows it
to function as a "light
well" (facing page, top).
The architect selected
1930s-style furniture—
his favorite period—for
the intimate living room
(left). The bathroom
repeats the motif of the
archaic Maghrebi home,
with a projecting arch,
a niche under an
arcade, and brick walls.
The walls are covered
with *tadelakt*, as
they would be in the
traditional *hammams* of
Marrakech. The architect
lavished particular
attention on this
room (facing page,
bottom).

CHARLES BOCCARA
AND THE ARCHAIC MAGHREBI HOUSE

Charles Boccara looks like an opera star; he has the corpulence and voice of a tenor. Along with Chafiq Kabbaj, Elie Mouyal, Jacqueline Foissac, and Karim el-Achak, he is one of the leading Moroccan architects to have fully developed his personal style. He has spent the last twenty years working on some of the largest construction projects in Morocco (including the recently built Opera in Marrakech). He approaches architecture like a composer creating a musical score. "Basically, an architect should not invent, but should compose." Charles Boccara doesn't invent anything, and bases his designs on tradition, which he feels is the source for everything. Tradition determines the floor plans. Once again, he draws a parallel with music: "I don't have to worry about designing a floor plan, so I am completely free to imagine an *andante* entrance for a *riad*, with an *allegro* patio and a *furioso* corridor. All I have to do is create a third and fourth dimension."

Charles Boccara's only reference is the archaic house of the Maghreb. His own home in the Palmeraie is a perfect illustration of this concept. His goal is to return a structure to this original condition. "This was the world's first house design, dating from a time when people marked out their property with a wall and a door to conceal the paradise behind. From the entrance, you move from the profane to the sacred, from the street to the courtyard. The air is scented with oranges, waters murmurs quietly, and no street noises penetrate inside." He believes that this layout, a source of natural well-being, was the quintessential bioclimatic home, comfortable in every season. "In summer, the courtyard fountain provides cool air for the lower levels, while in the winter, families live in the upper rooms." As a strong supporter of tradition, he promotes and renovates earthen structures. His villa is built of *pisé* and terra-cotta bricks. The traditional decorative elements consist of *tataoui* (thin strips of painted laurel arranged in specific patterns) for the ceiling and *tadelakt* for the walls.

Charles Boccara was born in Tunisia and is intimately familiar with the vocabulary of hot climates and homes with interior shutters and pools. His home is imbued with this Mediterranean and Maghrebi ambience (as are most of his designs). His architectural studies in Paris reinforced his attachment to tradition, while he learned to work with classical concepts such as symmetry, axes, and so on. Influenced by Greek and Roman art, he wanted to pursue a single concept: "To use this classical vocabulary in the noble sense of the term." The facade of his home is defined by a Greek-style pediment with two thick columns capped with capitals in the form of stylized human figures. It recalls a Dedalian style, with rigid, symmetrical, and almost geometric faces. The immense columns look like kouros figures, and suggest the monumental proportions of his interiors.

The architect is fond of domed ceilings that rise in a continuous line from the walls, arches, galleries, and barrel vaults—like the dome that rises high above the living room, bringing light into the room. All these elements have become inseparable features of the Boccara style. "I have been telling the same story for nearly thirty years: I want a room to shine because of the quality of the space, the height of the rooms, and their size, not because of the materials used, because I favor the simplicity of natural, earth, and clay bricks." He believes that a house is just a succession of modules; each one functions independently and is self-sufficient, yet remains open to the others. This was the guiding principle for the design of his own home. "My windows and extensions are designed to suggest ideas for moving through the interior of the edifice." Hence his use of passageways and galleries running the length of the rooms, which are often lined with white canvas curtains. You move from one house, the entrance; to another, the dining room; and then to yet another, the bedrooms or utility rooms. "It's a mosaic of constructions. You know, traditional homes were something like small villages by themselves."

Charles Boccara learned his trade working for wealthy Moroccan and French clients. He still looks back nostalgically on these large homes. He wants to perpetuate this "style of living within luxurious dimensions." And, as someone who appreciates good food, he makes constant comparisons with cooking, adding a number of ingredients that are essential to the overall effect of the furnishings, the *moucharabiehs*, silk, curtains, and pillows. He has a soft spot for the 1930s and its characteristic dark wood furniture, which he places in prominent spots. His home therefore offers space and the freedom to enjoy time. He likes to recall the wise Muslim definition of the three phases of life: learning, production, and contemplation. "We planted olive trees and we sit down to watch them grow. I have learned a great deal about using time in Morocco. Each activity must be accomplished with respect." Charles Boccara experiences each phase of his projects with intensity and passion: "I love my work and Marrakech!" he says. "My enthusiasm has not been dulled and I am still as fresh as ever."

Viewed from the outside, this house clearly demonstrates the classical principles underpinning Charles Boccara's design. The facade looks almost like a Greek temple, with a pediment supported by two columns and capitals crowned with stylized human figures. The impressive proportions prefigure the immense spaces that lie within. For the architect, "the quality of the space, the height of the rooms, and their size" is of primary importance (left). The placement of the home, which has been constructed in a vast garden in the heart of the Palmeraie, best exemplifies his preference for large spaces. Charles Boccara's architecture is most amply expressed when placed in a landscape equal to the scope of the building, as here, with palm trees rising like columns to the sky (facing page).

This small room is certainly the most Oriental-inspired space in the house, an effect obtained through the rich fabrics and range of bright, warm colors. The portrait of an Egyptian ancestor on the table reinforces this sense of identity (above).

IN MARRAKECH,
CLEAN LINES BY JACQUELINE FOISSAC

The architect and designer Jacqueline Foissac is one of the leading proponents of rehabilitating the architectural heritage of Marrakech, and it was only natural that she add her own unique touch of elegance to Dar Hathor. This respected designer is asked to work on all the "chic" projects, such as transforming old homes in the medina, or creating new ones in the surrounding areas. Virtually every European celebrity in Morocco—from actor to intellectual, artist, haute-couture designer, politician, and more—has contacted her to produce a home with her stamp on it. But Jacqueline Foissac has a personal code of ethics: she works only for friends or people she feels will become so in a short time. "I can only work with people I know well, in a sort of osmosis." Yehia Abdelnour, the Egyptian owner of Dar Hathor, is proof of this. Once the project was finished, the two became partners, and are now inseparable in their work. Without this relationship of trust, even abandonment, her talent cannot be fully expressed. His clients often give her a free rein, trusting implicitly in her judgement—even to the point of letting her choose the house to purchase for them. This trust is well rewarded: Jacqueline Foissac has unfailing taste and a talent for adding distinction to spaces, even in the least promising houses.

Initially, Dar Hathor was a newly constructed, poorly proportioned building, but it did have one asset: situated some ten miles from Marrakech in the middle of the countryside, it had a magnificent view of the Atlas Mountains and the *jahilat*, the Moroccan desert. Yehia Abdelnour, head of a company in France, had just bought the property. He had been captivated by the irresistible charm of the location, but he did not know how to proceed with the necessary renovation work. Jacqueline Foissac used her magical touch to transform a plain house into an attractive home. Each of her interventions revealed a grace that had been concealed and, in some places, nonexistent. Working closely with the owner, she decided to keep only the frame and to remodel the awkward proportions by dividing up the volumes. "I respect tradition, while modernizing it.

This passage (facing page), with a series of doorways cut in lancet-arched shapes, is a characteristic expression of Jacqueline Foissac's spare style. Sobriety in design is her trademark: the colors cover a natural palette ranging from gray to beige. Light underscores the gentle atmosphere. This room on the upper floor (bottom right) has the same range of colors, with a subtle reference to the nationality of the owner—a frieze of Egyptian hieroglyphs. Other details on the outside, such as a painted terra-cotta plate inlaid into the wall, or a wrought-iron gate with a frieze running above it (top right, center and right), demonstrate that her quest for purity does not necessarily exclude decorative elements. As for the small pavilion next to the pool (top right, left), it sparkles brilliantly white under the clear sky.

I eliminate a lot of elements. Initially, clients asked me to incorporate every possible traditional decorative device: copper, silver, *gebs*, *zelliges*, *tadelakt*. Finally, they end up clearing all this away on their own. For example, no one needs to have twenty-five objects, three is enough." Indeed, Yehia Abdelnour set the tone with his personal preference: "I want white, empty rooms." Completing his thought, Jacqueline Foissac adds: "I always give priority to the atmosphere; the rooms are peaceful and vibrant."

By remodeling the volumes, Jacqueline Foissac brought in space and light, one of the essential components of her serene style of architecture. "I love luminous houses." Naturally, then, the work started with the garden, a source of light, as a way of integrating the house into the landscape and using its major attraction, the surrounding decor. Yehia Abdelnour also loves gardens; he planted a long row of fragrant trees and a multitude of white roses. He created shady paths and viewpoints, dug a pool flanked by the green of a clipped box hedge and a lawn, and designed a white pavilion at the end of the pool, in front of which stands an arbor. This garden looks like an oasis surrounded by the silence of the desert, stretching in the distance just outside the door. This setting goes a long way to explaining why Jacqueline Foissac moved to the middle of the Palmeraie long before it became fashionable. In 1968, Jacqueline Foissac constructed a *pisé* house there, at a time when no one had even conceived of going beyond the wall of the medina. "At that time, everything had to be invented. Since then, a certain expertise has developed and new craftsmen have appeared." In the process, she met the young architect Elie Mouyal. The two worked together for a time exploring the techniques of *pisé* construction.

Foissac has been at work constantly since the 1980s, and has seen the popularity of Marrakech soar. She watched as the rural character of the Palmeraie was gradually subsumed under the vast wave of new construction projects. During the 1990s, remaining true to her avant-garde spirit, she became

The spacious proportions of this former *riad*, situated in the heart of the Marrakech medina, are unique. *Riads* are extremely popular nowadays and are getting hard to find— this one, with such a large building and garden, was a rare find. The austere architecture sets the tone for this house, now owned by the painter. The flowerbeds are filled with fragrant plants. Jacqueline Foissac designed a pond to add the traditional water element (right). The furniture, made of white marble, falls within the palette of neutral tones (top left). The towering doors are closed by bronze bars (bottom left). Inside, the ivory-colored chairs in the dining room repeat the color harmony. Monumental works by the painter cover the walls (far right).

This *riad* is governed by two guiding principles: white throughout the house and *bejmat* on the floor. The furniture in the living room comes from Syria, and is made of wood inlaid with mother-of-pearl. Draped fabric hangs over doorways between the rooms; this is one of the painter's favorite themes (facing page). Mint tea can be savored among friends in the living room (far left, top). The artist's office is also a library, with built-in shelves (far left, bottom). A series of three rooms, one leading to another, occupies the side of the house opposite the living room. The guestroom is simple; the only furniture is a Syrian chair, similar to those in the living room, and a magnificent chest (top right). The guest bathroom is covered with *tadelakt* and drenched in sunlight (bottom right).

the leading proponent of a new movement: a return to the medina. "Life is there, and I like that life, with the noises, voices, fragrances. I need it. It has a special charm."

She has, therefore, recently renovated a large *riad* in the medina. It was constructed in the early nineteenth century, probably at the same time as the Glaoui Palace, as it belonged to the family of a *caid* who was close to them. The client, a painter, placed the future of his home in Jacqueline Foissac's hands, asking her to find him a place that would be conducive to his work. She did not disappoint him, as she unearthed an absolute treasure: a *riad* with an unusually huge room facing north and running along an entire side. It is a dream location for an artist's studio, and the perfect place to spend the winter months.

The immense proportions of this *riad* is what strikes visitors first on entering the large inner courtyard. The garden is laid out in the traditional way, with four flowerbeds containing only palm trees, lemon trees, fées des neiges, and a white rose, plus an extraordinary cypress that rises skyward. Jacqueline Foissac designed a garden pool in the center, which also serves as a swimming pool. In the center is a large basin and fountain from Fez that seems to float above the water. The initial spaces were very beautiful, and they remain intact, but a few renovations were required. This *riad* originally had magnificent cedar ceilings that were reused with a few modern touches. In some cases, the cedar was sanded to remove the nine layers of paint that had been layered on over the centuries; in others, white lead was applied lightly.

This highly regarded professional does not have an architectural degree, but this has not stopped her from leaving her unique mark on Marrakech in the form of a certain *art de vivre*. Jacqueline feels a change in the air, and nowadays she works in Essaouira as well. "Marrakech will become a residential city, and everyone will have a beach house on the coast. The beauty of this country lies in its coastline, the Atlantic Ocean, and the deserted beaches."

The Majorelle Garden is a small piece of paradise in the heart of Marrakech. Pierre Bergé and Yves Saint Laurent revived the garden with the help of landscape artist Madison Cox. It provides unceasing pleasure to all those who wander along its pathways. An explosion of colors reigns here, between the famous blue indigo for which the painter is known, to the luxuriant green vegetation and blue water. Blue and green are closely linked here (left). Jacques Majorelle's studio at the end of the garden has been transformed into an Islamic Art Museum (facing page). A small kiosque has also been built in the private part of the garden (far right). This living area seems to float among the water lilies in the basin. The kiosque is highly appreciated for the shade it offers and is one of the most recent additions to the garden.

IN MARRAKECH, A HOME FOR ESTHETES

When Yves Saint Laurent and Pierre Bergé bought Jacques Majorelle's house in 1980, they inevitably linked their names to that of the painter, a famous member of the School of Nancy. They called it Villa Oasis, a reference to the title of a novel by Eugène Dabit. The house is also inseparable from the famous Majorelle Garden, created in the 1920s. The Villa Oasis may be private property, but the garden has been open to the public since 1956, and Yves Saint Laurent and Pierre Bergé continued to respect the former owner's wishes. This property thus unites the colors of both artists and brings together two different worlds.

Walking through this extraordinary garden is to plunge into deep blue and luxuriant green. Saint Laurent and Bergé acquired the garden with the intention of restoring it. They therefore hired the American landscape artist Madison Cox to supervise the overall project, using the existing layout of four intersecting pathways lined with a diverse variety of plants. The Moroccan botanist Abderrazak Ben Chaabane was given responsibility for carrying out much of the project; his task was to assess and entirely redesign the original plantings.

The overall result is stunning: the succulents are so sculptural that you could almost believe you were in the midst of an art installation. As you walk through this enclosed space, you're struck by the strong visual impact: the omnipresent agaves and bamboo plants reinforce the supremacy of the green, with blue providing an intense contrast. The cactus stand out against the blue walls of Jacques Majorelle's studio, which has been transformed into an Islamic Art Museum.

The paths lead through different areas, some dominated by blue, others by green. Glazed terra-cotta tiles on the ground blend the two colors. A warm, luminous space leads to a cool shady area. The desert plants grow skyward from the pebbly ground, hot under the brilliant sun. Farther along, a bridge stretches over a pond, under a curtain of light green liana dotted with pink flowers that cascades down into the water lilies. White jasmine flowers sparkle on the edge of a small wall bathed in blue and lined with ocher.

Architect Bill Willis designed this dining room and revamped the interior volumes of Jacques Majorelle's original house. Wood has been used everywhere in the interior decoration, which features paneling and painted ceilings (facing page). The wood is carved in places, which creates a lovely, muted ambience. One of the living rooms has a fireplace in a niche, while the wooden-paneled library has several lavishly decorated arches, with alcoves beneath (far left, top and bottom). The magnificent busts by Pradier are almost hidden under a profusion of amazonite and coral necklaces—a style that recalls the ethnic necklaces worn by models showcasing some of Yves Saint Laurent's fashions (top right). Detail of a palmette motif painted by Majorelle on a piece of original furniture (bottom right).

Jacques Majorelle was drawn irresistibly to the light and warm colors of the south. He designed his garden to be like an intensely colorful painting. After traveling through Spain, Italy, and Egypt, where he lived for four years, Majorelle was invited to Morocco by the French general, Louis Lyautey, in 1917. He fell in love with this country, and lived here permanently until his death in 1962. The small museum has a few of the works that he painted as he explored the Kasbahs in the Atlas Mountains. When Saint Laurent and Bergé purchased the property, their goal was first and foremost to conserve the garden. They wondered what to do with the villa for the better part of a year. By the 1930s, the painter was no longer living in the house and had given it to his wife. He then lived in various small houses around the garden, one by one, ending up in a house behind the studio. The villa had not been touched since it was built in 1922, and was in a terrible condition. For Bergé, "It had some element of modernity to it; we wanted to create rooms and continue the approach, colors, and original intent of Jacques Majorelle." The famous fashion duo hired the architect Bill Willis for the renovation and transformation work, and hired decorator Jacques Grange to select the furnishings.

The current appearance of the Villa Oasis is the work of the American architect who, without enlarging it, redefined the volumes. It still bears the influence of the Art Nouveau style, a movement Majorelle helped to pioneer. Bergé explains: "He treated Morocco in an admirable way, by reworking the Moroccan elements around him. But he was careful not to overdo the Moroccan spirit. There are, for example, no *gebs*." The Oriental influence is therefore present, but reinterpreted.

Bill Willis pursued this same philosophy. The house is laid out around a courtyard-style entrance with a central pool and, opposite the door, a living room installed in a raised alcove. Plunged into the dusky light, the visitor needs a few moments to adjust after passing through the sun-drenched garden. It's a simple passageway, but it sets the tone of the atmosphere and style within. Bill Willis also created a bookcase carved entirely from wood and placed it in a room that did not have any specific purpose when Majorelle lived there. It is very dark, yet illuminated throughout the day by the subdued lighting

from a lamp heavy with pendants and lanterns suspended under the wooden arches. Wall seats have been placed in these archways; above them on the walls are portraits of richly dressed sultans. The woodwork creates a muted decor featuring a garnet-red color with dark blue highlights, accentuated by the darkness. Many Oriental-style paintings hang on the walls. Several layers of thick carpets cover the floor. This peaceful space, created entirely by Bill Willis, is a lovely illustration of Orientalism in design.

For Yves Saint Laurent, Marrakech is synonymous with relaxation. The haute-couture designer was born and grew up in Oran (Algeria). When he is not in Marrakech, he's often in his house in Tangier, where he enjoys another facet of Morocco.

IN RABAT,
CHAFIQ KABBAJ'S ORIENTAL HOME

Chafiq Kabbaj belongs to the brilliant generation of Moroccan architects who cultivate their own vision of the Moroccan identity. His decision to work in Rabat was a deliberate return to his origins and his home town—although he actually spent very little time there during his childhood. His father was a diplomat, and Chafiq Kabbaj grew up in Rome, Vienna, Dakar, and Paris, where he studied architecture at the École des Beaux Arts.

He had lived in dozens of different places, but to his great regret, never in a Moroccan home, with the exception of the times during a few vacations when he visited his grandmother in Rabat. He finally returned to Morocco, with a diploma in hand and an irresistible desire to own a Moroccan house. Since he began his career, he had also wanted a client to ask him to do the design for this type of project: "A contemporary home, not a pastiche." In the end, he decided to create this home for himself. He spent many long years looking for the perfect house: "I didn't want to build a new house, and I wanted to live in the medina."

Chafiq Kabbaj finally found his dream home in a quiet street within the walls of the medina. It is both close to the busy life of the souks and just steps from the peaceful Oudaias Kasbah, the charming village-like neighborhood that lies along the waterfront. When he first visited the property, there was a shop on the ground floor and apartments on the upper levels. Yet he knew immediately that it was exactly the house he was looking for. "It wasn't very big and belonged to a family of modest means; there were therefore no embellishments, no *zelliges*...." The architect could see the great potential of this house.

He decided to keep the original decorative and architectural elements in order to underscore the authentic charm of the original house, which dated from the nineteenth century. When you enter the covered courtyard, you can't help but admire the magnificent and finely sculpted arches, made of Salé stone, which are brilliantly showcased by a

Faced with a choice between tradition or modernity, Architect Chafiq Kabbaj opted to use the initial volumes of the house. He created a terrace on the rooftop, a traditional Morocco element (facing page, top left), while on the ground floor, he covered the patio to make a huge entrance space. A wrought ironwork balcony, which he bought in Paris, has been converted into a console table (facing page, bottom). The mirrors in the sitting areas under the arches (made of Salé stone) on the ground floor create multiple effects of perspective. For the floor, Chafiq Kabbaj selected highly polished black granite stones, with intersecting lines of shiny stainless steel, repeating the mirrored motif (left). This is a sophisticated world, with contemporary, Oriental-style furniture (facing page, top right).

Chafiq Kabbaj's room is modeled after the design of a Marrakechi *hammam*. The *tadelakt* on the walls runs in horizontal stripes. This highly original room represents the achievement of one of the architect's dreams: for years he has wanted to have a bedroom reflecting the colors of Marrakech. It looks surprising in Rabat and is more reminiscent of the ambience of southern Morocco (facing page). The two large pivoting doors, situated behind the bed's headboard, separate the bedroom from the bathroom (far left, bottom). The floor is covered with a braided mat made specially for the room and trimmed with braid for a perfect fit (far left, top). The decorated dish in the small sitting area on the terrace is used for offerings at weddings. The cushions repeat the *zellige* pattern (right).

minimalist play of light that was designed with an almost surgical precision. Tiny metal lamps were mounted on rails and carefully oriented to best illuminate the arches. "I wanted to use things from my era to try to be more contemporary, to move forward. I did not want to use lanterns; pastiche and folklore were out of the question."

Chafiq Kabbaj spends most of his time living and working in this space. He greets his guests in the small rooms under the arches surrounding the patio. The furniture is a combination of styles from the 1930s and contemporary pieces, the only two styles, in his view, that are perfect for an Oriental interior. An extremely contemporary Knoll daybed with a curving frame recalls the forms of traditional decoration. This refined and eclectic decor is often used as the backdrop for a number of official dinners, as the architect is a close friend of the king's. Ministers appreciate the intimacy and the luxurious setting, which is harder to find in the restaurants of Rabat. For informal events and other impromptu gatherings, the black granite floor becomes a perfect dance floor; guests can then retire to the smaller room upstairs, which is lined with comfortable wall seats. Finally, at night, the rooftop, with its open-air living room, is an ideal place to enjoy dessert and to relax.

With a multitude of living areas, Chafiq Kabbaj's house is first and foremost an immense area for social gatherings. To his great regret, he cannot accommodate his friends overnight, but he has been restoring a pied-à-terre in the Oudaias Kasbah to serve as a guesthouse. Chafiq Kabbaj has achieved his goal of creating a Moroccan house that brings together tradition and modernity. His Arabic friends, regardless of which country they come from, all find something familiar here, as his aim was also to go beyond Morocco. "I designed this house as I felt it should be, imbued with the Moroccan spirit. Indeed, it is more an Oriental house than a purely Moroccan house. It is the Orient that interests me. This house is both authentic and modern."

The objects that fill this Tangier apartment all have a unique presence. Each one contributes to the dream world of the Orient. Shells are dotted around the furniture in the form of mother-of-pearl (far left, top). Seeming to reign here as master of the apartment, the bust of an Arab sheik greets visitors to the living room (top left). Régis Milcent's dark red room seems inhabited by the presence of several women (bottom left): in the black-and-white portrait from the 1950s, his mother looks like a movie star. There is a portrait of his aunt, too, who also has an aura of glamor about her. Other women from his family are presented in medallions; they grace the room with gentle smiles. The entrance area (right), which has striped fabric on the walls and striped drapes hanging in the doorway, sets the tone for the visit.

MOROCCAN NIGHTS IN TANGIER

It's best to visit Régis Milcent's apartment in Tangier at night, when the muted light, the principal element of the decor, works its magic to create the intimate atmosphere. The glass doors in the main room—the living room—lead to a balcony overlooking the famous tearoom, Porte. Sounds filter up from the street below. The neon lights flash sporadically. This is Régis Milcent's world. He wanted to have an apartment in the city designed for the night; indeed, it wouldn't even occur to visitors to come during the day. This screenwriter abandoned his career to live in Tangier. He started working as a decorator, bringing along with him the thousand and one objects that fill up this cozy apartment.

The entrance is somewhat dark and introduces the half-light, half-dark ambience that reigns here. The eye is immediately drawn to the lights in the living room, visible beyond the entrance. The windows are filled with vases, books, and antiques, providing a glimpse into the collector's personality. You first have to cross a round room, circumnavigating the table in the middle, to reach the luxurious living room. Régis Milcent sometimes places an immense, brightly colored bouquet in the center of this table. The floral composition acts as a powerful magnet, inevitably drawing your attention. With no flowers on the table, the eye is drawn to the walls covered with red- and green-striped Empire fabric and lined with framed paintings and photographs. This striped fabric reappears in several places, creating a specifically Oriental tone, skillfully orchestrated throughout the various rooms of the apartment. It reveals a nostalgia for a certain era in Morocco, where Régis Milcent was born and spent the first four years of his life. At the time, his father occupied the prestigious position of prefect, or chief administrative officer of the region. His framed memories, consisting of landscapes and portraits, present a fresco of the colonial period. One photograph portrays his great-great grandfather posing in an Algerian naval uniform. A watercolor on another wall reveals his artistic talents: he dabbles in painting. Régis Milcent is particularly fond of a view of a coastal region bearing a striking resemblance to Tangier; he likes to believe that it is really a depiction of the city he has chosen as his home. He also likes to display work by certain local figures, such as Marguerite McBey, by exhibiting one of her nudes. He says that she started to paint after the death of her husband, himself a painter. The eye is constantly drawn to one framed work or another, each with a story to tell.

Finally, you reach the heart of the apartment, the living room, which comes to life each evening under the illumination of standing lamps, candleholders, chandeliers, wall lights, and fake candles. Lighting here is a true art, certainly a legacy from Régis Milcent's moviemaking past. The immense living room is the main gathering place in this apartment and consists of two sections. The first is a smaller area arranged around a chimney facing the balcony, with an elegant Syrian overmantel purchased at the local Socco market, one of Régis Milcent's favorite places to wander. This is where he hosts his guests for pre-dinner drinks. The second area is a long room with a beautiful wall seat made of Cuban mahogany and covered in crimson red velvet. The room is bathed in a number of different lights; this creates the ambiance of a nineteenth-century opera box, which permeates the entire decor. A surprising gallery of miniature portraits of ancestors sporting blond curls and angelic smiles, placed in tiny Venetian frames made of multicolored pastel shells, is exhibited on a small Moroccan table.

Everything about the decor makes you feels as if you've gone back in time. The nineteenth-century fashion for all things Oriental can be seen in Régis Milcent's choice of furniture: low tables with mother-of-pearl inlays and a multitude of small, finely crafted metal objects. A beautiful bust stands on a chest of drawers; it has been attributed to Friedrich Goldscheider, a highly popular artist from the 1850s through the 1890s. It has a strong seductive power: the figure, with a proud and haughty bearing, piercing expression, velvety black skin, and fine features, seems to rule over this territory as his own. Finally, small bowls filled with Asilah coral, which Régis Milcent collects (along with giltwood pieces), are placed here and there around the room.

SIDI OSNI,
A CONTEMPORARY PALACE

E veryone in the Tangier Kasbah knows about Sidi Osni, as this is the name of the small marabout situated at the entrance. It is a place of worship and legend, and also remains strongly linked to the history of the medina. Indeed, this house once belonged to Barbara Hutton, the American heiress whose extravagant and unhappy life was acted out in the glare of publicity. In the 1940s and 1950s, this American heiress, dubbed the "million-dollar baby" and famous for her elaborate parties, became infatuated with Tangier and Sidi Osni, where she proceeded to create a living legend for herself. She used to receive her guests dressed as the glamorous Dutch spy Mata Hari; she would be seated at a throne, radiating the type of cool seductive powers for which the Swedish-born American actress, Greta Garbo, became famous.

The current owner has only half of the former property, which was once the size of a palace. The current style of Sidi Osni—decidedly contemporary and minimalist—has nothing in common with the one chosen by the fantastic goddess-figure who preceded this modern, hospitable man. The interior is laid out according to a succession of levels. As you visit it, you gradually move upward toward the top floors, where the terrace rooftops overlook the Strait of Gibraltar and a surprisingly quiet medina.

The entranceway sets the tone, or rather the tones, of a calm minimalism that exists throughout the house. There are no *zelliges* here, no stucco embellishments, no arabesque ironwork, and no carved ceilings. Nothing disturbs the rigorous order of the decor: everything is in tones of black or white, expressed through pure geometric lines that have nothing to do with the Moorish style that you might have expected to see here. This overall effect is the work of the decorator Jean-Jacques Demignot, who used to own the house. He had already totally redesigned the interior, and had eliminated every element of the traditional decorative decor created by Barbara Hutton.

Minimalism is the guiding principle for this small palace in Tangier. It offers a contemporary version of the geometry that underlies much of traditional Moroccan decor. Here, the colors have been simplified and reduced to just two: black and white, which extend from the patio entrance to the rooms on all the upper floors. The wooden balustrades and trellises repeat a stylized version of the word "Allah" in a square pattern (facing page). The purity of the lines on the terrace extends to the whiteness and round shape of the nearby mosque. The three domes at the top, each with a crescent and a star, soar skyward. A succulent, the color of which echoes the green of the mosque behind it, was set here on the ground to accentuate the link between the two (left). This attention to detail permeates the entire house.

A few steps lead up to the lavish double entrance door, which is completely gilded, like a piece of Chinese lacquerware. The Oriental style of Sidi Osni suddenly takes on nuances of Asia. This elegant note is repeated in other pieces of furniture, setting off the two-tone color scheme. The Asian-style entrance leads straight to the covered courtyard. The checkerboard-patterned floor, star-studded central fountain, and the chairs repeat the strict black-and-white decor. You could easily imagine this to be the contemporary interior of a triplex apartment in some major Western European capital, if the overall structure and archways did not immediately pull you back into the Islamic world.

A simple decorative element is repeated throughout the house like a leitmotif, confirming that this is, indeed, a traditional *dar*: the backs of all the chairs, arranged symmetrically at the base of each arch, have the same geometric motif, a stylized version of the word "Allah." This same pattern is repeated on the bedspread in the terrace room, the staircase banister, the *moucharabieh*-style wooden screens on the bedroom doors, and the balustrades around the courtyard—all emphasizing the strong identity of the house. This signature seems to be an obvious choice given the geographic location of Sidi Osni. As you climb the staircase to reach the upper floor, you are struck by a singular sight: as you move higher, the enormous dome of a mosque appears in the windows of the living room. This blindingly white and perfectly round dome fills up the entire view, and it is so in keeping with the spirit and colors of this home that it looks as if it were placed there as a modern sculpture.

The owner designed a room he calls his "studio" on this floor. This is where he stays when he is alone, preferring this to the other rooms. A living room and bedroom occupy the same rectangular space, which is separated widthwise by an immense gilded screen, like the one at the main entrance. This Art Deco piece is the main decorative element in the room. A white bed in the bedroom, concealed behind the screen, is flanked by gilded lamps on the bedside table.

The wood panels with openwork designs in the dining room are modern, reinterpreted versions of the traditional *moucharabieh*. The stylized name of "Allah," the decorative leitmotif of the house, can be seen on the backs of the chairs in the dining room (left) and on the bedspread of the summer bedroom (right). The bed looks away from the terrace but faces an immense mirror, which offers a panoramic view over the Bay of Tangier. The winter bedroom is part of a studio and has an entirely different type of decor. A screen separates the bedroom from the sitting area. The gold panel (far right, top) uses the same material as for the entrance to the *dar*. The living room is a model of minimalist rigor in design. The gilded motif reappears on the low tables and candlesticks (far right, bottom).

A desk faces the windows that overlook a teak terrace, sheltered by the dome. The small pool here looks as if it has been built to fit into the upper deck of a yacht.

The upper floor consists of a series of superimposed terraces, which rise above the rounded forms of the mosque. The bedroom, also on this floor, is as meticulously composed as the other rooms in the house. The terrace side is a single wall of windows fitted into barrel vaults. Another wall on the inside is taken up by an immense mirror that reflects the view of the Tangier harbor and the dome. From the bed, this spectacular sight can be enjoyed endlessly in the mirror. The only reason to leave this room is to go to what the owner calls the "magic square," a square living room under a pergola. When the east wind starts to blow, he repairs to his usual place under the *caidal* tent set up on the upper terrace. His greatest pleasure is to contemplate the stars at night during the cool August evenings.

Life at Sidi Osni revolves around the sky. You could almost forget the time if the muezzin did not provide a rhythm to accompany the idyllic days.

IN TANGIER,
A PALACE IN THE KASBAH

The house that belongs to interior designer Laure Welfing is situated in the heart of the Tangier Kasbah, hidden in the labyrinth of steep, winding alleyways. The entrance to this small palace is recessed back from the street and is hidden from prying eyes like a secret passageway. The doorbell rings with an old-fashioned metal twang, worthy of a grandiose home. The heavy entrance door opens and you are pulled into the darkness of the vestibule. It's impossible to get an overall view of the house, but the height of the ceilings, the familiar scent of an old home, and the formal portrait of the emperor of Austria and king of Hungary, Franz-Joseph I (1830–1916), which hangs at the entrance, all augur a noble dwelling. Souvenirs, personal objects, and all manner of acquisitions are arranged throughout the room as part of the family legacy, perpetuating a shared memory from generation to generation. This is very much a family home, where you will find people of all ages.

The house is filled with history. It served as the base for the Spanish consulate in the nineteenth century, during Tangier's golden age, when its residents were able to enjoy the prevailing cosmopolitan ambience. It then became a Koranic school and, finally, the home of a holy man, Cherif Ben Sadek, whom everyone here speaks of with great admiration. His tomb is located just next door. Laure Welfing and her husband purchased this house from the widow of Ben Sadek's last disciple.

In addition to its diverse and historic past, it also has a breathtaking location. Seemingly suspended on a cliff, it overlooks the entire medina and the harbor at Tangier. From its rooftop terraces, there is a spectacular 360-degree view over the surrounding neighborhood. From the outside, it's impossible to imagine that the small dark passageway could lead to such amazing vistas.

In the dining room, a generously laden fruit bowl forms the centerpiece of the table. Cut-crystal carafes, colored stemware, and flatware of all kinds are arranged on a red batik tablecloth, which drapes down to the floor, and which matches the color of the walls (right). Portraits of Berber women, painted by a Moroccan ancestor during her youth, grace the walls (top). A detail of one of the doors in the dining room, with a shell motif (above).

The home offers other eclectic surprises. A strange marble statue in the opening of a narrow door in the corridor stands in front of the bottom of a concealed staircase. As you continue to walk down the dark corridor, your eye is suddenly drawn to a ray of intense red light coming from the dining room. A round table, behind a set of eighteenth-century Rococo-style doors covered with thousands of shells, is set for some mysterious guest.

The corridor leads to the courtyard, which acts as a well of light. But your curiosity will be piqued along the way by yet another door, leading to a library that is filled floor to ceiling with old books; the smell of old leather and yellowing paper assaults the senses. The library contains collections of encyclopedias, travelogues, poetry, and literature. The owners love to explore markets and secondhand shops and are constantly returning to the library with diverse and varied acquisitions. They have a slight preference, however, for more eccentric works. An enormous volume is always displayed open on a bookstand. This book is a thick compilation of collages, an unidentifiable object that is part-travelogue, part-diary, and part-chronicle of days gone by. It is meant to be consulted at will, perhaps to decipher its mystery.

The covered courtyard, just past the arches, is filled with light. This part of the house was totally redesigned, but it was done so skillfully that it looks as if it were part of the original design. The owners had to remove an awkwardly placed and unattractive staircase, replacing it with a black-and-white checkerboard floor and a small pool lined with green *zelliges*. The moss-covered fountain looks as if it came straight from a Florentine garden.

Alcoves all around the archways have small Moroccan-style sitting areas, perfect for enjoying a glass of mint tea or a snack when the mistress of the house prefers to serve an informal meal here rather than to seat everyone in her dining room. Tall mirrors over the pillows and wall seats reflect back different views. An immense portrait of Louis-Philippe's queen, Marie-Amélie, reigns over one of these sitting areas. Under another

The full extent of the reigning eclectic style of this house is illustrated by this portrait of Queen Marie-Amélie, placed above a Moroccan wall seat (top right). These two, seemingly distant worlds come together again upstairs in the gallery of portraits depicting famous aristocratic figures. This gallery leads to a room decorated in pure Moroccan style (left). A *haiti*, a traditional piece of fabric, is hung behind the headboard. During the colonial period, baldachin beds such as this one were manufactured in England and sent to Arab countries. But the prize for decoration must go to the master bedroom (bottom right), with a diverse collection of objects brought back from trips abroad: binoculars, gamebags made in the Rif, mule pack saddles, shields from an Italian opera, coats of arms, seals, and heraldic devices.

This Tangier palace is clearly also a family home. The collection of souvenirs, the acquisition of antiques, and the accumulation of portraits of people who could be ancestors; all give a historic bent to the home. A series of several rows of court paintings, portraits of kings, and historical works form a gallery on the upper floor (top left). It is placed directly under the high skylights in the lateral walls, casting bright lighting on the works below. The effect of these paintings is somewhat reminiscent of the works by French painter Hubert Robert, depicting the creation of the Grande Galerie in the Louvre Museum. The gallery is a room of imposing size. African chairs stand at the end of the room to complete the eclectic style that reigns throughout.

archway, like a remnant of some architectural ruin, is a gigantic thumb by the sculptor César. This courtyard is a synthesis of the eclectic spirit of this small renovated palace, in which different styles come together to create a single, homogenous entity.

This eclecticism reaches its apogee on the upper floor. An impressive gallery consisting of several rows of portraits of aristocrats and noble ancestors and their illustrious contemporaries are exhibited under the immense ceiling. Your eye is drawn upward to the rooftops and lateral windows, which provide a constant stream of light. It looks like a work by French painter Hubert Robert depicting the creation of the Grand Galerie in the Louvre Museum. But the comparison ends there: these princes, monarchs, and beautiful ladies, frozen by protocol, are deployed in African chairs with lion-shaped armrests. There is, to say the least, a striking diversity of styles between the giltwood frames and the rougher, unfinished wood.

One floor up, the master bedroom and office are a perfect illustration of this quirky blend of personal objects and family heirlooms. Objects of all kinds coexist with heraldic ornaments in a clutter worthy of a young bachelor. A series of framed works, devoted to heraldic devices, coats of arms, and seals, makes this look like the private domain of a gentleman-adventurer, who has been a world traveler, explorer, geologist, esthete, and even scholar. Hundreds of trophies from multiple travels hang from a panel, like a mihrab, that separates the bed from the rest of the room: this chaotic collection consists of a pair of binoculars, gamebags woven by Rif farmers, and pack saddles for mules; on the floor are piles of stones or larger pieces of rock; above, shields from an Italian opera—not to mention, of course, the stacks of books scattered throughout the room.

The only view from this treasure trove, which is lined with straw mats and carpets, is the immense ocean; this can be seen from every window. When the wind blows really hard, sea mist fills the room. This room is like an impregnable ivory tower, yet escape is possible via the small concealed staircase that leads to the terrace.

On the rooftop, the stepped and linked terraces offer in themselves an entirely different living area, open to the sky and fanned by the sea air. The palace suddenly seems to be like a citadel, with crenellated walls and watchtower. The small pavilion with arches and open windows seems to plow through the sea like the prow of a ship. This unique observation post is devoted entirely to rest and relaxation. Benches have been placed among a tangle of shimmering, brightly colored fabrics, pieces of embroidery, and sequins, creating a lavish setting. The brilliant white walls are almost blinding under the burning sun. There are too many things to look at: the to and fro of the ferryboats and trawlers in the harbor, the bustling medina, or merely the endless stretch of sea. Infinity feels very close indeed.

The windows of the sitting room face directly on to the Strait of Gibraltar (facing page, bottom). The waves break below and the sea mist streams down the walls. The interior, however, is sheltered safely by thick curtains, and there is no hint of the tumultuous sea and wind. Quite the opposite, in fact: this is a muted world of peace and quiet. In the foreground, a photograph of the grandmother's wedding leans against a bust. And in the corner are pictures of Berber women, immortalized in the 1930s by an artist who made quite a name for herself by being one of the first to exhibit her works at the prestigious Mamounia Hotel. In the early years of her marriage, she lived in a fortress in southern Morocco, where she forged close links with remote groups of people, especially with the women, who agreed to sit for portraits. To the right of the kitchen (above) is a collection of traditional shelves; to the left, glasses for tea are hung .

La Vieille Montagne, surrounded by a magnificent swath of unspoiled nature in the old part of Tangier, is home to Désirée Buckingham. Her house is hidden away among the lush vegetation. A surprising sight awaits the visitor at the end of a thickly wooded path: the green coast with the sea stretching as far as the eye can see (right and below).

THE OLD-WORLD CHARM OF TANGIER

Désirée Buckingham's house is a small paradise on earth. Yet it is impossible to imagine it exists at all when you are standing in Tangier's harbor or walking through the tiny streets of the medina. Exploring this house is like traveling back in time to the golden age when Tangier was a light-hearted playground of a city. First, though, in order to find the house, you have to go to the old part of town, La Vieille Montagne, at the edge of the busy city. Here, Désirée Buckingham, known as Daisy by all her friends, is continuing a fascinating legacy.

An idyllic vision of a rural paradise stretches behind the door like a vision of casual spontaneity. It sums up the charm of this property, where nature reigns supreme. The beauty of the site is due more to the matchless location than to the architecture, which is invisible at first. You have to continue down the sloping path before you can make out, hidden by plants, the three small houses in a row. A tiny path runs along them; this is overhung by a thick arbor, which is covered in bignonias in bloom with long, pale pink, bell-shaped flowers.

A completely unexpected sight appears once you emerge from the end of this tunnel of greenery: suddenly there is a clifftop view and the blue sea lying below.

Nothing has really changed much here since the 1930s, when Désirée Buckingham's parents moved into these three identical small houses (each had a kitchen, bathroom, and two rooms). They belonged to the French company that was building the harbor at Tangier and they were used to house workers. Désirée's father, Winthrope Buckingham, an American heir to a family of bankers, was nearly ruined by the 1929 stock-market crash. He decided to tour Europe and try to live a simpler life. He met his wife, the daughter of an English pastor, in Grenada. They traveled to Tangier, where they became part of the world of dilettantes that gravitated here during the city's most famous times.

The author Paul Bowles lived many years in one of their small houses. He even brought his piano and used to sing classics from Broadway musicals. The American writer Truman Capote also visited often. At the time, the couple ran a small hotel on the same property. The large white building behind the thick vegetation is still visible. The El-Farah Hotel (meaning "joy" or "happiness" in Arabic) became the gathering place for a generation of artists, writers, and archeologists.

This past is displayed in the family photographs that lie scattered around the various rooms. The furnishings and layout of each room do not really obey any overall decorative plan. Things seem to be where they always have been, as they were initially placed. As for the garden, visible from every window, it has invaded the house in the form of the freshly cut flowers that stand in every room.

Irregular steps lead from the terrace, enclosed with an English-style wooden gate, to the roof of the adjoining house, where Désirée was born. The roof has not been remodeled into a terrace, even though it is used as one. The floor is made of slightly cracked rough concrete. A rusty metal chaise longue looks to be abandoned under a rickety umbrella held up by a string. Yet this perch offers a magnificent view over the bay. Désirée Buckingham's house is unpretentious, offering the simplest pleasures in the world.

All you have to do to find Daisy Buckingham's small piece of paradise is to follow her instructions: "When you see the sea in the dip as if in a glass of champagne, take the path that goes up." This is start of the climb to La Vieille Montagne. We take the steep, winding road that passes by sleepy villas scattered among the foliage on the hill, against the backdrop of the blue sea. We then turn off at a curve in the road. A small dirt path wanders through the damp undergrowth and drops suddenly to the gate. The property has not changed at all since Désirée Buckingham's childhood. She has done very little to the decor and everything is original—somewhat old-fashioned, but full of life and memories. Nothing has changed in the Bohemian atmosphere, which is, after all, the charm of this unique site (right).

NEAR ESSAOUIRA, A SIMPLE VACATION HOUSE

All that's visible from the outside of Joël Martial's house in Ghazoua is a solid white wall. But the charm of Ghazoua, a small isolated village (*douar*) several miles from Essaouira, is tempting enough. Indeed, a number of adventurous vacationers seeking peace and quiet have chosen to live here.

To find the house, you'll have to get off the main street leading to Agadir, turning off opposite the restaurant, Chez Kébir, which is Joël Martial's exclusive supplier of lemon tarts. After bumping down a rocky track amid clouds of dust, you reach the heart of Ghazoua without even realizing you have done so: it lies between the fountain—surrounded by thirty donkeys—and Hassan's tiny grocery store. Joël Martial's house is right here, at the edge of the path. This is where he decided to settle, giving up his career as a makeup artist for the Parisian fashion world to open a rental agency, Essaouira Homes Collection, which offers houses specially selected for the quality of their interior decoration.

Completely whitewashed, this house appears to be identical to its neighbors. But any comparison stops at the studded, bluish-colored door. No sooner have you stepped across the threshold than you plunge into a courtyard tiled in a faded black-and-white checkerboard pattern, steeped in a cloud of fragrances. The heady nocturnal scent of the belle-de-nuit is familiar; this plant opens its petals at dusk, filling the air with a lovely fragrance that lasts until dawn. In the center is a flowerbed designed by Joël Martial. He made no effort to create a formal composition, but in his enthusiasm he planted plants with fragrances and colors that reflect his instinct and his particular preferences. The blue-gray tones form a striking contrast with the pale yellow of the belle-de-nuit.

Two shapes stand out in this flowerbed: an olive tree and a palm tree. A table is set up farther away, in the corner of the courtyard. It stands under the shade of an enormous bougainvillea, which is in riotous bloom, the flamboyant flowers cascading down from the upper floor.

Joël Martial's house is a
perfect vacation home.
There is only one order
of the day: rest and
relaxation. The
Moroccan style of
lounging about is best
experienced in the
central courtyard, by
sitting comfortably in
one of the reed chairs
around the table under
the cascading
bougainvillea flowers
(facing page). This is
where Joël Martial and
his regular guests often
spend the greater part of
their time. Another
possibility exists,
however: the rooftop
terrace and the upper-
level extension above a
bedroom is like a
solarium (right). A
ladder leads up to the
top space, so that there
are two different areas
devoted to the sun,
siestas, reading, or
endless conversations
among friends. The
warm colors of the
walls and the bright
blue decorative details
underscore the resort-
like atmosphere
of this vacation house
(far right).

If you're looking for sun, take the staircase climbing up from the lower courtyard. It leads directly to the roof, which is covered with a pale pink ocher wash. The large rectangular space is surrounded by four walls, including one that leads to a bedroom and another to a small Moroccan sitting room. It is a place entirely devoted to the enjoyment of the sun and to relaxation. It looks like a solarium. Chaise longues are the only furniture here, and they offer delightfully tempting places for naps. Joël Martial and his friends can relax here in total peace, sheltered from any outside disturbance, as if they were secluded in a bubble. They can spend entire days lounging on the chairs, lost in books, or engaged in lively discussion. They come here to live a long lazy summer among friends, far away from their daily urban lives. There is another terrace above the bedroom at the top of the house that can be reached by a ladder. Joël Martial has built a pergola here and planted a young bougainvillea.

The interior of the house is, of course, whitewashed. This color reflects the light and is repeated in the fabric used throughout the rooms of the house: on the curtains drawn between the two rooms to separate the ground-floor rooms, as well as on the bedspreads and the pillowcases. Joël Martial finds all his materials in the medina. The textiles come from Essaouira workshops, which are well known for their simple striped or colored cotton and wool weaves. In most of the rooms he has opted for white to emphasize the sensation of coolness and light.

The two rooms on the ground floor face the sun-drenched patio. Filtered by the ironwork on the window frames, the light creates lovely patterns on the beds. The overall tone is natural simplicity. "I did not want a 'thousand-and-one-night' palace, like you see in Marrakech," confirms Joël Martial. When he first arrived, the comfort was minimal. Hot water and electricity from Ghazoua are fairly recent additions. But Joël Martial continues to light candles and carry lamps throughout the house.

This sitting room on the upper level is one of the few rooms in the house that is not inundated with light. This, then, is where Joël Martial decided to arrange a Moroccan sitting room. The muted light forms a space that is decidedly different from the rest of the decor in the house. Here, white is not the color of choice; instead, the room is decorated in a range of intense deep greens and reds. As opposed to the relative simplicity that marks the rest of the interior decoration, this room radiates a certain opulence, reflected in the sofa covered with pillows, the paintings on the walls, the lanterns, carpets, and candleholders arranged throughout the room. This is an ideal place to spend some quiet time. It is at the end of a corridor that leads only to this room. The traditional ceiling is made of *tataoui* (right).

The bathroom, located between the two downstairs bedrooms, is a voluptuous place, and has a lighting style borrowed from that of the *hammam*. Light comes from the roof via glass tiles placed in the floor of the terrace above. They provide a gently filtered light to the round shower room. A small bench, built into the wall, offers even more comfort. The bathroom is screened off by a piece of finely woven fabric bought during a trip to the East.

Joël Martial could not find furniture to his taste, so he decided to design his own. The grocer, Hassan, his close friend from the beginning, agreed to make them. The metal table in the dining room with its small folding chairs, the patinated wooden desk in the entrance, the blue bookcase in the living room, the red armoire in the bedroom, and the painted wooden closet doors all contribute to the decidedly rural style of this vacation home.

An air of happiness and contagious tranquility reigns here. And it is good to know that the house is available for rent when Joël Martial is not at home.

After crossing the patio to re-enter the house, you reach the dining room. A wide arch links this room to the kitchen, while another one leads to the living room (above left and right). The tone here is set by the simple furniture and refreshing colors. This is where friends meet up; it is basically the nerve center of the entire house—indeed, for Joël Martial, cooking up meals for his guests is an essential part of any vacation.

IN ESSAOUIRA,
BETWEEN THE SEA AND THE SKY

I t would be hard to find a better lookout point than Jack's house. Constructed on the imposing crenellated ramparts of the *sqala*, the front-line citadel of Essaouira, it offers a magnificent view over the sea, over the Purpuaires Islands (the name comes from the purple that was once extracted from the shells), and over the harbor. But to reach the point from which you can appreciate this superb panorama, you have to embark on a long climb. From the bottom of the narrow street, squeezed in by the walls, you don't have the slightest glimpse of the blue sea. The door to the house leads to a tiny entrance; the only way to go is up the narrow spiral staircase that seems to climb endlessly. At the top is a landing, where you enter the world of Jack Oswald and his wife, Azziza, and their children Karim and Rayan. For Jack, this house symbolizes everything that is fascinating about Essaouira: it is a historical eighteenth-century building and it faces the breaking waves.

When the door opens, you are immediately struck by the size of the rooms and the impressive height of the ceilings. This was once the headquarters of the British Consulate, when the cosmopolitan city of Essaouira housed embassies from many foreign powers, in keeping with the desire of Sultan Sidi Mohammed Ben Abdellah (reigned 1757 to 1790) to forge diplomatic and trading relations throughout the world. It was during his reign that Morocco recognized the newly formed United States of America. Nowadays, the property belongs to Jack, known throughout Essaouira by his first name, because it is the name of his businesses: Jack's Bookshop, the essential daily stop for everyone who travels through Essaouira, and his rental agency, Jack's Apartments. His priority for the renovation work was to emphasize space and light.

The entrance leads directly to the living room, which is two floors high with a mezzanine. You immediately sense the presence of the sea. The tall windows look directly past the

The bed in the master bedroom faces the sea (above). All the walls on this floor are painted white. This makes them highly reflective; they mirror back the light from the sea. Looking through the windows at the changing colors of the sky is like watching a film.

ramparts, above the rocks, and beyond to the sea. Jack Oswald had these windows enlarged. Initially, however, the house had a specific type of architecture: the windows facing outward were more European than Moroccan. Jack guesses that they were designed by an English architect and made by Moroccan *maalem* (master craftsmen). Open one of them, and a gust of sea mist fills the room.

The house is battered by the winds that blow constantly, and echoes to the never-ending sound of the sea. It gives you the feeling that you are at sea and no longer on solid ground. The most interesting sights are outside, not inside; the decoration is simple and the sofas all face the windows, the

Jack Oswald fell in love with this house, once the headquarters of the British consulate in Essaouira: "It was this link between history and geography, nature and culture that first attracted me," he says. "A friend had bought it, but he never really lived in it, and he offered to show it to me. It was at night, there was no electricity, and we could hear the waves breaking against the rocks. I first discovered it by candlelight. It was all so huge and enigmatic, like a haunted house or Dracula's castle!" He designed the banister with the motif of seagulls in flight (top left and right). This all-yellow triangular room sticks out into the sea like the prow of a ship. You can no longer see the ground from this level, and the bed on the floor near the windows seems to be floating in the air (right). Waking up in the morning here must be quite amazing.

better to watch the action. In any case, it is impossible *not* to look at the sea. Yet you feel safe and sheltered inside, ready to spend long hours contemplating the passage of clouds scudding across the sky and the changing palette of the sea. There is still one more, higher level to this home. This time, we're on the top of the house.

The Essaouira medina stretches out below. Seagulls glide overhead, carried by the wind that blows so hard that you almost want to spread your wings and take to the sky yourself. The birds land for a moment on the charming small white tower of a nearby house, before taking to the air once again. No home has ever seemed so close to the elements.

IN CASABLANCA,
A HOUSE WITH A CONTEMPORARY FEEL

S ophia Tazi, a young Casablancan interior designer, found the home of her dreams for her family, which means her two daughters, Serena and Shaden. It is a small colonial house from around 1940, situated in a calm residential neighborhood created during the Protectorate. What she like about it was the fact that it had a village-like Bohemian feel, and that recently this neighborhood has started to become more popular with young couples, who are slowly starting to invest here.

It's hard to get an overall idea of Sophie's simple white house at first. Hidden away among lush vegetation, it hides its charms. You can't see what it looks like from the outside, as it is completely concealed by plants; furthermore, the garden is very small, so it's hard to get any perspective on it. To reach the main door, you have to walk through a tunnel of greenery. Sophia made sure she kept as much of this unspoiled natural plant-life as possible; she didn't want to cut a single one of the old trees or prune the flowering shrubs. The atmosphere is almost tropical, especially as the trees are all

This sitting room on the ground floor is also where the owner entertains her guests. "Everything happens in this large room," says Sophia Tazi, who spends most of her time here (far left, top). Chairs designed by Tom Dixon, with arabesque backs, are placed in a small corner sitting area and around the dining-room table. Sophia Tazi wanted this room to have a contemporary loftlike feel to it, by keeping the maximum amount of open space. Behind the staircase is a screen painted by her mother (top left). The rooms upstairs reflect her vagabond spirit, with fabric from Bali used as a bedspread. She knocked down a wall between two rooms to create a single, large room (bottom left). The small guestroom has a bedspread made out of fuchsia-colored fabric that she found in India, pillowcases covered in madras cloth, and a brightly colored seat (right).

somewhat exotic: two large trees—a jacaranda and an Australian gresilinia—tower over the old climbing roses and the bougainvillea filled with birds' nests. Beautiful palm trees and three varieties of bamboo top off this rich tableau of sounds, scents, and colors. Finally, tiara flowers add a note of lovely tropical fragrance at the threshold of the main door.

Nothing remains of the original interior of the house as it was when Sophia Tazi first bought it. "There were two suspended ceilings, just 12 inches (30 cm) around the beams, with round laminated brown forms around the pillars, a brown floor that made the main room very dark, and green tiles. In short, it left much to be desired! I got rid of everything." An interior architect, she radically changed the style of the house to make it look more like a loft. She created another window facing the garden to bring in more light. She removed the tiles and had a tinted concrete floor poured. The floor is surrounded by *bejmat*, the traditional Moroccan terra-cotta bricks. She bleached and patinated the wooden doors, as well as the spiral staircase leading to the upper floor. Finally, she painted the walls in two colors "like in the old whitewashed medinas," she says.

For the decoration, Sophia Tazi opted for a personal style of furniture. This means a combination of objects that she designed herself, others that she has brought back from her travels, and still others from the Moroccan tradition, such as the *mida*, a round table with a lip: couscous used to be eaten from these tables. Finally, she has also included contemporary designer furniture, such as a Fortuny lamp, Tom Dixon chairs, and a Bugatti table.

The large living room on the ground floor is used as a dining room and reception room. A double bed covered with brightly colored pillows sits on a platform around a chimney. Sophia and her children often cuddle up here to read stories, under the watchful eye of her mother and sister, whose portraits look down from the fireplace. Opposite the fireplace is a screen depicting a scene from a medina, painted by her grandmother. In these gentle, intimate moments, it's as if every generation of women has gathered together around the warmth of the fire.

A VICTORIAN VILLA IN TANGIER

General Beaufre, a major figure in the French army, loved Morocco. After he died, his wife Geneviève, their son Roland (a photographer), and their daughter Florence Denarnaud decided to honor the general's memory and his love for Morocco by moving to the charmingly bucolic neighborhood of La Vieille Montagne in Tangier.

As soon as you step over the threshold, you enter three distinct worlds. This first is the large house, with Madame Beaufre's apartment on the ground floor; her son's fief is on the upper floor. At the end of the garden is the small house that belongs to Florence and Jacques Denarnaud and their two daughters, Eugénie and Blanche. "The house is always very lively, and we love it because we're all together, but everyone is autonomous, has their own space, and lives according to their own rhythm," explains Roland Beaufre.

The large house was built in the early nineteenth century and shows the clear influence of its Spanish past. The two benches flanking the entrance are covered with ceramic and placed under an overhang that is characteristic of this style. From here, several archways connect the various rooms. The interior corridor continues in this same spirit, with a nineteenth-century Spanish medallion tiled floor. This is the ground floor, in the apartment that belongs to Madame Beaufre. The dining room is a very Spanish-style room, with pinkish-ocher walls. The room is large, and a long table takes up most of the space. A seventeenth-century tapestry covers one section of a wall. The effect is a cozy one, and you feel more as if you're in a comfortable Parisian apartment than a house in Morocco. Just past the dining room is the large living room, separated from a smaller one by an archway.

A boudoir just outside Madame Beaufre's bedroom serves as an antechamber and gives a foretaste of her private world. A daybed covered in red silk damask nestles in an alcove; this is the same fabric that is used in the Paris Opera and the Comédie Française. But the woodwork of the bed comes from a nineteenth-century mosque and provides a more exotic note. Finally, the bedroom appears behind a faded pink curtain held back by a Napoleon III giltwood element—illustrating Geneviève Beaufre's passion for this era.

Roland Beaufre's apartment on the upper floor is designed around two main areas: his bedroom and the terrace. The former is painted bright yellow, which sets off the Moroccan-style decoration. An early twentieth-century copper bed is covered with a piece of fabric that is traditionally given in Morocco at a marriage. Above the bed is an embroidery from Rabat. A *haiti*, or typical Moroccan decorative fabric, hangs behind the headboard. This particular piece of fabric is unusual in that it is made of silk. Roland Beaufre has pinned a collection of ex-voto hearts to it that he brought back from Greece, South America, and other countries. The bed is framed on either side by a silk *haiti*. But Roland Beaufre spends most of his time on his terrace. "As soon as the weather is nice, I spend my life in the shade of the reed screens, because the terrace is always in the sun. It replaces the living room. I set up braided plastic *haitis* the entire length of the terrace, and raffia or plastic mats on the floor, covered with cushions. I also planted a yellow bougainvillea and a pepper tree that's growing over everything."

From up here, the photographer has the only view of the city offered by the house, which is otherwise totally surrounded by plants. It also overlooks the lush garden filled with roses, lilies, laurels, a plombago, and a climbing jasmine that has reached the terrace. "I am inundated by this scent; I love it." An umbrella pine and a hedge of cypress trees conceal his sister's house from view. Sheltered behind the thick vegetation, Roland Beaufre likes to organize open-air parties on his terrace, unless he opts for an evening out, exploring Rabat's nightlife. Returning at the break of day, he often meets up with his mother, an early morning gardener. They share this love of profuse vegetation. "She is so persistent that she has managed to grow a bed of hydrangeas!"

At the beginning of the winding road leading toward La Vieille Montagne, you'll see this large blue and white gate, over which flies the Moroccan flag (facing page, left). The Beaufre family display the Moroccan colors, proudly proclaiming their links with the country. The entrance hall is devoted to the memory of General Beaufre (facing page, right). A Napoleon III-style boudoir reflects the tastes of the mistress of the house (top right). When Roland Beaufre is not on his terrace watching the stars, he spends his time in his Moroccan-style bedroom, which is punctuated with a few kitschy elements, such as these ex-voto hearts pinned to a *haiti* (bottom right). From the age of ten years old, he spent every vacation in Morocco. Since then, he has become a resident of Tangier, which he considers to be his first home.

A PIED-À-TERRE IN ESSAOUIRA

Christophe Girard is deputy mayor of Paris, responsible for culture, and is also director of strategy for the fashion sector of the LVMH (Louis Vuitton-Moët Hennesy) group. As a businessman and politician, he only has a limited amount of time for vacations. For him, a second home can only be a place he passes through. Therefore, he would never have imagined that on his first trip to Essaouira he would return to Paris with the keys to a new house in his pocket. His friend, the interior designer Didier Gomez, showed him around this seaside town, and he instantly fell in love with a small *dar* just steps away from a hotel, the Villa Maroc. Christophe Girard made up his mind "on a whim," and he proposed a deal: he would buy this "small house" and Didier Gomez would take care of the decoration. In exchange, the designer would have a room of his own in the house.

The good thing about the house was that it was in good condition and didn't require any major renovation work. The interior designer, a devoted admirer of Havana, used the beautiful black-and-white tiling in this *dar* as the natural base from which to create a Cuban-inspired home. "The idea was to create a sober, 1950s style. Didier Gomez started with what he had at hand and emphasized it," explains Christopher Girard. He therefore kept the tiling, which became an essential decorative element, like a motif that runs through the entire house. He also kept the same layout, but added a few windows for better air circulation.

The traditional staggered entrance, decorated with African masks, leads to a patio with a magnificent banana tree—again, the Cuban influence. In the main room, the original system of doors with metal frames, extremely characteristic of the 1950s, introduce the style of choice. "Didier Gomez's stroke of genius was that he didn't try to convince me that having a Moroccan house meant trying to create a palace. I didn't want anything sumptuous, luxurious, or affluent. Indeed, Essaouira is a town of fishermen and life is hard; this kind of house goes with the town. This house does not pretend to be anything other than what it is: a small

The interior designer Didier Gomez got a room in Christophe Girard's house in exchange for his work. For the walls of his bedroom, Didier Gomez selected striking black-and-white photographs that depict everyday life during the colonial period. Warm earth tones are provided by the African fabric, which is used for bedspreads and for carpets. Christophe Girard's room is similar to Didier Gomez's, and repeats the same motifs (facing page). The same is true of the two bathrooms: the layout of both is identical, although the colors are different. The bathroom wall is lined with enameled terra-cotta tiles in the ocher and brown tones reminiscent of *tadelakt*. The series of arches (left) are among the few decorative elements that underscore the Moroccan style of this house.

"It's Havana!" cried the decorator Didier Gomez, a fervent admirer of all things Cuban, when he discovered the black-and-white tiled floor and the courtyard filled with luxuriant banana trees. This tiling became the central motif for the entire decoration of the house, which is very 1950s (right). The original system of glass doors with iron uprights, also in the 1950s style, confirmed him in his design choice. He kept a few elements, such as the two-tone painted ceiling (top left) and the other painted ceiling above the dining area, which is designed to accommodate the maximum number of guests (bottom left). Christopher Girard wanted a house that would be inviting to all his friends. "This *dar* is wonderful, because it's not a country house or a seaside house. It is in the town and we can enjoy all the activity around us."

house in a small Moroccan town." The property consists of one-quarter of a *riad*, laid out in an L-shape. It was the modest size of the house that attracted Christophe Girard in the first place. The entire *dar* consists of a living/dining room and four bedrooms upstairs.

The central room is bathed in light. The sofas and wall seats were designed by Didier Gomez, as were some of the chairs with braided seats placed along the glass doors. The original fireplace with faïence tiles was renovated somewhat, because the two men wanted to retain some traditional local elements, such as the two-tone ceiling in the living room and the painted ceiling over the dining area. But the 1950s-style chairs immediately set the tone of the overall decor. They were unearthed at a flea market in Paris. Another nostalgic touch is in the form of a series of photographs depicting everyday life in the Maghreb and sub-Saharan Africa during the colonial period. These magnificent black-and-white photographs underscore the contemporary-style white wall seats just below, alternating with wall lamps and canvas shades. Austerity is the watchword in this house.

These images reappear in Didier Gomez's room, where the walls are ocher *tadelakt* with brightly colored African fabrics. "This house is beautiful because it has so many colors," explains Christophe Girard, whose room echoes that of the designer. Only Girard's bathroom displays a different decor: instead of a bathroom wall tiled in a predominantly blue tone, he selected tiles all in shades of brown. His son's room is "like a monk's cell!" The tiny size and lack of light are nevertheless offset by the luminous sky blue of the walls. Two single beds, placed side by side and covered with white sheets, lodge themselves in the narrow room.

In good weather, everyone moves up to the terrace, where the balustrades are painted in the famous Essaouira blue, as are those on the upper floor and the shutters. "This is in keeping with the local tradition," says Christophe Girard. The view from the roof stretches over the entire city, and you can see that the house sits between a bank, a mosque, and a *hammam*. "A balanced life. In other words: economic, spiritual, and sensual activities," says the politician.

This simple country house is in total harmony with nature. It appears perfectly integrated into the rocky landscape, because it is constructed of the same material; in other words, dry stone walls (right), with trunks of argan trees and agave branches for the ceilings. It has not been modified at all. There is no electricity, and the owner uses candles for light. In the main room (center), *canouns*— small barbecues— are used for cooking.

NEAR ESSAOUIRA: LIFE IN NATURE

B ert Flint's house lies at the end of a rocky track, behind a dry stone wall. The Dutchman is a renowned specialist in popular Moroccan art, and owner of the Maison Tiskiwin, the museum in Marrakech that houses his fantastic personal collection. He left his luxurious city dwelling, where he lived on the second floor, without a backward glance, preferring instead the simple life at Ghazoua. Totally in harmony with its surroundings, the building blends happily into the rocky landscape. "This house perfectly suits my need to escape culture and spend more time in nature," he explains.

Refinement and luxury are excluded here. This rural, single-floor building is the very embodiment of simplicity. Visitors are immediately struck by the rough local material used in its construction: trunks of argan trees and agave branches form the ceilings, while the dry stone walls match those that separate the surrounding fields.

The house is surrounded by vegetation that grows wild in nature, and the owner refers to it as a "field" rather than a "garden," even though small stones seem to set off a packed earth path between the succulents. Electricity and running water only reached the village recently, but Bert Flint prefers "the taste of my well water and the flame of my candle." Cooking is done on small barbecues, or *canouns*.

He adds that "here, luxury is in the large interior spaces that seem to be part of the outside, without doors or windows", an effect made possible by the gentle climate and the location, which is sheltered from the north wind. The interior decoration is extremely simple and consists of nothing more than the absolute minimum. The main room is used as

a dining room, living room, and kitchen. Beige mattresses in the corner are used as wall seats, with a few pillows covered in brightly colored woven fabric. Part of this room extends outside under the overhang of the roof, under which sits a table and stools. Terra-cotta containers and pitchers placed throughout the house, either inside or out, accentuate the authenticity and rustic character of the house.

The stables were renovated to create a guest room, which has a single bed covered with a *haik* and a rough wooden chair. The bathroom is an open-air space. The water in the rooftop cistern is heated by the sun. The large mirror on the ground, framed in thuja, offers a lovely example of the typical wood craftsmanship of Essaouira. For Bert Flint, nothing beats the pleasure of a shower enjoyed in the open air, except "relaxing in the midst of weeds and tiny flowers, which I love more than the tulips of my native land."

RENDEZVOUS

Morocco is renowned for its traditional hospitality, and whether the accommodation you choose is simple or more refined, you will be given a warm welcome. There are many different kinds of places to stay, each with its own special charm: picturesque hotels, guesthouses, rented *dars* and *riads*, or palaces like the Amanjena (preceding pages). Visitors are traditionally greeted with mint tea. Here, at the Dar el-Ghalia, which belongs to an old Fez family, the art of hospitality has been handed down through the generations. Tea is served in the main courtyard (right). In Meryanne Loum-Martin's new villa-hotel in Marrakech, archways lead from one patio to another (facing page).

DARS, *RIADS*, AND LEGENDARY HOTELS

Travelers have long been fascinated by Morocco. At first they came in search of the exotic; now they may come looking for a complete change of lifestyle. In the past, visitors to Morocco tended to be either adventurers, artists, or members of the privileged classes, but today's tourists come from all walks of life. Everyone is captivated by the mystery that is Morocco; some people have found themselves unable to leave. Of those who stay, many have decided to renovate traditional residences, turning them into guesthouses. This formula has proved so successful in Marrakech and Essaouira that it is gradually spreading to the southern reaches of the country—along the Dadès Valley, for example, where earthen fortresses (rather than urban dwellings) have also been converted. Visitors can rent refurbished *dars* and *riads* in Marrakech and Essaouira, which enables them to live Moroccan-style for a few days and experience local life to the full, either in the heart of the medina or in a little *douar* (village). In Fez, some of the Moroccan dignitaries who have inherited splendid family homes also open their doors to guests.

One of the charming things about Morocco is its traditional hospitality; visitors are treated like distinguished guests, and Moroccans readily invite travelers into their homes for a glass or two of mint tea or a meal. More and more foreign residents are opening guesthouses, to share their passion for this hospitable land and to help perpetuate the tradition of welcome.

The type of accommodation available to tourists plays an important part in the irresistible appeal of Morocco. Many of these places afford a precious insight into the Oriental art of living: sometimes simple, sometimes refined, it is always full of charm. The legendary Moroccan hotels are surviving evidence of the elegance of the past; other, more recent establishments propose an updated but equally attractive version of Muslim architecture and the gentle way of life that goes with it. Sometimes these places are in fabulous spots off the beaten track—maybe near the ocean, or in an oasis at the gateway to the desert. Or you can opt to view stunning landscapes while trying out the nomadic life—or a luxury version of it—in a bivouac worthy of the film *Out of Africa*. Trips can be taken to the middle of the Atlas Mountains or the foot of the dunes: romance and enchantment guaranteed.

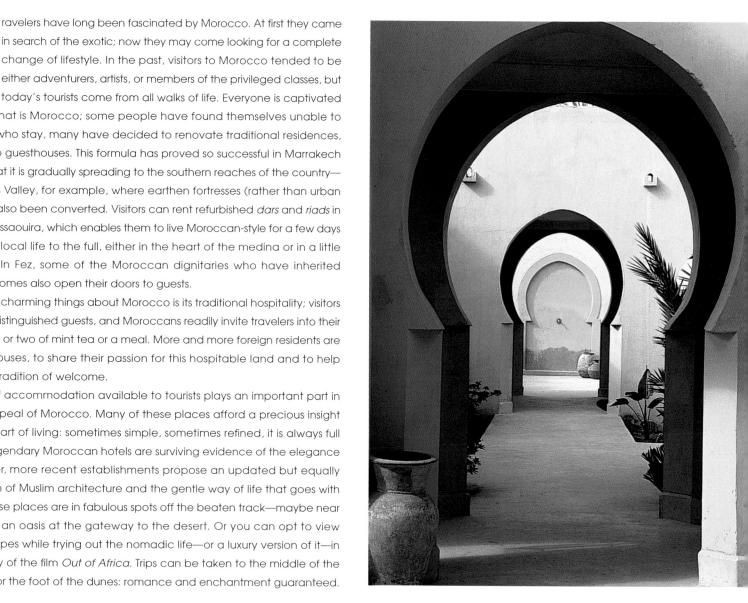

Simplicity is of the essence at the Dar Ouali, as in many of the houses that have been renovated by architect Quentin Wilbaux and interior designer Valérie Barkowski. The courtyard is typical of the Islamic architectural tradition: it has a central pool, with rooms situated all around it (top left). The furniture in the dining room is modern and elegant; it was handmade by local craftsmen, using traditional skills, such as wrought ironwork, for the chairs, table legs, console, and mirror (bottom left). From the rooftop terraces, there are splendid views of the town with its minarets, and the Atlas Mountains in the distance. A simple tent, like a Saharan bivouac, creates a lounge area (right), a perfect place for relaxing in the shade.

LIVING MOROCCO-STYLE

Why not live in Marrakech for a few days or a few weeks? Not as a tourist, but "at home" with friends or family, in a rented *dar* or *riad* where you can enjoy life Moroccan-style, with all the comforts of a hotel but none of the constraints. What better way to get an authentic taste of everyday life in another land?

QUENTIN WILBAUX'S *RIADS*

Belgian architect Quentin Wilbaux is the founder of an unprecedented movement to restore the *riad* houses in Marrakech. At the same time he has also opened the Marrakech-Medina agency, with the aim of renting out renovated places such as Dar El-Qantara and Dar Ouali.

This unusual success story began about ten years ago with what amounted to a treasure hunt: Quentin Wilbaux and Abdellatif Aït Ben Abdallah, who worked closely together from the very beginning, had noticed that the *riads* and *dars* in Marrakech were deteriorating at a fast rate. The Moroccan middle classes were deserting the medina, and country families, victims of the drift away from the land, had begun to take possession of the abandoned houses, places so vast that they would promptly divide them up. "All this architectural heritage was disappearing," Quentin Wilbaux remembers. "At the same time, my friends wanted to live in the medina or buy a house there and rent it out."

Encouraged by this synergy, the two friends therefore started out on an enthusiastic *riad*-hunt: "No survey had ever been done of housing in Marrakech," says Wilbaux. "We knocked on doors with no idea of what to expect." They ventured into alleyways and dead-end streets in the secret hope of finding hidden gems, and went from one surprise to another. "When we came upon a *riad*, we could never tell how big it was going to be."

The renovation work was the opportunity to rediscover traditional crafts, which were often in danger of dying out, along with the *riad* themselves. Quentin Wilbaux and

At Dar Ouali, the
bedrooms are furnished
in the simplest of styles.
For the floor coverings,
bedding, and cushions
Valérie Barkowski has
chosen textiles in natural
colors. The principal
decorative feature of this
room is its painted
ceiling (above).
In this bathroom (left),
the mirror is cleverly
positioned in order to
create an effect of
perspective.

The courtyard at Dar Ouali, seen from behind the decorative wrought-iron balustrades of the second floor; it forms the heart of the house (right).

Abdellatif Aït Ben Abdallah relied on the experience of old *maalems* (master craftsmen), and never wavered in their aim to respect the original architecture, sticking to a working drawing and using authentic materials. They founded Marrakech-Medina in 1995, in order to manage this huge undertaking (Abdellatif Aït Ben Abdallah was later to leave).

Nowadays the agency has fifty or so renovations to its credit, and has twenty *riads* and *dars* available for rent. Quentin Wilbaux entrusted the decoration of the properties to his compatriot Valérie Barkowski, renowned for her successful household linen and clothes business (Mia Zia). Her aim was to decorate the renovated *riads* in a style that suited their architecture. Her keywords were simplicity, refinement, and modernity, with all ornamentation, opulence, and Oriental sophistication reduced to a strict minimum. The result is refreshingly understated, with no room for superfluities. The idea is for visitors to enjoy private accommodation, but also be provided with all the services and facilities of a hotel. Guests therefore rent the whole *riad*, both accommodation and service, and can stay in the heart of the Marrakech medina as tourists, while still feeling quite at home.

Quentin Wilbaux has lived in the medina himself for fifteen years. In Marrakech, he finds "the kind of magic you find in Istanbul, which gives you a feeling of peace and strength, and makes you want to stay. It's not an anonymous place: it's a joyful city. That's the result of being a place first created by caravans, then acquiring a cosmopolitan atmosphere by welcoming people from Timbuktu and elsewhere. It's a multicultural civilization, so there's plenty of exchange. This is why I want to stay—plus I felt I had a job to do here, in safeguarding this fragile heritage."

Visitors to Dar El-Qantara feel they are staying in a kind of second home, as if they were not tourists at all; they can make themselves perfectly comfortable, in the courtyard or in a living-room recess. In this modest-sized *dar*, which has no particular ornamental features, Quentin Wilbaux chose the oxblood color which is characteristic of such places to paint the shutters and balustrades (left). Another pleasant place to unwind is the lounge area on the second floor, with its stuccoed ceiling painted in bright colors (facing page, top). The elegant white crockery is by Charlotte Barkowski. The furniture is of exclusive design—like this table and armchairs (facing page, bottom).

Ouardaia villa is part of Dar Tamsna, the first luxury residence designed by Meryanne Loum-Martin in the Marrakech Palmeraie. Dar Tamsna comprises two such villas: Nakhil and Ouardaia. The latter, set in the heart of a lovely garden (right), illustrates the designer's idea of luxury: all the space, tranquility, and privacy of a house which is yours for the length of your stay, plus attentive hotel service, so you have none of the usual practical details to worry about. Dar Tamsna has become a great classic in Marrakech. Loum-Martin adopted the same formula—but on another scale and in a different style—with Jnane Tamsna. This vast residence was designed like a Moorish hacienda (which explains the series of arches). It comprises ten spacious bedrooms, with living and dining areas; the atmosphere is like that of a large country house (facing page).

TWO VILLAS IN MARRAKECH

Meryanne Loum-Martin, a successful businesswoman with a flair for style, has been running a remarkable enterprise over the last ten years. It all began with Dar Tamsna, an ongoing success story: forerunner of the vogue for luxury holiday homes, the property has become a great classic in Marrakech. The estate comprises two luxurious villas, Nakhil and Ouardaia, which nestle discreetly in the Palmeraie.

Meryanne Loum-Martin has a gift for creating places with character. She used shades of pink to color these houses, in which the play of light is an important feature. The whole range of local crafts were used, including the age-old technique known as *tadelakt*, which is what gives the walls an exceptionally warm and lustrous look. The floors are made of Ifrane marble, decorated with *zelliges*. Meryanne Loum-Martin also salvaged original wooden elements from palaces, such as doors and *moucharabiehs*.

Dar Tamsna is not intended merely as a means of conserving traditional techniques, however. The main house, Nakhil, is sober in design and built along strict geometrical lines. There is a wide stone staircase in the entrance hall, with a 1930s-style metal banister that imitates thuja-burr wood; it is a lovely feature of the house, which embodies this pleasing combination of tradition and modernity.

Meryanne Loum-Martin found this rather cubic architecture somewhat lacking in traditional Islamic character, however, and added a gallery of lancet arches, thereby creating a veranda that faces the gardens. The pillars are constructed of handmade bricks, in perfect harmony with the *bejmat* floor. The whole Dar Tamsna estate has a charm and character all of its own.

Meryanne Loum-Martin continued to innovate by opening a restaurant-gallery-boutique—Riad Tamsna—in the Marrakech medina, in an old house that she decorated like a private mansion. Then, ten years after her initial success, she created Jnane Tamsna. This is an enormous house in the Palmeraie which looks like a Moorish hacienda. It comprises ten rooms. You can rent each room separately, or the property as a whole, and it has the benefit of hotel facilities.

The property is centered around a series of patios and arches, which combine to create an impression of space and, at the same time, a monastic appearance, rather like a cloister. The atmosphere of the place is extraordinarily peaceful. Despite its Moorish style, the character of the Jnane Tamsna estate is unique in Marrakech, because it is situated on hilly ground—a rarity in the Palmeraie, which is mostly flat. It therefore enjoys exceptional views of the surrounding area, the Palmeraie, and the mountains.

Meryanne Loum-Martin wanted to take advantage of the excellent location to give the property a rural feel. "At first it was like the garden of a large country house," she remembers, "only the house was missing, so I had it built!" She planted a vegetable garden on the 6 acres (2.5 hectares) of land; olive trees, fruit trees, and hundred-year-old date palms were among the treasures already there. In the entrance garden, thyme, rosemary, and lavender mingle with dwarf palms. Inside the house, the first patio gives off delicious fragrances, with its profusion of white flowers: daturas, gardenias, white jasmine, and stephanotis. The second patio has olive trees and large, decorative artichokes, which underscore the rural character of the property.

The bedrooms are designed to look like large private apartments, and all the walls from the living areas to the dining rooms—and even the bathroom—are entirely covered in *tadelakt*. Meryanne Loum-Martin explains her choice: "Jnane Tamsna was not inspired by the land, either in colors or in design." She wants her guests to feel as if they're in a large family house, in which they can enjoy total privacy and freedom for the duration of their stay.

Meryanne Loum-Martin's houses are holiday residences with a difference: she wants visitors to feel as if they are special guests in a large family home. The walls may be freshly painted, but the impression is one of a place with a past, thanks to the choice of antique-style furniture. Meryanne Loum-Martin has a distinct preference for Syrian or Syrian-inspired furniture, inlaid with mother-of-pearl. She often adds furniture of her own design to complete the Moroccan decor, as in this bedroom (above left). The walls at Jnane Tamsna, the vast mansion in the Palmeraie, are coated with *tadelakt*, as are the walls in the bathroom at Dar Tamsna (center left). This gives them a beautifully lustrous finish. Cozy touches are added, like the paintings and photographs that hang on the living-room walls (far left).

Nakhil Villa at Dar Tamsna has a wonderfully spacious interior. Meryanne Loum-Martin went around the local antique-dealers in order to furnish it. She chose oriental furniture for this salon—a Syrian wardrobe inlaid with bone and ebony, kilims, and artifacts, ceramic vases from Fez, and hookahs (left). She demonstrates her talents as a designer at Riad Tamsna, her restaurant-gallery-boutique (above).

According to its owner,
the atmosphere at Riad
Enija is one of harmony,
with its balance of yin
and yang (expressed by
the double meaning of
the word "enija"). In the
evening, the guests have
only to step outside their
rooms to dine on this
patio, with its twenty-
three varieties of palm
(above and right).

GUESTHOUSES

The guesthouse formula is currently in vogue in Morocco. It works for both homeowners and guests, and owners appreciate the trend because it gives them the opportunity to refurbish mansions, build houses of character inspired by tradition, or revive a family heritage. Those paying for accommodation, too, appreciate being received like distinguished guests, with a personalized welcome that is a far cry from the anonymity of a hotel. It is an opportunity for people to meet and exchange viewpoints and life stories. A stay in this type of accommodation is made memorable not only by the surroundings, but also by the owners' personality.

THE RIAD ENIJA IN MARRAKECH

The Riad Enija is located within walking distance of the excitement of Djemma el-Fna square. In Greek and Arabic (*Hnia*), the word "enija," means balance and tranquility, which augurs well for your stay. Enija is also the first name of the owners' daughter. Her parents are remarkable characters: her father, Björn Conerding, is a Swedish architect (specializing in historical monuments), and a highly original personality. His quirky wife Ursula Haldimann is a Swiss interior designer. Not surprisingly, their guesthouse is as non-conformist and exuberant as its owners. Riad Enija is totally different from any other guesthouse in Marrakech: its decoration is uncompromising and audacious, marrying old and new in defiance of all current rules of style.

Björn Conerding collects works of contemporary art and design, and many of the finds he has brought back from Europe now furnish his three-hundred-year-old *riad*. The resulting atmosphere is a cross between an art gallery and a fairy-tale castle, with pieces by designer Tom Dixon, strangely shaped painted furniture by Chantal Saccomano, and amazing baroque mirrors by Alain Girel. In the bedrooms, there are extravagant beds with gigantic ornate headboards under huge center lights with crystal trimmings by Pier Lorenzo Salvoni.

Björn Conerding wanted the architecture of the place to respect "the historical style." The famous blue and white Fez

zelliges in the courtyards have now been restored to their original status: Björn Conerding found a specialist craftsman in Fez itself to do this job. He was equally determined to respect tradition when renovating the sumptuous coffered ceilings, and the colors of the sculpted plaster decoration are now as bright as they used to be.

Björn Conerding has been uncompromisingly faithful to the past; his respect for the original architecture is such that he has not added so much as a partition. The proportions of the narrow, infinitely long rooms seem odd, but he intends to keep them that way. He has also kept the small room adjoining the bedroom that traditionally served as a dressing room. It has been converted into a bathroom, with the partition wall left intact: "The guests in the rooms that face the garden have to go outside to get to their bathrooms. They just slip on their *babouches* and bathrobes," explains Björn Conerding. In the evening, they only have to step out of their bedrooms to dine by candlelight in the garden, which is planted with twenty-three species of palms.

"The guests in the rooms facing the garden have to go outside to get to their bathrooms. They just put on their *babouches and* bathrobes. They're quite happy, they feel they're at home!" explains Björn Conerding, who has faithfully preserved both the atmosphere and the architecture of the past. The traditional room adjoining the bedroom (which used to be a dressing room) is now used as a bathroom (above).

The ornamental pool in the patio at Riad el-Mezouar reflects the lovely little palace. From the water in the pool to the surrounding greenery and the green silk drapes, everything is a harmony in shades of green (right and far right).

A TAJ MAHAL IN MARRAKECH

Jérôme Vermelin and Michel Durand have also created an original atmosphere at the Riad el-Mezouar. When you enter their dazzling white palace with its lancet arches you might think yourself in India. They wanted white, they explain, because "the medina outside is full of color and commotion; when you step in here, you need calm."

When you emerge from the dark entrance hall and see the immaculate patio bathed in light, you certainly get a wonderful feeling of serenity. The central pool with its still, dark-green water reflects the surrounding architecture. Jérôme Vermelin and Michel Durand found their inspiration in the layout and proportions of *medersa* courtyards, so it is hardly surprising that the atmosphere they have created is conducive to contemplation.

Michel Durand has lined the edge of the pool with two rows of planting. This is what he has nicknamed his "crazy garden;" he has indulged his whim to grow simple meadow grasses and other wild grasses there. These dance in the slightest breeze, mocking the impassive, traditional orange trees. He brings these finds home from the royal nurseries, which are, unsurprisingly, among his favorite places.

Michel Durand set out with the express intention of having fun with Riad el-Mezouar. Unable to resist the appeal of Morocco, he put his Parisian lawyer's robe away and became an interior designer in Marrakech. In doing so he not only changed his lifestyle, but also went back to his roots—

although at first he didn't know it. "The things we do are always connected to our family history, even though we don't intend them to be," he laughs. In his case, the proof is contained in a series of black-and-white photos exhibited in the upstairs gallery (which is to be converted into a library). These show his great-uncle, who was ambassador plenipotentiary and delegate to the resident commissary-general during the Protectorate ("In fact, he was the country's political leader during the war.") We see him in his official capacity, alongside the king, at various "fabulous feasts."

It is probably no coincidence that Jérôme Vermelin and Michel Durand ended up buying the historic Mezouar *riad* (the *mezouar* being the chief of protocol at court). In his role as interior designer, Jérôme has all he could wish for in this princely eighteenth-century residence, where the present *mezouar* was born. It has all the characteristics of a prestigious palace; here he has found the pleasing, traditional proportions he was looking for. "You can tell this is a palace, because the rooms are so long and narrow," he observes. During the year-long renovation work, Michel Durand was determined to restore the original layout and proportions, with two long narrow rooms upstairs and downstairs. He also placed the staircase back in its original position.

When it came to decorating, Jérôme and Michel began to introduce other styles. "In fact, we spent a lot of time studying beautiful homes all over the world—Indian or Italian palaces, for example—and found our inspiration there." It's no surprise, therefore, to find a Medici vase in the gallery (this had formerly been part of the decor at the legendary La Mamounia hotel in Marrakech); neither does it seem odd to see the exotic contrast of whitewashed walls and sea-green silk drapes that echo the pool outside.

Riad el-Mezouar is a very personal place. The owners even designed some of the furniture themselves: a sober line of consoles, wardrobes, armchairs, daybeds, small bedside tables, and wooden or patinated-metal writing desks. For Jérôme Vermelin and Michel Durand, this *riad* represented a springboard to other projects: they now use their talents to restore other places in Marrakech in their own inimitable style.

Jérôme Vermelin has decorated his *riad* with Chinese *objets d'art*: crackleware and oxblood vases, ginger jars and bronzes, and so on. The Riad el-Mezouar, a beautiful eighteenth-century palace, took a year to renovate. It is a very personal place: the owners even designed some of the furniture themselves. The result is an elegant line of wooden or patinated-metal consoles, wardrobes, armchairs, little bedside tables, as well as the writing desk and daybed that you can see in this room (above). This passageway (left) is a harmony in white, and is typical of the palace. The French author Pierre Loti would have approved: "The slightest time-worn arabesque over an ancient doorway—even mere whitewash, cast like a shroud over a tumbledown wall—plunges me into dreams of a mysterious past."

A FAMILY HOUSE IN FEZ

It feels like a privilege to stay in Dar el-Ghalia. This eighteenth-century residence is in the heart of the medina, in the Ras Jnane district where Arabs and Jews settled after being driven out of Andalusia. Also known as the Palais Hadj Omar Lebbar, it has been converted into a guesthouse but is still home to its owners, an old Fez family. This private place is imbued with the history of the many concubines who once lived here. El Ghalia was Hadj Omar Lebbar's favorite; she was both feared and admired for her strong personality.

By opening their home, the descendants invite you to share their memories and enjoy the nostalgia of the traditional way of life. Each bedroom is named after its former occupant, so the palace is rather like a portrait gallery: Dada Fatima's room is a tribute to one of the first concubines to succeed El-Ghalia after her death; and El-Guamma (the moon) honors Fatna Lebbar, wife of the founder's eldest son. She was given her nickname because of her beautiful pale complexion, blue eyes, and round face. The Lala-Rkiya suite is dedicated to the present owner's mother.

Delicacy and hospitality go hand in hand here. There are not many rooms and only a few suites, so guests feel all the more privileged. One of the suites (and surely the most beautiful) goes by the evocative name of Laaziza (the Beloved). A stunning canopied bed with a shimmering counterpane takes up a large part of the bedroom. The living room has richly brocaded seats placed around the fireplace (where a fire is lit as soon as the weather gets wintry). This second-floor suite opens onto the courtyard. When you wake here in the morning, and open the stained-glass windows and doors, you feel you are part of the history of Fez.

This *dar* is constructed according to the traditional layout, with a central courtyard that still has its original decoration of *zelliges* (now chipped by the passage of time). The courtyard is a haven of tranquility, where you can enjoy a leisurely meal—all year round, as it is covered in winter. The adjoining rooms (El-Yacout, Fathzot, and El-Anber) have been converted into a dining room, which is perfect for romantic dinners. Dar el-Ghalia is an exclusive address, with plenty of Moroccan mystery.

Dar el-Ghalia is an exclusive address, where you are welcomed like privileged guests by the Lebbar family. You can perceive something of the mystery of Morocco in this eighteenth-century palace. The ornate bedroom doors face the courtyard, where meals (including breakfast) are taken; the courtyard is covered in winter. The adjoining rooms have been transformed into a dining room, perfect for romantic dinners. In this lovely Fez home, the staff will make your stay a truly luxurious one (above and right).

A RED HOUSE NEAR ESSAOUIRA

Baoussala is a red house that stands out on a rough track among an ocean of gorse bushes that ripple in the wind. It's the last building in Ghazoua village, near Essaouira; there is nothing beyond it but a stony track that leads toward windswept Sidi Kaouki beach. The house's name means "compass" in Arabic, so its position is significant. Visitors come here to enjoy the great outdoors—which is why its owner, Dominique Maté, first bought it.

So Baoussala is red. Nothing like the minimalist "little white square" that Dominique had first imagined as being ethnically appropriate. She had been captivated by many of the houses she'd seen on her travels, in Sardinia, Chile, and elsewhere, but had never dared take the plunge and buy one. Strangely enough, she eventually decided to purchase a place in Essaouira, even though she certainly did not fall head over heels in love with the town on first sight. In fact Dominique had been on a camping expedition in the desert and was feeling elated; her subsequent arrival in Essaouira toward the end of her vacation was actually something of a disappointment after the exhilaration of the desert.

Finally, however, she decided to buy a plot of land: a eucalyptus wood on the outskirts of a remote Berber village. When she began to dig a well, she was quick to find water, which seemed to be something of a miracle. Hers is the shallowest well in the village. The delighted proprietor decided that this was a good omen, and, as her doctor husband, Bruno Maté, was keen to try his hand at architecture, the plans got under way.

The first stone laid was for the "marabout," which is the name Dominique gave to a little building at the entrance to the property, where she lived when she was overseeing construction work. Nowadays, she and her young assistant Marie take turns living there when the main house is full. It is a monastic residence, which consists of a single bedroom and bathroom—in fact it probably comes close to the minimalism Dominique Maté first dreamed of for her property.

But Baoussala itself turned out to be round and ocher-colored, with a central patio—a convivial place in which visitors can enjoy breakfast or perhaps take a siesta in the shade of the huge parasol. There are four bedrooms, all situated around the patio.

From the outside, Baoussala looks surprisingly like a Kasbah; its thick, windowless walls are reminiscent of the earthen fortresses in the southern expanses of Morocco. Inside, it is full of the dazzling colors of a hacienda, and you can feel the sun everywhere.

THE ESSENCE OF MOROCCO IN ESSAOUIRA

Who would guess that the quintessence of Morocco is hidden behind the blue door of Dar Loulema? This eighteenth-century house was first inhabited by rich Jewish merchants, then by fishermen's families who hadn't the time or money to maintain it. Luckily, Dany and Raymond Lami came along. This French couple renovated the *dar*, transforming the abandoned ruin into a charming guesthouse. They used traditional crafts to best advantage: *tadelakt* and wrought iron from Marrakech, sculpted stone from Rabat-Salé, *bejmat* and *zelliges* from Fez.

Their goal was to share the magic of Mogador with their guests, and to make their stay as delightful as possible. They decided to favor space over accommodation: of the *dar's* 5382 square feet (500 sq. m), just over 3200 square feet (300 sq. m) are reserved for living space, and a little more than 2000 square feet (200 sq. m) are devoted to amenities: the result is a lovely, spacious house in which guests can enjoy their surroundings to the full. A fountain plays in the courtyard, which is filled with the trill of birdsong. Inside the house, there are three living rooms on the first floor: perfect for evenings around the fire. The upper-floor garden is a lovely, peaceful place in which to unwind, among the hibiscus, bougainvilleas, jasmine, geraniums, and bignonias—a special treat in Essaouira, whose Atlantic climate means there are few green spaces. From the rooftop terrace, there is a marvelous panoramic view of Mogador Island, the port, and the beach.

The bedrooms are like a concentrate of all the beauty and refinement of Morocco under the same roof: "Mogador" is blue and white like the city; "Marrakech" is red-ocher like its ramparts; "Souira" is beige like the sand dunes. "Agadir" is contemporary in design with burgundy-ocher tones; "Majorelle" is blue (an allusion to the painter); and "Todra" is decorated Berber-style. The furniture was designed by the lady of the house, who found her inspiration in Moroccan tradition and entrusted the work to local craftsmen. Raymond and Dany Lami put their hearts into this renovation; they have created a stylish guesthouse, and they give it extra warmth with their hospitable attention.

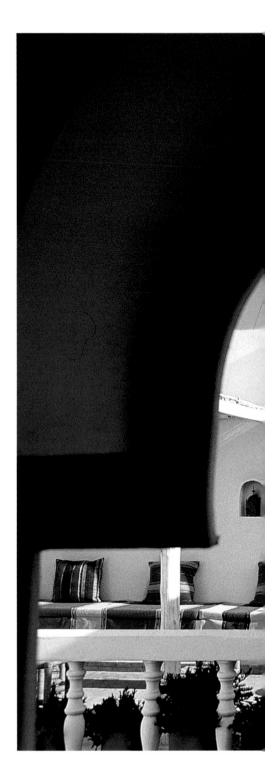

At Dar Loulema, the rooftop terraces are a wonderful place to enjoy life. Choose your spot in the sun or the shade, and relax on one of the brightly colored bench seats. From up here, you can admire the panoramic view of the port and islands (left and facing page, top). Each room has a personalized bathroom (facing page, bottom). The terrace is decorated with great attention to detail, such as this lovely decorative vase (above).

The Kasbah Ben Moro is a historical monument, which was restored with the help of the Moroccan Center for Restoration and Conservation of Earthen Architecture (left and far left, top). It was founded in the twelfth century, but stood in ruins for a long time. The natural earth colors of the walls need no ornamentation apart from the decorative incisions; the new owner of the Kasbah, Juan De Dios Romero, chose minimalist decoration to highlight this simplicity. The furniture is rectilinear (echoing the geometric lines of this architectural style); it was designed by Patrick Hyvert in Marrakech. Headboards, consoles, mirrors, and chairs are of wrought iron, which looks good with *pisé*, as you can see in this room (far left, bottom). It also gives the place an African look— Skoura is in the far south, after all. The natural-colored fabrics are the work of women from the Todra Valley.

A FORTRESS IN THE DADÉS VALLEY

The Kasbah Ben Moro stands out in the splendid setting of the Skoura palm grove. It was founded in the twelfth century during the Almohad dynasty, by a Berber tribe who gave it their name. The fort was in ruins for a long time, before being bought and converted into a guesthouse by Juan De Dios Romero, an Andalusian who feels he has returned to his roots: the Kasbah was built by a Moor, driven out of Andalusia during the Reconquest of Spain.

Skoura is a historic site, and the fort's new owner was determined to respect that, and to adhere to the local traditions. He kept the initial layout: a square base, with a tower on each corner. The first impression it gives is one of great solidity, with walls as thick as those of a fortified castle. There are geometric patterns along the upper part of the facades, and a series of decorative incisions ornament the *pisé* (earth mixed with straw) surface. The crenellated towers stand out against the pure blue sky.

It is almost completely dark inside the fort, and delightfully cool as well. Like every Kasbah worthy of the name, Ben Moro has very few openings to the outside world, and all its windows are narrow. The central courtyard, which has four massive pillars, is light and bright, however. There are three bedrooms on the first floor, five on the second, and five more on the third floor, which open onto the rooftops with four interconnected terraces, one for each tower. The view of the surrounding palm grove is magnificent: "It's almost paradise!" says Juan De Dios Romero.

The owner wanted to retain the harmonious combination of nature and architecture. He liked the natural color of the earthen walls, and opted for minimalist decoration to show off the simplicity of the place to its best advantage. The furniture is plain and rectilinear, echoing the geometric-style architecture. Juan De Dios Romero wanted to create the kind of house he would have liked to find when he was traveling throughout Morocco and exploring this region: an exceptional place, like this, in extraordinary surroundings. He has certainly—and most successfully— achieved this goal.

At the Palais Salam hotel, the pasha's apartments have been converted into bedrooms, which face onto the patios (top left). The Moroccan-style lounges in the old wing are decorated with *zelliges* from floor to ceiling; armchairs with distressed-leather backs contribute to the relaxing atmosphere. In the bar there is a fireplace, surrounded by a gorgeous mosaic panel (bottom left). The pasha had his home designed with alternating indoor and outdoor areas in which to enjoy a constant change of scenery. Strolling through the series of courtyards, patios, and alleyways is like coming upon one treasure after another— and feels rather like exploring a jungle: there is luxuriant vegetation everywhere, which either highlights the building or merges with it (right).

LEGENDARY HOTELS

In the past a trip to Morocco was a real adventure: the ultimate in exoticism. Certain prestigious hotels have preserved something of the glory of the past, and they have now become legendary institutions, possessing a quaint Oriental charm that still has the power to fascinate. Although these luxury establishments are often pricey, they are well worth a visit, even if you are only going to have a drink in the courtyard, or enjoy dinner in the restaurant.

Certainly, even though some of these places have lost their former luster, many of them have become more accessible, and are still full of nostalgic charm. Worth a special mention is the majestic Amanjena, which has managed both to integrate and to modernize the timeless splendor of Muslim architecture, and to elevate the whole to a level of luxury that is rarely attained elsewhere.

A PASHA'S PALACE IN TAROUDANT

Inside the famous red ramparts of the Kasbah at Taroudant, the Palais Salam hotel with its splendid gardens is waiting to be discovered. Its imposing door stands out against the thick ocher walls; a few horse-drawn carriages are always waiting outside, ready to leave on a tour of the walls. To get to the reception area, you walk along a wide passageway, covered in *zelliges*; it is lined with tall plants and the atmosphere is as humid as a greenhouse, heralding the lush vegetation to come. Once past the lobby, you reach an extraordinarily dense tropical garden, with a diverse number of plant species, some of which are nearly two hundred years old.

This residence, built by a pasha in the nineteenth century, epitomizes the Moroccan art of living. Vegetation is omnipresent, indistinguishable from the construction itself. Hundred-year-old branches and trunks are entwined around vaulted archways that face the courtyards of the two ancient *riads*. Inside, thick foliage masks the walls. The huge leaves of banana trees hang down over the fountains, and as they sway in the breeze, their shadows shift over the black-and-white checkered floor.

The tropical garden at the Palais Salam hotel is extraordinarily dense. Greenery is everywhere: there are banana or palm trees, with the occasional hibiscus or amaryllis to create a bright splash of red. The vegetation finds its way into courtyards, along passageways, as well as between the walls of the ramparts; indeed, nothing seems to stop it (left).

The pasha's private apartments were laid out around these two *riads* with their luxuriant courtyards. Nowadays, all the hotel bedrooms open out onto this fabulous greenery. The Moroccan sitting areas in the old wing are decorated in *zelliges* from floor to ceiling; the atmosphere is intimate and cozy, reminiscent perhaps of a gentlemen's club, with comfortable tanned-leather armchairs in which you can relax. It is here, too, where you will find the bar, situated under huge ceiling lights. There is a fireplace set into one wall; this is surrounded by a beautiful, elaborate mosaic panel. The whole area is a contrast with the outside—it is a place where you can linger in the shadows for a while, if you can resist the appeal of the gardens that beckon through the wrought ironwork at the windows.

The style of architecture in the newer wing is much less ornate and sophisticated. It has the stark, rectilinear outlines of an earthen dwelling, and the feel of the place is almost monumental, with high ocher walls forming alleyways that look like a miniature medina. The whole thing—palm trees included—seems to soar skyward. In both *riads*, the vegetation seems to be incorporated into the architectural design, and the result is enchanting.

Visitors to the Amanjena are invariably impressed by the overwhelming majesty of the place, with its series of elegant lounges (facing page, top right and bottom). It is centered around the huge, 646-square-foot (60-sq.-m) central basin (formerly used as a reservoir for use in irrigation), and canals (right, and facing page, top left). Architect Ed Tuttle has used his remarkable mastery of composition to create a truly magical atmosphere. The Amanjena is not just a replica of a Moroccan palace; it has something of the monumental perfection of Karnak temple, and the fascination of the Taj Mahal. It belongs to the hotel group "Aman Resorts," one of the most prestigious in the world, whose trademark is absolute refinement. This is the first Aman resort to be built on the African continent. Ed Tuttle has created a monument in which to enjoy a life of luxury.

PEACE AND PLEASURE IN MARRAKECH

If there could only be one hotel in Marrakech, it would have to be the Amanjena ("peaceful paradise"), which must be the ultimate in Moroccan luxury. Its setting is fabulous for several reasons: it's in the heart of the Palmeraie—that oasis of palms and olive trees; it faces the High Atlas Mountains; and it's on the edge of a verdant golf course.

What makes the Amanjena especially luxurious, however, is its total discretion. Even its entrance is hardly visible from the road that snakes through the palm trees, and it is enclosed like a palace, kept apart from the outside world. It's a sumptuous, elitist expression of the regal lifestyle—designed by Ed Tuttle. The architect aimed at perfection, so although the proportions seem inordinately large, they are nevertheless harmonious. When you walk through the entrance gallery and come upon the huge central basin (traditionally used for collecting rainwater from the mountains) you feel both small and elated.

The Amanjena is a particularly attractive interpretation of Moorish architecture. Ed Tuttle respected the great traditions of Islamic construction by using the whole range of arches magnificently—Roman, Moorish, lancet, and trefoil arches—together with long colonnades that are designed to amplify the effects of perspective.

The grandeur of the complex is magnified by the immense, square basin, which mirrors the dusky pink facades. The basin measures 646 square feet (60 sq. m), and was originally used to collect water from the Atlas Mountains for use in irrigation. The layout creates an oasis of harmony and serenity that is conducive to contemplation—and even meditation. The water is like a focal point that unifies the diverse elements of the huge estate.

Six two-story "pavilion-maisons" are arranged around the basin; a further thirty-four single-story pavilions are scattered around the waterways and swimming pool. The latter has a huge, green-tiled dome at one end; the floor of the pool is covered in the same mosaic, which is also reflected in the architecture (shades of the Blue Mosque in Esfahan, Turkey). The Amanjena draws its inspiration from the

essence of Islamic art, to create a magnificent ensemble. Palm trees rise up like columns all around the grounds, echoing the elegant lines of the buildings.

The interior design of the pavilions is similarly grandiose and luxurious, but on a more intimate scale. Each has its own private garden and *menzeh*—a gazebo that faces the golf course and mountains. The living-dining area is the perfect place for an aperitif at sunset, when the High Atlas Mountains are all aglow.

OLD-WORLD CHARM IN MEKNES

The Hotel Transatlantique looks down on the medina from its hilltop, where it seems to be in a world of its own. It is almost as if the years had slipped by and left no trace on this jewel from the past—a past it shared with La Mamounia (the old part of the Hotel Transatlantique is an exact replica of La Mamounia as it was before its renovation). The Transatlantique has acquired a new wing, but the original character of the place seems not to have changed at all. If you stay at the Hotel Transatlantique, you will find out what La Mamounia must have been like in bygone days.

The colonial age is over, and the hotel is no longer the height of fashion—but it still has plenty of charm. The elegant facade comes into view at the end of a long alleyway: a beautiful construction of pleasing proportions with its two stories, adorned at regular intervals with painted shutters. It is almost as if something intangible, like a ghost from the past, had decided to take up residence here forever.

The bedrooms in the old wing are situated along seemingly endless corridors. There is still the original 1930s furniture: dark wooden armchairs, tables and beds, inlaid here and there with stylized flowers in mother-of-pearl. The simple,

elegant design looks surprisingly modern nowadays. The wood trim echoes these floral motifs, and is also used to frame panels of blue and white *zelliges* in simple geometric designs.

You can get from one balcony to another through wooden side doors, which match the painted shutters. The balconies overlook the gardens and offer a panoramic view over Meknes. This is a marvelous place to take an evening stroll, before enjoying an aperitif under the white archways of the terrace, when the medina begins to sparkle in the setting sun. The Hotel Transatlantique will take you back in time—and its wonderful views will make that journey an unforgettable one.

A FIN-DE-SIÈCLE HOTEL IN TANGIER

The Hotel Continental is in the heart of the medina, overlooking the port. Its vast terrace juts out like a stage, and is a good place for watching the hustle and bustle of the port below—just settle comfortably on one of the dark green, 1900-style iron chairs, and peep through the dense thicket of palm leaves. It is a place of extraordinary, almost other-worldly serenity: even though it is in the town center, it manages to keep a kind of distance, the nature of which it is difficult to define. Could it be its air of solidity that sets it apart? Or the old-fashioned charm? In any case, it seems to advance resolutely through the years like some formidable lady, caring nothing for passing fashions, and determined to do things its own way. Ever since it was built in 1870, the Hotel Continental has opted for a certain discretion, in comparison with the more luxurious Minzah, for example, with its constant round of celebrities. It is proud to be different—and the same can often be said for its clientele.

This independence of spirit is what gives the place a certain freshness, which it expresses with a choice of wonderfully bright colors. The green shutters on the facade are framed with lemon-yellow; the windows of the first-floor terrace have multicolored panes; behind them is a bright pink corridor, leading to a dining room of the same color. The atmosphere of the dining room is rather like that of an old boarding house, where the tables and chairs have always been arranged in exactly the same way. Opposite the reception area is a beautiful staircase leading to the upper floors, with an antique clock and old prints for decoration. Recent renovation work has made the colors brighter, so the old-fashioned furniture is all the more distinctive. Some of the bedrooms have *caidal* beds, with brass bedposts and canopies: the famous model was designed in Great Britain for use in Arab countries.

The Hotel Continental certainly has character. The French artist Edgar Degas succumbed to its charm, and stayed here for a long while in 1889. The Italian writer-director Bernardo Bertolucci was also sensitive to its fascinating atmosphere, and shot scenes of his 1990 film, *The Sheltering Sky*, here.

A COLONIAL HOTEL IN RABAT

La Tour Hassan Meridien has been more than just a hotel since it was built as a Glaoui palace in 1914—it is a part of the history of Morocco. In 1925, when it was just a little colonial hotel with seven bedrooms and a view of the sea, it became the place where matters of state were discussed, and thereby witnessed history in the making. General Lyautey, who was appointed first resident-general, made his Rabat headquarters here, since it was ideally located, just a quarter-mile away from the embassies. Nowadays extensions have been added to the hotel, but this older part is still the soul of La Tour Hassan—the hotel's Moroccan restaurant, La Maison Arabe, is still here, with the original decoration of *zelliges*. The bar is on the other side of the staircase; it has a neo-Moorish atmosphere, reminiscent of the Protectorate, and in this nostalgic, elegant environment it is easy to imagine the diplomatic dealings of the past. The architecture has not been changed, and the original multicolored stained-glass windows are still in place. The fine, slender columns support decorative arches, with openwork foils carved in Salé stone; you can sit here and sip your drink— and spare a thought for French novelist and pilot Antoine de Saint-Exupéry, a regular guest in the Andalusian wing. This was added to the hotel in the 1940s, providing seven more rooms.

The hotel is in downtown Rabat, but has managed to preserve a peaceful haven of green that contrasts with the hustle and bustle of the town. Most of the bedrooms overlook the garden, which is of Andalusian inspiration and creates a link between past and present.

The rooms overlooking the garden at the Hotel Palais Jamaï in Fez (left) were once the apartments of the Grand Vizier Jamaï. He served as prime minister under Sultan Moulay el-Hassan (reigned 1873–1894). British statesman Winston Churchill was among those who stayed at La Mamounia. In 1935 he wrote to his wife, Lady Clementine: "This is a wonderful place, and the hotel one of the best I have ever used…. I have…a wide balcony, looking out on a truly remarkable panorama over the tops of orange trees and olives…." He was an amateur painter, and used to go from one balcony to another to paint the sun as it set. The "Churchill Suite" was named after this regular visitor. The garden caters to all tastes, with flowered pathways (facing page, top left), a huge swimming pool (facing page, top right), and a buffet for refreshments (facing page, bottom).

SULTANIC SPLENDOR IN FEZ

The Palais Jamaï hotel in Fez is a place of stunning beauty, without doubt one of the most breathtaking in Morocco. Its charm comes from its unique position and fascinating history.

The palace is located uphill from the ramparts, overlooking the imposing medina with its intricate network of buildings, souks, *medersas*, mosques, and alleyways—yet despite all the hustle and bustle, no noise from the medina comes to disturb the sanctuary of the palace. The fountains' gentle murmur is enough to muffle any other sounds, while the hundred-year-old trees scattered throughout the gardens lull the visitor; and, to add to the sensual atmosphere, a cool breeze blows down from the hills where the last Merenid sultans were buried.

This restful climate is the reason why the Palais Jamaï was constructed on this site. The building has a fascinating past: in 1879, the Grand Vizier Jamaï, prime minister under Sultan Moulay el-Hassan (reigned 1873–1894), decided to construct what is generally called a *menzeh*—a garden pavilion that can vary enormously in size from modest gazebo to vast house. This construction was actually a palace in Arab-Moorish style, a jewel among the residences belonging to the high dignitaries of the Jamaï family. The vizier designed his apartments and a harem, then an Andalusian garden. Staying in the Palais Jamaï is an exotic experience that conjures up a past full of sultanic splendor.

If money is no object, then in order to enjoy this evocative experience to the full, you should stay in the royal suite, which used to be Grand Vizier Jamaï's apartments. The decoration and layout have hardly changed at all since this residence was converted into a luxury hotel in the 1930s. It still boasts all its original pomp: the living room with its shimmering fabrics, the *zelliges*, the stucco ornamentation, and so on. A king-sized canopied bed on a mezzanine-platform overlooks the bedroom and gardens. The restaurant (which is also in the vizier's wing) still has its original decor, too—bench seats in alcoves, ideal for romantic tête-à-têtes—and you can enjoy traditional Fez cooking here, said to be the most refined in Morocco.

A PARK IN THE HEART OF MARRAKECH

The hotel La Mamounia gets its name from its gardens, which were formerly called "Arset el-Mamoun." All the charm of this legendary palace is concentrated in its fabulous park, a haven of tranquility in the heart of Marrakech. The surrounding walls, covered in bougainvillea, form a rampart against the clamor of the town.

The two-hundred-year-old garden has a history of its own: it once belonged to Prince Moulay Mamoun, fourth son of Sultan Sidi Mohammed Ben Abdellah, who reigned in the eighteenth century. The custom at that time was for the sultan to give his sons a house and garden outside the Kasbah when they married. For his wedding present, Moulay Mamoun was therefore given this park, to which he gave his name; he had it designed in the purest Moroccan tradition. Its magnificence is due to the great variety of plant species that create a number of different atmospheres. In an area of almost 18 acres (7 hectares), visitors can stroll along paths planted with olive trees, orange and lemon trees, or palms, then suddenly arrive in wild, tropical thickets of bamboo, banana trees, hibiscus, and yuccas, followed by fragrant rose bushes, mimosa, and verbena.

La Mamounia hotel itself was built for the Moroccan railway company in 1922; its architects were Prost and Marchisio. Their idea was to combine elements from the Moroccan architectural tradition with the latest Art Deco designs. Art Deco furniture was made exclusively for La Mamounia, and the hotel became famous for this style. Its "M" logo was applied to its crockery and other everyday objects. The hotel originally had 100 rooms, and it was successively enlarged in 1946, 1950, and 1953. In 1986 it underwent major renovation work, and it now boasts 200 bedrooms.

Over the years, La Mamounia became a favorite with statesmen such as British prime minister Winston Churchill, French leader General de Gaulle, and U.S. President Franklin Roosevelt (after the Casablanca Conference, January 14th–24th, 1943) but also attracted filmmakers, who found this exotic palace a perfect environment for filming on location.

Alfred Hitchcock made his 1934 film *The Man Who Knew Too Much* here, and it was also here that Austrian director Eric Von Stroheim filmed *Alerte au Sud* (1953). After the war, wealthy Europeans and Americans flocked to the hotel in search of the Moroccan south, opting for the discretion of Marrakech rather than the frenetic pace of Tangier.

The Hotel el-Minzah is part of the mythology surrounding Tangier. Visitors who come to Tangier looking for traces of its bygone golden age stay at the Minzah, to soak up the atmosphere in its lounges, bedrooms, and corridors (far left, top and bottom). In the 1930s, the hotel attracted glamorous European socialites; after the war, wealthy Americans stayed here. The charm still works. The hotel's location is enchanting: bordered with palm trees, it overlooks the Bay of Tangier (right). If you stay in one of the rooms facing the sea, you can admire this magnificent view while relaxing in a reclining chair on a terrace shaded by colonnades (facing page). The Moorish architecture is an added attraction. The building was built in the 1930s by a Scottish lord, who dreamed of owning a Moroccan palace.

A LEGENDARY 1930s HOTEL

Tangier has another legendary institution: the Hotel el-Minzah. In the 1930s, when Tangier was renowned for its exciting atmosphere, it was here that Europe's wealthy socialites and vacationing dilettantes took up residence. After the war, Americans stole the show by making the Minzah their headquarters in Tangier. The establishment still retains its former glamor and charm, and is a must for visitors to Tangier who come looking for a taste of the legendary past.

The Minzah is located downtown, on a busy street near the medina; it is most imposing with the white, Hispano-Moorish facade, enormous iron-studded wooden door and voluted gates. The lobby is dimly lit by lanterns, but as your eyes adjust you can distinguish the wall hangings, carved ceilings, and doors with traditional Gothic Moorish arches. The heart of the hotel is its famous patio with blue and white arcades: the perfect meeting-place. You can happily wait in the shade of the columns, lulled by the murmur of the central fountain, soothed by the beautifully decorative *zelliges* that cover the floor and walls, and refreshed by the omnipresent greenery. From the patio you can move on to the garden and swimming pool; the vegetation is luxuriant, with banks of rose bushes and bougainvilleas and palm trees that reach gracefully toward the sky. Suddenly you come upon an unexpected panoramic view: below you lies the Bay of Tangier, which encompasses the old town, with the Strait of Gibraltar visible in the distance.

The hotel itself has never been renovated; it still has its original charm and chic, and its rooms are still decorated with the same unpretentious elegance. This impressive building dates from the 1930s, when it was built by a Scotsman, Lord Bute, who dreamed of having his very own Moroccan palace. There is a portrait of him in the bar, where the atmosphere is reminiscent of an English gentlemen's club. You can have a drink there in the evening in calm and comfort, and soak up something of the atmosphere that must have prevailed when Tangier was the place to be.

The Hotel des Deux Tours, tucked away in the Palmeraie, is the perfect place to pamper yourself. The wooden entrance is flanked by the two towers that give it its name (top left). It has an exceptionally beautiful *hammam* (far left, bottom) and tempting swimming pool (bottom left). The historic Jardins de la Medina hotel is splendidly regal; the lovely gardens are the heart and soul of the place, and all the bedrooms overlook this greenery. The elegant white columns at the entrance to the building are vestiges of its prestigious past (far right, top), and are succeeded by slender columns painted almond green. At the bottom of the garden is a lounge area, like the one at the entrance, with an extra floor (right). The edges of the swimming pool are shaded by palm trees (far right, bottom).

PICTURESQUE HOTELS

Each of these hotels is unique—and all are charming. They are an expression of Moroccan diversity, with their various locations and architectural styles, including traditional earthen dwellings on the edge of the desert, updated versions in the Marrakech Palmeraie, renovated *riads* in the medina, and houses standing near the ocean. They are all wonderful places to stay, which will add to the fascination of your trip.

IN THE PALMERAIE OF MARRAKECH

Famous architect Charles Boccara is a fervent defender of tradition. He refurbishes earthen dwellings, and a marvelous example of his work is the Hotel des Deux Tours. This hotel is tucked discreetly away in the Marrakech Palmeraie. Its *pisé* walls give it the characteristic dusty-pink color, while its massive wooden doors are framed by the two towers that gave the hotel its name. Charles Boccara used the whole range of local architectural features in his renovation work: terra-cotta bricks, terraced roofs, connecting rooms, and central patios. He also kept the ruins of the old village's *pisé* ramparts, which he has incorporated as a feature in the swimming pool. There is a long basin filled with emerald green water, which is at grass level and merges into the surrounding vegetation. Prickly pears, bougainvilleas, and papyrus are dotted among the palm trees.

Six villas were built at first, and two more were added later in order to meet the demand for accommodation at this increasingly popular address. Apart from the traditional *zellige* mosaics and *tadelakt*, Charles Boccara used decorative touches such as ceilings in painted *tataoui* (oleander branches arranged in a criss-cross pattern). The highlight is probably the *hammam*, which is extraordinarily beautiful: it is a masterpiece of harmonious design, with a dome over the pool that lets the light filter in through astral motifs and an openwork brick dome over the massage area. Les Deux Tours is more than a hotel: it is a world of its own, in which you can pamper yourself to your heart's content.

A HOTEL FIT FOR A PRINCE IN MARRAKECH

The hotel Les Jardins de la Medina incarnates the definition of the word *riad*, which means "garden" in Arabic and, by extension, a garden within the walls of a house. This princely residence, now a hotel, contains impressive rows of orange trees; few *riads* have such extensive gardens. It is located within walking distance of the Royal Palace; until recently it belonged to the king's entourage, and it is of incomparably regal elegance. The hotel has therefore inherited a tradition of refinement. At Les Jardins de la Medina, you will enjoy a stay in exceptional surroundings, with a lush garden planted along geometrical lines for harmony and symmetry.

The hotel Les Jardins de la Medina is in the city center, but it is hidden behind high walls. It comes as quite a surprise to discover such an expanse of greenery in this quiet little street inside the ramparts. Michel Sautereau, his sister Annie Rigobert, and André Bos initiated the renovation project, which they entrusted to the brilliant young architect, Karim el-Achak. Their express intention was to preserve the *riad* as a symbolic representation of paradise. They were aware that they had found an extraordinary treasure, and they were determined to preserve its authenticity: the hundred-year-old palms were left untouched, as were the olive trees that filter the dappled sunlight as it passes toward the restaurant terrace—it's as though the terrace had found its way among the trees in order to enjoy their precious shade.

Besides the garden, Karim el-Achak retained the existing buildings and their original functions. At the entrance, the *menzeh* is still used, as it was traditionally, as a kind of summerhouse in which to spend many a pleasant moment. It has a restaurant and a shady terrace. At the bottom of the garden is a second *menzeh*, to which an extra story has been added. The ground floor of this is still used as a summerhouse, a place of relaxation. The buildings that now link these two original constructions have bedrooms overlooking the garden. At the edge of the swimming pool, the architect has created another, completely independent construction,

consisting of two *dars*, each with its own courtyard; this structure faces away from the garden, and is intended for guests who prefer the privacy of their own accommodation. Karim el-Achak wanted these various constructions to create a kind of dialog between indoors and outdoors. The bedrooms have their own private outdoor areas—patios, balconies, or terraces.

La Maison Bleue, in the
Fez medina, built in
1915, was once the
sumptuous home of a
professor at the famous
Qarawiyyin University,
who was also a
renowned jurist and
astrologer. His
descendant, Mehdi el-
Abbadi, restored it and
converted it into a luxury
hotel, but kept the
original decor. He has
just restored another *riad*
on the ramparts, built in
1880 by another great
jurist and scientist,
Si Mohammed bel Arbi
el-Alaoui. The style of
the Riad Maison Bleue
is rather different; it
has an open, flowered
courtyard planted with
orange trees, unlike the
blue patio at La Maison
Bleue. The two houses
form an ensemble
(visitors can stay at
the Riad Maison Bleue,
and enjoy hotel service
provided by its sister
house). Behind the rich
brocades, the splendor
and attention to detail i
n this sumptuous home
is reflected in this lovely
courtyard (left).

LA MAISON BLEUE IN FEZ

La Maison Bleue in the Fez medina was once the splendid home of Mohammed el-Abbadi, a well-known jurist and astrologer. The renovated and refurbished *dar* has been transformed into a luxury hotel. It takes its name ("the Blue House") from the color of its *zelliges*.

Guests can stroll at their leisure around the lovely courtyard, which is paved with marble and *zelliges*, and admire the fine plaster decorations and stained-glass windows. There is also a library, which houses the precious collection of scientific, theological, and philosophical works that once belonged to the master of the house.

The floors of suites between the courtyard and the rooftop terrace are decorated in a historical style with beautiful antiques and precious materials. The walls are hung with paintings by Moroccan artists. The heir to La Maison Bleue, Mehdi el-Abbadi, has recently restored a *riad* on the ramparts, which provides an alternative to its sister hotel and another version of the Fez lifestyle. It is rather smaller, with fewer rooms, and the whole building can be rented by a family or group of friends, with hotel service provided by La Maison Bleue. The terrace is the perfect place for a meal, with a spectacular view of the Merenid hills, and a more intimate view of the courtyard and the swimming pool, which is bordered by orange trees.

The atmosphere is decidedly Oriental. High windows face the courtyard and let plenty of light into the house. Mehdi el-Abbadi has also converted a long, narrow room into a bar, where you can enjoy an aperitif before climbing up to the terrace for dinner. He has furnished it with warm-colored bench seats and thick rugs, and given it subdued lighting; *moucharabiehs* filter the daylight and create a warm, relaxing atmosphere. There's a cozy area in the extension with a table and benches. If you study the decor of the house more closely, you'll see a dresser and writing desk that once belonged to Lyautey (the French resident commissary-general in Morocco)—more evidence of the rich and varied history of Fez, of which it is so rightly proud.

NEAR TANGIER, A HOTEL ON THE WATERFRONT

Eleven miles (18 kilometers) from Tangier is a hotel with a particularly appropriate name: Le Mirage. It looks quite unreal, as if it were floating on the sea. Facing it, the vast, deserted coastline stretches away as far as the eye can see. This spectacular location makes Le Mirage a fabulous place to stay. Its gardens slope down toward the water: they are flanked by white balustrades with friezes of *azulejos* (decorative painted tiles) that end in flights of steps. The whole thing has a markedly Iberian feel. The bottom steps are carved directly into the cliff, and go right down into the sea. On your way down the steps, you will see some hollows in the rock which could be used as shelters. Le Mirage is not far from the famous Hercules' Caves, a series of natural caverns, filled at high tide, where the legendary hero is said to have rested before attempting one of his labors: picking the golden apples in the garden of the Hesperides.

As the hotel is well away from the city of Tangier, it is a favorite with those who love the great outdoors. The accommodation is in bungalows, dotted around the swimming pool among the clumps of palm trees, hibiscus bushes, clusters of bougainvilleas, and hedges of rose bushes. Lower down are several suites that overlook the sea. They have large picture windows, which take up the whole of one wall and provide such an impressive view that it makes you feel almost dizzy.

Roger Schwarzenberg, the hotel's genial owner, entrusted the decoration of the bungalows to the Tangier designer Régis Milcent. Little by little, he has renovated the entire establishment; he has stamped it with his trademark Oriental style, thereby creating a striking contrast between the sophisticated, cozy interiors with their subdued colors and the natural landscape where the elements run wild. He also designed a bar, which is decorated English-style: it is a cozy place to shelter when the wind is raging outside.

The Mirage seems to be floating on the sea. Most hotels in such extraordinary locations are built parallel to the shore, but the Mirage is practically on the beach, perpendicular to the sea itself. Sea spray is all around, so the gardens here are especially fragrant; it is a delight to walk in them, breathing in the heady perfumes and enjoying the sea air.

A LIFE OF EASE IN ESSAOUIRA

The Riad-al-Madina's card invites you to "live in the eighteenth century": so it comes as no surprise to find that this house was restored with respect for its historical character. Its major attraction is its courtyard, an elegant place that has lost nothing of its former luster. It is surrounded by beautiful freestone columns and arches that stand out against the white walls, and the floor is decorated with antique *zelliges*. It is the focal point—indeed the heart—of the entire hotel. First-time visitors who come across the idyllic sight of this flowery, luminous courtyard are readily convinced that life is sweet in the Riad-al-Madina. The pasha who had it built must have had wonderful flair, because his residence still works its charm on today's visitors—and there are plenty of them! There is a marvelous feeling of comfort and well-being here, which has appealed to many famous guests in the past: Jimi Hendrix, for example, appreciated this relaxing atmosphere, and many other musicians followed in his footsteps.

It is easy to feel at home in this *riad*, as it is relatively small-scale; indeed, you may soon feel so much at home that time will slip by unnoticed. The hotel is situated right in the heart of the medina, in a street with plenty of small stores, so you can stock up on local handicrafts without having to carry them too far. What's more, the beach is only a short walk away, so when you come back, you can settle comfortably near the fireplace in the lounge-bar and relax in the pleasant warmth. The bedrooms around the courtyard also create a relaxing environment: they are decorated in blue, white, and matching tones, and furnished with all kinds of antique objects that the owners have collected over the years. The result is exquisitely simple and harmonious—and just outside is the glorious haven of the courtyard, with two fountains full of rose petals.

THE COLORS OF MOGADOR

It did not take long for the Villa Maroc in Essaouira to become a veritable institution and a favorite meeting-place for artists, writers, and all manner of esthetes. When the lovely blue and white Atlantic city of Essaouira suddenly became a popular

The patio at the Riad-al-Madina is the heart and focal point of the house (left). It's sunny and spacious, perfect for relaxing and much appreciated by guests who come here to enjoy breakfast or to take a break between trips to the medina. The patio at the Villa Maroc is more hemmed in and shaded. If you want a place in the sun, you just climb up to one of the many rooftop terraces. Both the patio and terraces are decorated in bright blue and white, accentuating the structure of the building (facing page, right and far right, top). The bedrooms and sitting areas are mostly white and bright (far right, bottom). The Villa Maroc, which was built in the eighteenth century, has become an institution in Essaouira; it is a favorite among artists and writers, who enjoy its "marine" theme and luxuriant garden.

tourist destination, this eighteenth-century property was converted into a charming hotel. The Villa Maroc, which comprises two houses, opted for a decorative style which echoes the traditional colors of Mogador and has made them its own. Its "marine" theme set the tone for a whole series of *dars*, which were restored and converted into guesthouses.

Not surprisingly, the front door is bright ocean-blue. It is hidden away in a little street, hemmed in by the high ramparts of the old part of town, and so discreet that you might almost walk past without seeing it. The Villa Maroc is typical of the kind of tall Moroccan house, several floors high, that reveals nothing from the outside: everything is turned inward, centering around the inner courtyard, which is the focal point of the residence. The whole downstairs area is cool and dark; the light shaft is not filled with sun for very long, and the surrounding rooms get precious little light. The Villa Maroc, however, is famous for its brilliant blue, splashes of which adorn the doorframes and archways. White is predominant in the downstairs lounge areas, with its whitewashed walls; but, as you climb to the upper floors, you get nearer and nearer to the sparkle of the ocean. On your upward climb, you are not alone: the plants in the courtyard climb up with you. They create a kind of miniature jungle around the building, climbing up the columns, wrapping themselves round the blue balustrades of the courtyard, threading their way across the ceiling, and hanging down in creepers from one floor to another. Plants are everywhere, making the hotel look like a greenhouse with a tropical garden. The city of Essaouira is full of sea spray; the hotel courtyard benefits from this humidity, which is why the vegetation is so luxurious. And if you want to enjoy the sea air, too, you only have to climb up to the terraced roofs between the two houses, for more delights in blue and white.

A KASBAH IN THE WESTERN SAHARA

Lost between the Drâa and Dadès valleys, facing the austere Jebel Sahro mountain range that leads to the Sahara Desert, is a village called N'Kob. N'Kob is remarkable in more ways than one: it overlooks a magnificent palm grove—and it has dozens of Kasbahs.

A wealthy local entrepreneur realized how precious this legacy of Kasbahs was, and he decided to renovate the Kasbah Baha Baha. The rehabilitation work was carried out with the utmost respect for traditional Moroccan architectural techniques. The result is a typically massive *pisé* construction, with windows accentuated in white. The same rules were applied to the furnishing of the Kasbah: authenticity and rural simplicity were the watchwords. The furniture, therefore, is woven in palm fiber, and the rugs, blankets, cushions, and other textiles are of a very sober range of colors. The Kasbah walls are impressively thick, with narrow openings that let through just a small amount of light. These buildings were originally designed to protect from cold, heat, and danger. The result is a fortified construction, with four towers. It used to be divided vertically in two, with one side reserved for the men's apartments, while the other housed both the women's apartments and the communal dining room.

The restored Kasbah Baha Baha is managed and generally looked after by the young people of N'Kob. When they are dressed in the traditional garb of their ancestral "Ait Atta" tribe (white cotton *djellabas*, plaited sandals, and headscarves), you feel you are among some kind of brotherhood. Indeed, this is not so very far from the truth, as life here is indeed rather monastic, with its vegetable and herb gardens, which are cultivated around the well. The Kasbah Baha Baha is not like any other place.

The kitchen alone is worth a visit. With its oven fed with palm leaves, its hard-packed earthen floor, and the light diffused over the ceiling, it is exactly like the kitchens that are still part of many village homes in Morocco today. You will have the opportunity to watch age-old rituals, such as the baking of bread or the preparation of couscous: a flavorsome kind of history lesson.

N'Kob overlooks a superb palm grove and has dozens of Kasbahs—one, the Kasbah Baha Baha, was restored by the villagers and converted into a hotel (top left). It comes as a surprise to find this place so far off the beaten track. It has plenty of charm and character, and is managed by young people from the village. A space is reserved as a washing area in the bedrooms, with an urn full of fresh water (bottom left). The Auberge Derkaoua has has small outdoor sitting-dining areas under the trees, in the shade of the eucalyptus and olive trees, protected by thick walls (right). This little island of greenery is just a few kilometers away from the desert dunes. A swimming pool has been added, to turn this place into a real oasis (facing page, top). The cloister was inspired by the officers' quarters in desert forts (facing page, bottom).

LAST OASIS BEFORE THE DUNES

When you leave Erfoud for the dunes of Erg Chebbi, you start out on the long, dusty road to Merzouga. There is nothing to indicate that there will be a Kasbah, so coming upon the Auberge Derkaoua is like seeing a mirage. Behind the boundary wall of this unlikely construction is a huge mass of greenery. All this is the work of one man, Michel. He is an elderly gentleman now, with plenty of personality: it took a lot of nerve and tremendous willpower to build an inn in the middle of nowhere and to plant more than two thousand trees.

Michel has been a desert enthusiast ever since he can remember; it was only logical, then, that he should spend his retirement here. He felt attracted to the Sahara even as a little boy; perhaps he was inspired by a photograph of his grandfather before the First World War, sitting on a dromedary at Ain Salah, an oasis in the south and the hottest spot in the Algerian Sahara. At the age of forty, Michel became a teacher, like his grandfather, and promised himself that he would one day rebuild Meribel fort, where his grandfather had lived.

Derkaoua is the reconstruction of a world that Michel was able to piece together by consulting the archives at Ain Salah and comparing them with family photos. The main body of the building looks like a cloister; Michel explains that he wanted to rebuild the officers' quarters here. The atmosphere of the place is somewhat austere, with bedrooms along two covered galleries that face each other across a long narrow courtyard. The *pisé* architecture is spartan and functional.

Michel dotted a few bungalows here and there among the lush vegetation, with a swimming pool to emphasize the sense that one is in an oasis. Nowadays, Derkaoua is full all year long, and you have to reserve to be sure of your room in paradise. "The oasis is Allah's paradise," he explains. "A world of beauty. The nomad can endure certain rigors, because he knows that there is this delight to come." The dry air full of dust is there to remind us that we're in a kind of bubble, in this island of greenery only a few kilometers away from the dunes; it will make you appreciate your stay all the more. So whether you're setting out on an expedition to the desert, or already on your way back, a stay at Derkaoua is a must.

Campers enjoy lunch in the open, after a night in a Saharan tent on the edge of an oasis (top left). These luxury bivouacs, in Morocco's most beautiful sites, present their own version of the perfect vacation. Near the Sahart Foundation's encampment for artists, caravans come to this well to replenish their supplies, and dromedaries come to drink (bottom left).

CAIDAL OR SAHARAN TENTS

Desert landscapes are the most beautiful in the world, so for a once-in-a-lifetime experience, why not try sleeping in a tent in the desert? When you find yourself face to face with vast stretches of sand and sky, you will get an understanding of the kind of sensations nomadic peoples have always experienced, feel in harmony with the natural elements, and experience emotions you have never felt before.

A SAHARAN PATRON OF THE ARTS

Imagine this: you leave Rissani, the last "civilized" town on the outskirts of Morocco and the frontiers of Algeria, and travel for three hours along a desert track. Then, in the middle of nowhere, you come across an artists' encampment. You have arrived at Sahart, where art and the Sahara come together.

The Sahart Foundation provides bed, board, and laundry-service for artists; in exchange, when they leave the camp, they leave a work behind as a record of the inspiration they found in Morocco. Meanwhile, they are invited to continue their work

at the foundation's headquarters in Marrakech. These artists can be painters, sculptors, photographers, storytellers, land or installation artists, poets, musicians, or writers. For the last four years, groups of three artists at a time (a dozen a year) have been experiencing the desert in the camp's five tents, under the tranquil gaze of Youssef, the camp's guardian angel.

The story began when a group of artists met Youssef, and the first tent was set up. The group was traveling in southern Morocco when one of its members got out of his automobile and found a gold coin in the sand, on the gold road that leads from Sijilmassa (now Rissani) to Timbuktu. He looked up to see Youssef (a nomad who had settled here) with his wife and, behind them, the ruins of a village dating from the times of Leo Africanus (a sixteenth-century Moroccan explorer). This village, called Oubaghelou (which means "the site of grandfather's well") used to overlook a lake. There is still a well here today, where you can enjoy a refreshing shower at nightfall.

The aim of the Sahart Foundation is to take a different approach to works of art, and give them another dimension. It welcomes creators of all kinds, and has no esthetic prejudices. The only criterion of selection is the following: "The artistic approach must be intellectually interesting."

A LUXURY BIVOUAC

Who has never dreamed of the ultimate romantic experience, worthy of *Out of Africa*: a romantic and elegant candlelit dinner in breathtakingly beautiful surroundings? Atlas Sahara Trek can make such dreams come true. This travel-agency-with-a-difference sets up camps in the middle of nowhere, against a backdrop of dunes, mountains, oases, and stars.

Bernard Fabry and his team take care of everything. This outdoor-enthusiast and desert-traveler crossed Algeria, the Niger, and Libya, before settling down in his home town of Marrakech. He knows all the most thrilling sites in the Moroccan desert. From mid-September through mid-April, he heads off to the desert and the dunes near Mhamid or Merzouga. At the end of April, his destination is the Atlas Mountains—the Ait Bougmez and other forgotten valleys. Each program he prepares is personalized, so all manner of tastes are catered for.

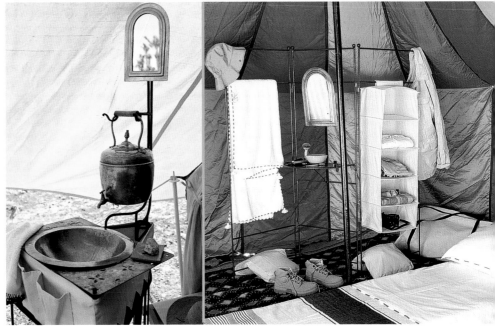

If your style is contemplative you can opt for a fixed bivouac, but if you're more sporty you may prefer to trek. Your bags will follow in a Land Rover, or be carried by camels and mules as you walk along beside them. Whatever you choose, your trip will involve at least two daily highlights: sunrise and sunset.

Bernard Fabry does not merely send you to the ends of the earth; he also sets the scene for you, with the made-to-measure tents that were designed exclusively for Atlas Sahara Trek. You can choose the style that suits you best: *caidal* (white with black motifs) or safari (unbleached linen). Candles and lanterns are arranged around the bivouac in the evening. Dinner is served under the stars, or in the mess tent if it's cool. Bernard Fabry has also designed portable furniture worthy of colonial expeditions: wooden and canvas camp beds, metal wardrobes, and copper washbasins. There are woven fiber and leather Mauritanian mats or rugs on the floor. Last but not least there is the shower tent, with large duckboard and towel rack (hot water is brought in pitchers). Absolutely nothing is left to chance, and the evening ends around the camp fire—with entertainment courtesy of the shooting stars.

The so-called *caidal* tent, exclusively designed for Atlas Sahara Trek, brings luxurious living to the desert, with its cozy camp bed, canvas shelves, woven fiber rug, and portable washbasin (above left and right). Camping trips are a fantastic way of experiencing the world's natural wonders. You can head for the desert, or for the Atlas Mountains, setting up camp under the stars near dunes, mountains, and oases (left).

The oven in the Kasbah Baha Baha kitchen (see page 194) is fired with palm leaves, for baking bread (left), and for making couscous the traditional way (far right, top). For a touch of refinement, the semolina can be flavored with cinnamon, raisins, or almonds (near right, top). Tagines, the spicy stews that are so popular in Morocco, are well simmered before being served in the cooking dish of the same name (near right, bottom; center right, middle). Tagines vary according to regional or family specialties: chicken tagine, for example, can be served with lemon (center right, top), or with prunes (far right, bottom). Salads are often accompanied by olives or preserved tomatoes (near right, middle; center right, bottom). Green tea, sugar, and mint are the essential ingredients of an age-old ritual (far right, middle).

GASTRONOMY

Moroccan cuisine is a subtle mix of sweet, savory, and spicy, which will give your trip an unforgettable flavor. It is the best expression of the traditional hospitality and generosity of a people who attach such importance to sharing and welcome. "Bismillah!" is the traditional word of blessing that is said at the beginning and end of a meal.

The national dish of Morocco is couscous, grains of semolina steamed until plump. Couscous varies greatly in the way it is presented according to region, family, and season. Sometimes, as a sign of wealth and refinement, it is flavored with cinnamon and raisins or almonds. The great classic is still to serve couscous with lamb or beef and vegetables, and flavorings such as coriander, saffron, and cumin, but on the coast you will find a variation with fish, and in the mountains you may have couscous with meatballs and boiled eggs.

Tagine comes in a similar range of flavors. This stew, made with red meat, chicken, or fish, is steamed for hours with whatever fruit and vegetables are in season. In the fall, for example, it may be served with quince. It is seasoned with preserved lemons and onions, olives, almonds, or prunes, and when it has simmered long enough it is served in the famous glazed earthenware dish of the same name, the tagine, with its distinctive conical lid.

Elsewhere, in more rustic mode, you may be served harira as a starter. This is a thick soup, of Berber origin, made of lentils, chickpeas, aromatic herbs, and spices (with or without lamb). It is so filling that it could replace the main course. During Ramadan, it provides an energizing daily meal, when served with dates or even honey pastries. It is eaten every evening when fasting is over.

There is not a great variety of desserts. You might try a sweet version of pastilla, which is just the flaky pastry topped with almond milk. Saffa is very fine semolina, which can also be served sweet, with icing sugar and cinnamon sprinkled on top. An orange salad, with orange blossom water and cinnamon, makes a refreshing end to a meal.

Mint tea is served with piles of pastries glistening with honey and sprinkled with almonds; these might include gazelle horns and bracelets (top right). They are usually made of phyllo pastry, and stuffed with dried fruits including dates and walnuts (bottom right). An elaborately carved metal tray is arranged with bunches of mint, green tea, and sugar on one side, the teapot and little gilt-decorated, multicolored glasses on the other. The host measures out the perfect quantities of sugar and tea, then he fills the teapot and glasses in turn. Finally, he raises the teapot very high over the tiny glasses, and pours the scalding amber tea in a long stream (far right). Marjoram, thyme, or anise is sometimes used to add their delicate flavors. In October, you may have a delicious salad of fresh pomegranates (center right).

This guide provides the addresses of all the hotels, guesthouses, and restaurants (Moroccan-style only) mentioned or photographed in the preceding chapters. Our museum selection is deliberately not comprehensive: we decided to include only the smaller, more intimate museums devoted to the decorative arts, local traditions, and regional art. Some of these museums are housed in beautiful homes or palaces.

More and more guesthouses are opening up in Morocco. Choosing accommodation of this type often allows you to discover private homes that have been restored tastefully and with attention to detail. Their owners are often happy to share their passion for Moroccan crafts and culture. For this book we have selected the more authentic, charming places that capture the real character of Morocco. Again, this is not meant to be a comprehensive listing.

Many of the people who produce crafts and artisanal goods work from small shops in the middle of a souk; in such cases, it is impossible to give a precise address. The name of the craftsman is sometimes all you need to find his shop. Often, someone will take you to the person you are looking for if you ask for help or directions once you are in the medina. Most of the larger cities have government-run craft centers, known as the *Ensemble Artisanal*. Here, you can generally find a wide selection of various local crafts, and sometimes objects from other regions of Morocco. The prices at these centers are set by the *Direction de l'artisanat*, the government agency that administers Moroccan crafts. A visit to one or more of these centers may be useful if you want to get a good, general idea of prices and quality before beginning the adventure of bargaining in the souks.

This guide is organized by city or region, and follows the suggested itineraries of the book. Addresses are then classified by category.

CHEFCHAOUEN

HOTELS

PARADOR
B.P. 3 Place El Makhzine
Tel.: 212 (0) 39 98 61 36/98 63 24
Fax: 212 (0) 39 98 70 33
E-mail: parador@iam.net.ma
This hotel is ideally located in the city center, with a magnificent view of the nearby mountains. This is a modest yet perfectly comfortable hotel, with friendly service and a pool. The exceptional beauty of the site makes this an excellent place to stay.

CASA HASSAN
22, rue Targui
Tel.: 212 (0) 39 98 61 53
Fax: 212 (0) 39 98 81 96
This lovely small hotel gives you the chance to experience a traditional Moroccan home, with rooms and lounges arranged around the central patio. This is a particularly charming place to stay. It also has a very pleasant rooftop terrace.

RESTAURANTS - CAFÉS

Take a break at one of the cafés or restaurants on the Place el-Hammam and enjoy the relaxing ambience.

ALADIN
A small, friendly restaurant just above the Place Uta el-Hamman, with a tiny terrace offering a lovely view of the square below and the mountains opposite.

CRAFTS

DAR CHEFCHAOUEN
Baba frères
Rue Jamma 17
Quartier Bab Souk
Tel.: 212 (0) 39 98 71 11
Factory and showroom for carpets and blankets made with the characteristic colors and patterns of the region.

FOUTAS
Rue Lalla El Hora, n° 56
This is the spot to purchase one of the famous *foutas*, the striped pieces of fabric woven and worn by the women of the Rif. You will find a wide selection of all sizes and colors to remind you of the bright shades of the Rif region.

TANGIER

HOTELS

EL-MINZAH
85, rue de la Liberté
Tel.: 212 (0) 39 33 58 85
Fax: 212 (0) 39 33 45 46
(see page 187)
E-mail: elminzah@tangeroise.net.ma
A classy, legendary hotel situated in a lovely building downtown. It was patronized by European celebrities who traveled to Tangier during the golden age of the 1930s, and by Americans later on. The myth of the hotel lives on today. Even if you do not stay here, stop by to enjoy a drink on the pretty blue and white patio.

HÔTEL CONTINENTAL
Dar Baroud 36
Tel.: 212 (0) 39 93 10 24/37 58 51
Fax: 212 (0) 39 93 11 43
(see page 182)
E-mail: hcontinental@iam.net.ma
This is a charmingly old-fashioned turn-of-the-century hotel in the heart of the medina, with a view overlooking the harbor. Edgar Degas stayed here, and Bernardo Bertolucci did some filming here, too. The relaxed atmosphere attracts a laid-back clientele. This is one of Tangier's oldest hotels.

LE MIRAGE
Les Grottes d'Hercule
B.P. 2198 Tanger
Tel.: 212 (0) 39 33 33 32/33 34 90/33 34 91
Fax: 212 (0) 39 33 34 92
(see page 191)
E-mail: mirage@iam.net.ma
Just 9 miles (15 km) from Tangier, this hotel consists of a series of individual bungalows hidden away in a lush garden. It has a spectacular view of the sea and the immense beach below. The decor was designed by Régis Milcent. It provides the perfect seaside stopping place, invigorating but relaxing, where you can also enjoy the excellent cuisine, particularly the fresh fish specialities.

GUESTHOUSES

À LA KASBAH
Tel.: 212 (0) 62 11 27 24
Philippe Guiget-Bologne
A charming guesthouse, situated in the heart of the Kasbah.

RESTAURANTS

SAVEURS
2 escalier Waller
The speciality in this popular restaurant is fish: you will have a choice between fish tagine, sautéed fish, steamed fish, and so on. They close fairly early in the evenings, so lunch is probably your best option.

And here are two other unpretentious and friendly places to enjoy authentic Moroccan cuisine:

AGADIR
21, avenue du Prince-Héritier
Tel.: 212 (0) 61 53 89 48

LACHIRI
Ksar es Seghir
Rue principale
Route Tanger-Ceuta

CAFÉS - BARS

EL-MINZAH
85, rue de la Liberté
Tel.: 212 (0) 39 33 58 85
Fax: 212 (0) 39 33 45 46
(see page 187)
E-mail: elminzah@tangeroise.net.ma
This famous hotel is also a perfect place for a cocktail; try the cozy English bar or enjoy a drink during the day in the shade of the colonnades.

CAFÉ HAFA
Quartier Marshan
(see page 21)
Once a favorite haunt of Paul Bowles, Jean Genet, and other local celebrities, the café clings to a clifftop overlooking the Strait of Gibraltar. The natural terraces and gardens offer a stunning setting to enjoy a glass of mint tea while you contemplate the horizon. The café has been open since 1921; it still does not have a sign, but everyone knows how to reach it by the path along the coast.

TANGERINE
1, rue Magellan
One of Jack Kerouac's hangouts and a favorite with the Beat Generation. Unchanged since the 1960s, it is always a surprise: sometimes packed, sometimes deserted, and you never know when it is going to close.

MUSEUMS

DAR EL-MAKHZEN and THE KASBAH MUSEUM
This palace, on the Place de la Kasbah, was built in the seventeenth century by Moulay Ismail and enlarged several times over the years by subsequent sultans. This beautiful building now houses a museum devoted to traditional Moroccan arts, and an Andalusian-style garden filled with flowers and lemon and orange trees. You can admire the garden from the Riad-Sultan tea room on the upper floor.

LE PALAIS DES INSTITUTIONS ITALIENNES
Rue Mohammed-Ben-Abdelouahab
This is a magnificent site. It houses an immense garden and a palace, with a long series of rooms with Florentine marble fireplaces. It can be visited on request by contacting the Italian Consulate in Casablanca, Tel.: 212 (0) 22 20 84 45. The Moorish-style building was constructed between 1908 and 1914 by Sultan Moulay Hafid, then sold to the Italian government in 1929. It was transformed into a training institute, and is now the headquarters for an Italian cultural association. It feels slightly run-down today, although this only adds to its charm.

SHOPPING

LA LIBRAIRIE DES COLONNES
54, boulevard Pasteur
This was the local haunt for the leading lights of Tangier's literary world, including Paul Bowles, Mohammed Choukri, and others. The shop sells the works of these authors, even rare editions, along with a great selection of books about the city.

PARFUMERIE MADINI
14, rue Sebou en médina
This Tangier institution has been run by the Madini family for generations. They distill essential oils and can prepare any type of perfume on request, including copies. Their clients, particularly from the Arab world, come from all over for their products. Barbara Hutton used to shop here.

BAZAR TINDOUF
Rue de la Liberté
Situated opposite the Hôtel Minzah, this is a great place to browse around for all

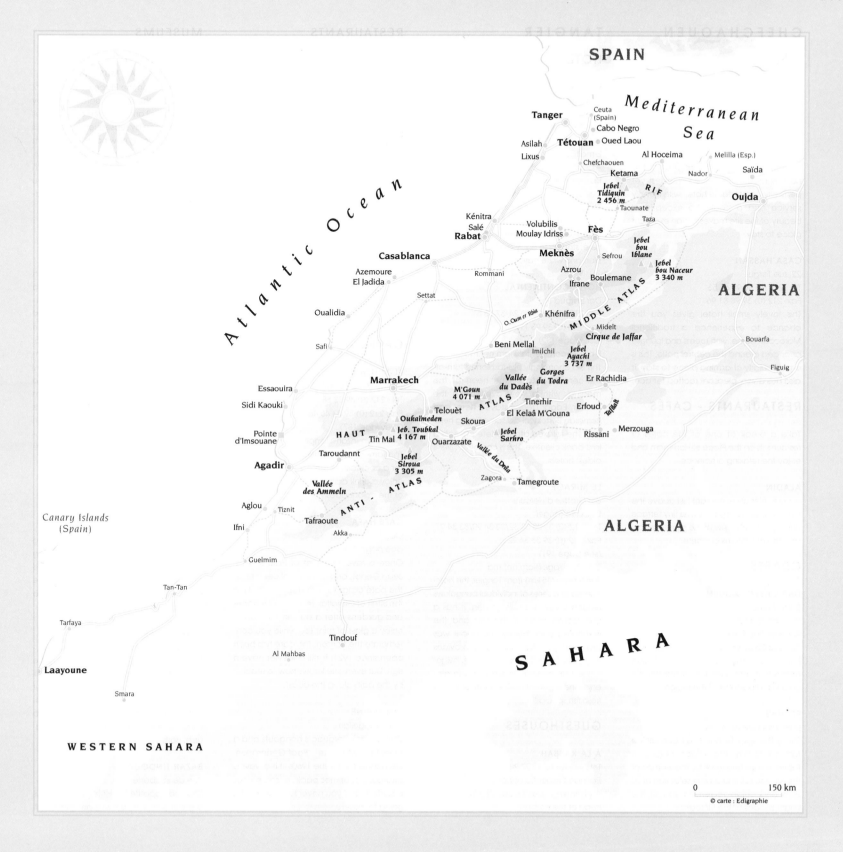

kinds of objects (lanterns, pottery, old traditional clothes, fabrics, furniture with mother-of-pearl inlays). It is also one of the city's most beautiful stores.

MAGID
6, zankat el-Mouahidine
An antique dealer with a good selection of jewelry, fabric, and old carpets.

THE BERBER CRAFTS SOUK
Rue des Almohades
A good place to shop for a selection of high-quality carpets.

NIGHTLIFE

MOROCCO PALACE
Rue Moulay-Abdellah
This nightclub has an incredible decor that looks like something out of a Hollywood film, overlaid with a touch of the 1960s. This is a good place for a memorable evening out; a rai band livens up the dance floor.

ASILAH
RESTAURANTS

CHEZ PEPE
Place Zellaka
A pretty setting to enjoy fish specialties, situated just opposite the Kasbah.

CASABLANCA
RESTAURANTS

LE CABESTAN
90, boulevard de la Corniche
Phare d'El Hank
Tel.: 212 (0) 22 39 11 90
This French-run restaurant serves the best fish in Morocco. The menu offers a selection of Moroccan and French specialties.

LE MÉDINA
50, rue Normandie
Tel.: 212 (0) 22 25 25 13
This lovely house nestled in the Maarif quarter offers Moroccan specialties among antique furniture and traditional crockery.

RIYAD ZITOUN
31, boulevard Rachidi
Tel.: 212 (0) 22 22 39 27
A lovely small restaurant in a charming setting, decorated with zelliges and traditional wooden latticework.

PASTRY

PÂTISSERIE BEN HABOUS
2, rue Fkih-El-Gabbas
Tel.: 212 (0) 22 30 30 25
This is Casablanca's best pastry shop. Try the cornes de gazelle, briouates, fekas with almonds, and other Moroccan specialties.

DESIGN

A DÉ
37, rue Assilm
Quartier Racine
Tel.: 212 (0) 22 95 01 13/22 95 03 47
Fax: 212 (0) 22 95 01 14
E-mail: stazi@wanadoo.net.ma
Internet: www.studiumcasa.com
(see page 144)
This home decor shop run by the talented young interior architect Sophia Tazi offers a selection of her furniture prototypes that are available on order. Her original designs are contemporary, creative, and almost playful. A talented representative of a new generation of designers.

FABRICS

BENCHEKROUN
50, rue Souhail-Lahcen
This family-run shop in a kissaria (a shopping arcade) in the Derb Omar quarter specializes in fabrics. It has been passed down from father to son since 1949.

ANTIQUES

ABDERKADER
1, rue Cadi-Ayad
You can find the famous French pottery from Digoin (made in the 1920s for countries in the Maghreb) as you bargain-hunt in this eclectic jumble.

RACHID & JOUAD
30, rue El-Hadj-Lamfadal
This antique shop, right in the heart of the Habbous quarter, specializes in curios and Orientalist paintings.

EXCURSIONS

GT ORGANISATION
Tel./Fax: 212 (0) 22 23 26 49
E-mail: ja.guilbert@marocnet.net.ma
This agency organizes all sorts of custom-designed excursions throughout Morocco for small groups, as well as mountain-bike trips through the Atlas, treks on camelback, or airplane trips in search of Saint-Exupéry's body; he was declared missing after a flight in 1944.

MONUMENT

HASSAN-II MOSQUE
(see page 24)
Not to be missed for any reason, as this may be the only mosque you will be allowed to enter in Morocco, plus it is an amazing building. Commissioned by King Hassan II, it combines architectural tradition and technical innovations. The immensity of the building alone is breathtaking. Entrance fee.

MUSEUM

LA VILLA DES ARTS
Avenue Brahim-Roudani
This 1930s colonial villa, restored in 1999, houses the Contemporary Art Museum.

SAFI
CERAMICS

AHMED SERGHINI
7, souk de poterie
Tel.: 212 (0) 44 62 69 10
(see page 89)
Each potter in Safi jealously guards the secret of his own production. Serghini, a master potter from a family of potters going back seven generations, is the most famous; his output is as great as his reputation. He generally works with typical forms and traditional designs, although he is willing to integrate marine motifs (fish, stars, sun) on his pottery to keep up with the fashions of the time.

AHMED LAGHISSI
9, souk des potiers
Tel.: 212 (0) 66 12 21 62
(see page 89)
Ahmed Laghissi is another Safi potter. He is less productive and less widely known

than Serghini, but his work is distinguished by its extremely personal artistic style, characterized by unusual motifs based on ornamental scrolls and arabesques. His colors are intense and deep, a good reflection of his own artistic work. His work is a far cry from mass production; each piece is unique and is a true work of art. This potter, combing the past and the present in the art of terracotta, is definitely worth discovering.

ESSAOUIRA
HOTELS

VILLA MAROC
10, rue A. Ben Yassine
Tel.: 212 (0) 44 47 61 47 / 44 67 58
Fax: 212 (0) 44 47 58 06 / 47 28 06
E-mail: hotel@villa-maroc.com
Internet: www.villa-maroc.com
(see pages 192–193)
The charming Villa Maroc sets the standard for all the other hotels in the town. In recent years, this eighteenth-century house, decorated in white and blue, and located along the ramparts, has become the favorite stopover for artists, writers, and esthetes. The rooftop terraces offer stunning views over the city. In the evening, dinner is served at intimately set tables.

AUBERGE TANGARO
Quartier Diabat
B.P. 8
Tel.: 212 (0) 44 78 47 84
This has been a legendary establishment since the 1960s, as travelers flocked here in search of Jimi Hendrix, who lived for a time in the nearby small Berber village of Diabat. Today, visitors come to relax amid the unspoiled environment, and to enjoy panoramic ocean views, all just a few miles from Essaouira. The luxury of this auberge is only accentuated by its quiet, simple, candlelit interiors.

DAR MIMOSAS
Route d'Agadir
Tel.: 212 (0) 44 47 59 34
Fax: 212 (0) 44 78 52 74
E-mail: mimosas1@iam.net.ma
This charming hotel comprises eight villas, decorated in a predominately blue color scheme and set in a tree-filled garden. Run by Philippe Cachet.

VILLA QUIETA

86, boulevard Mohamed-V
Tel.: 212 (0) 44 78 50 04/44 78 50 05
Fax: 212 (0) 44 78 50 06
E-mail: villa.quieta@iam.net.ma
Internet: www.villa-quieta.com
Situated outside of the medina, just 150 feet (50 meters) from the beach, this hotel is ideally placed to enjoy the view of the ramparts and the ocean. This former private home was renovated by the owner's family, who kept the kitsch decor. It offers spacious rooms, suites with terraces overlooking the sea, large salons, and friendly service provided by Hymen, the mistress of the house, who looks out for your comfort and wellbeing.

HÔTEL RIAD AL-MADINA

9, rue Attarine
Tel.: 212 (0) 44 47 59 07/44 47 57 27
Fax: 212 (0) 44 47 66 95/44 47 57 27
E-mail: riadalma@iam.net.ma
Internet: www.almadina.com
(see pages 192)
The Riad al-Madina in the heart of the medina gives you the experience of living in the eighteenth century. This perfectly restored home, which once belonged to a local pasha, is laid out around the flower-filled central courtyard. The rooms in this idyllic spot are light and decorated in natural tones.

PALAZZO DESDEMONA

12–14, rue Youssef El-Fassi
Tel.: 212 (0) 44 47 22 27
Fax: 212 (0) 44 78 57 35
This elegant house is situated at the gates to the ramparts in Essaouira, and just steps from the harbor. It has been entirely renovated in Art Deco style, with a sophisticated touch in all the details. A very upmarket establishment.

GUESTHOUSES

BAOUSSALA

Douar El-Ghazoua
Tel./Fax: 212 (0) 44 47 43 45
Cell phone: 212 (0) 66 30 87 46
E-mail: dchoupin@yahoo.fr
Internet: www.baoussala.com
(see page 173)
This lovely, round building looks something like a Kasbah. Constructed by Dominique Maté and her husband, this guesthouse offers a hospitable stay in the midst of the countryside, on a small road between Essaouira and Sidi Kaouki. In this enchanting place, cut off from the rest of the world, you can take time to relax and enjoy the contagious good humor of the mistress of the house. There are not many rooms, and guests are welcomed like family. A Berber tent is set up in the garden during summer months.

DAR LOULEMA

2, rue Souss
Tel.: 212 (0) 44 47 53 46
Cell phone: 212 (0) 61 24 76 61
E-mail: rlami@free.fr
(see page 174–175)
Dany and Raymond Lami are like a number of couples who have fallen in love with Essaouira and decided to renovate a *dar* in the medina as a guesthouse. The rooms are laid out around the courtyard; each one is decorated differently using traditional techniques, beautiful brightly colored fabrics and *tadelakt*.

RIAD AL-ZAHIA

4, rue Mohamed-Diouri
Tel.: 212 (0) 44 47 35 81
Cell phone: 212 (0) 61 34 71 31
E-mail: Zahia@essaouiranet.com
Pascale Robinet and Alain Crozet put their heart and soul into the renovation of this typical old *dar*. The decoration is charmingly romantic, overseen by the mistress of the house.

RENTAL HOMES

ESSAOUIRA HOMES COLLECTION

Tel.: 212 (0) 44 44 75 00
Fax: 212 (0) 44 44 96 99
Cell phone: 212 (0) 67 59 60 27
E-mail: 1001prod@cybernet.net.ma
(see pages 138–141, Joël Martial's home)
Joël Martial, a former fashion makeup artist, fell under the spell of Essaouira, moved here permanently and opened up a rental agency. He offers a good selection of houses, including his own. They are all charming places to stay, with lovely decors and settings.

JACK'S APARTMENTS

1, place Moulay-Hassan
Tel.: 212 (0) 44 47 55 38
Fax: 212 (0) 44 47 69 01
E-mail: apartment@essaouira.com
Internet: www.essaouira.com/apartments
(see pages 142–143, Jack's house)
You ought not miss Jack Oswald in Essaouira. He opened up this agency offering houses and apartments to rent long before the town became so popular. He offers a large selection of accommodations in different styles and sizes, including some in the medina, some with a view of the sea, and even some for a single night.

RESTAURANTS

CHEZ KÉBIR

Situated five miles (8 km) along the road to Agadir, at the intersection leading to Ghazoua. Enjoy candlelit dinners and incredibly copious meals, topped off by one of the remarkable lemon tarts for dessert. This is a friendly, generous restaurant for a guaranteed great meal.

CAFÉS

TAROS

2, rue Sqala
place Moulay-Hassan
Tel.: 212 (0) 44 47 64 07
Fax: 212 (0) 44 47 64 08
(see page 28)
Breton owner Alain Kerrien named his literary café "Taros," after the name of one of the winds that blows through Essaouira. It is located in a two-hundred-year-old house. Lots of people come to browse through the many books, watch the action on the busy harbor from the sunny rooftop terrace, enjoy some of the famous stuffed sardines, or visit the exhibition of the moment. Decorated with *zelliges* and old bright yellow tiles, this pleasant cultural hangout is so friendly and relaxing, it may soon become one of your regular stopping places. It also functions as the headquarters for the Essaouira Festival.

CHEZ DRISS

10, rue Hajjali
Place Moulay-Hassan
This pastry shop has been delighting its clientele with hot *pain au chocolat* and croissants since 1925. Enjoy a wonderful breakfast on the tiny patio with toast and fresh orange juice. The French pastries are another great reason to stop by for an afternoon snack. A local institution for good, simple pleasures.

BOOKS

JACK'S

1, place Moulay-Hassan
Tel.: 212 (0) 44 47 55 38
Fax: 212 (0) 44 47 69 01
Jack Oswald's bookstore, located on the famous Place Molay-Hassan, is *the* meeting place for everyone in Essaouira. People come here for postcards and the large selection of books about the town. Stop by when you first arrive in Essaouira and you can pick up information about places to stay (*see also* Jack's Apartments).

SECOND-HAND SHOP

RIRI D'ARABIE

66, rue Boutouil
Tel.: 212 (0) 44 47 45 15
Cell phone: 212 (0) 61 15 17 46
Both the shop and the shopowner are worth the visit. The enthusiastic, good-natured proprietor knows how to find objects from all over, to the great delight of the antique- and bargain-hunters who stop by. You are sure to find all sorts of wonderful surprises here.

PAINTINGS

MICHEL VU

(By appointment only)
Tel.: 212 (0) 44 47 43 73
Cell phone: 212 (0) 66 07 65 41
Michel Vu, a painter who has been living in Essaouira since the 1970s, has a favorite subject: the *haik*. All of his work is based on depictions of the women wrapped mysteriously in this typical Essaouira fabric. Real painting aficionados can also experience the everyday world of this Bohemian artist by renting out rooms in his home, which is situated in the middle of the countryside.

FRÉDÉRIC DAMGARD GALLERY

Avenue Oqba-Ben-Nafii
Tel.: 212 (0) 44 78 44 46
Fax: 212 (0) 44 47 28 57
The gallery, run by a Dane, specializes in local painters. Their artwork ranges in style from Pointillist and Cubist to abstract, naive, and even primitive with African influences—all reflecting the diversity of the Essaouira culture. The extremely colorful and original paintings have received worldwide recognition.

WOOD

To really appreciate Essaouira's unique character, take a walk along the length of the citadel ramparts, where the distinct scent of *thuja* wood, carried by the sea mist, fills the air. The wood is transformed in the small workshops set up in the former munitions warehouses. Local craftsmen excel in the art of marquetry, and you can find objects ranging from tables to chests, numerous boxes, backgammon games, platters, and more. But you should bear in mind that your house will probably be much drier than the ambient humidity of Essaouira, and that this type of marquetry does not always react well to arid conditions.

ARABESQUE
Adelmounaim Rahmini
n° 5 Laalouj Road
Tel.: 212 (0) 44 47 60 66
Adelmounaim Rahmini creates standing lamps or wall lamps, using age-old techniques. His highly personal and inventive designs are distinctive and unusual.

WEAVINGS

LAHRI MOHAMED BEN LHOUSSAINE
souk El-Ghazel n° 181
Tel.: 212 (0) 44 47 28 77
You can find a large selection of lovely cotton or wool blankets in this shop. They come in varying thicknesses and in a wide range of patterns and colors. Different sizes are available, and you can also commission specific items.

CERAMICS

AICHA HEMMOU
place aux grains n° 115
Tel.: 212 (0) 61 77 52 09
This shop is unusual in that it belongs to a woman potter, not a common sight in Morocco. She makes simple dishes with a white or lovely yellow background, which she decorates with graceful Berber patterns. Her tableware is also availabe for purchase at Taros (*see above*).

LAMPS

BOUDLAL AFIF
12, rue de la Sqala
Tel.: 212 (0) 44 47 64 29
The ubiquitous goat-skin or lamb-skin lamp, decorated with henna, has found its master in Foued. Afif is known for his wide selection of stylized ethnic motifs (sometimes the same as those painted on women's hands) and beautifully detailed designs. You cannot help but appreciate the quality and beauty of his work, especially after seeing other, less accomplished examples of these lamps.

JEWELRY

ZAROIL
53, rue Laartine
Tel.: 212 (0) 44 47 62 55
Zaroil's designs are surprisingly modern, yet as timeless as their simple motifs, such as the spiral medallion, a symbol of life. If you like ethnic jewelry, this selection of work is bound to please.

TAROS
2, Sqala
place Moulay-Hassan
Tel.: 212 (0) 44 47 64 07
It is not enough for Alain Kerrien to own Taros, the literary café of Essaouira. He also designs silver rings for men and women, characterized by a powerful, austere beauty: interlacing rings, rings with onyx stones, and engraved silver rings. All these original designs are on display in the exhibition space of the café, along with an interesting selection of other craftwork from Essaouira.

RAPHIA
Rafia Craft
82, rue d'Agadir
Tel.: 212 (0) 24 78 36 32
E-mail: rafiacraft@yahoo.fr
Miro is back in Essaouira after creating shoes for Agnès B and a number of other Paris designers. He continues to create elegant, sophisticated, and natural raffia footwear. His mules and other open shoes are all braided and handmade in his small workshop, which is filled with every possible color of raffia. He also produces a line of multicolored lampshades. This is high-quality craftsmanship.

FOUM JEMAÂ

RIYAD CASCADES D'OUZOUD
Tel.: 212 (0) 23 45 96 58
Internet: www.ouzoud.com
The Riyad Cascades, just two hours from Marrakech on the road to Fez, overlooks the most beautiful waterfalls in Morocco. The building is laid out according to the classical floor plan of traditional homes in the region. The painted ceilings and *pisé* walls are inspired by the Berber tradition, yet the house also incorporates the joys of modern comfort, with a fireplace, air conditioning, and *hammam*. There are a total of seven rooms, including one in a tent for an experience not soon to be forgotten.

LEGZERA

CHEZ ABDELLAH
Six miles (10 km) before Sidi Ifni on the road from Mirleft.
An unmarked road leads about a third of a mile (500 meters) to this inn on the banks facing Legzera island. This establishment is worth a stop, if only for the beauty of the unspoiled site and the lack of other visitors. On the deserted beach is a series of four red rock arches. If you are looking to spend a night on the beach and enjoy a fish dinner, this simple, bright pink inn offers fairly basic comfort, but is wonderfully welcoming. It is hard to beat the pleasure of a candlelit dinner.

TAROUDANT

HÔTEL PALAIS SALAM
Tel.: 212 (0) 48 85 25 01
Fax: 212 (0) 48 85 26 54
B.P. 258
E-mail: salamtaroudant@groupesalam.com
Internet: www.groupesalam.com
(see page 178–179)
This nineteenth-century palace once belonged to a pasha. It adjoins the famous red ramparts of the city, and boasts numerous courtyards and a stunning garden with a lush, diverse vegetation. The new wing with pink houses fits seamlessly into this idyllic setting. One of the hotel's pools is located at the base of an old rampart and is surrounded by plants.

LA GAZELLE D'OR
Tel.: 212 (0) 48 85 20 39
Fax: 212 (0) 48 85 27 37
This is a discreet temple of luxury. The Gazelle d'Or embodies the quintessential refinement of the palaces of yester-year, long before the advent of mass tourism. It should therefore come as no surprise that this hotel is so popular with a range of celebrities in search of anonymity and relaxation. Thirty bungalows, each with private gardens, are scattered throughout the Eden-like gardens, where fragrant, luxurious roses compete with the pervasive scent of jasmine, and where ornamental grasses, cacti, and orange trees flourish. Everything here is designed to contribute to an overwhelming sense of calm and comfort.

The lobby, bar and restaurant are decorated in a delightfully casual style, and create a perfect backdrop for the pianist and the blend of Italian-Moroccan cuisine. Many of the ingredients are produced on site: the owner personally oversees production of oil, wild honey, jams and preserves (tomato, grapefruit, orange), and fully organic vegetables, which are grown in the huge kitchen garden.

Lunch alongside the pool provides a romantic interlude far from the hustle and bustle of daily life. The *hammam* and massages available to clients only prolong the sense of wellbeing that permeates this establishment.

OUARZAZATE

DAR DAÏF MAISON D'HÔTES
Désert et Montagne Maroc
B.P. 45
Tel.: 212 (0) 44 88 51 46
Fax: 212 (0) 44 88 63 52
Internet: www.dardaif.ma
This guesthouse, run by a Basque-Berber couple, recreates the rural Berber lifestyle of Morocco. It is a good place to stay if you are eager for contact with local residents. The house has a distinctive character that reflects the owner's genuine love of Morocco.

DADÈS VALLEY

GUESTHOUSES

KASBAH AÏT BEN MORO
Oasis de Skoura
Tel./Fax: 212 (0) 44 85 21 16
E-mail: hotelbenmoro@yahoo.fr
(see page 177)
Juan De Dios Romero, from Andalusia, has renovated this Kasbah, fully respecting

the simple, clean lines of this type of earthen structure. The pefect opportunity to stay in an authentic Kasbah.

DAR AHLAM
Palmeraie de Skoura
Tel.: 212 (0) 44 85 22 39
E-mail: darahlam@Leverderideau.fr
Dar Ahlam is a traditional Kasbah consisting of eight suites and three independent apartments. The gardens were designed by Louis Benech. The guesthouse offers a *hammam*, jacuzzi, swimming pool, and massage rooms.

HOTELS

KASBAH TIZZARIOUINE HÔTEL
Boulmane du Dadès
Tel.: 212 (0) 44 83 06 90
Fax: 212 (0) 44 83 02 56
This hotel is particularly recommended for the originality of its rooms, some of which are built directly into the rock, with a spectacular view stretching over the valley and the palm grove below. The owner, Brahim Lemnaouar, organizes excursions and camping trips in the area, and can tailor-make trips to suit your needs and interests.

FROM THE DRÂA VALLEY TO MERZOUGA

KASBAH BAHA BAHA
N'Kob village
Zagora Province
Tel.: 212 (0) 44 83 90 78 / 44 83 84 63
Fax: 212 (0) 44 44 67 24 / 44 83 84 64
Internet: www.kasbahbaha.free.fr
(see page 194)
This Kasbah is very different in character than all the others and has the added advantage of being off the beaten tourist track. It has been restored and decorated by the residents of N'Kob in keeping with the pure tradition of earthen architecture. It is managed by the young people of the village, who are extremely keen on providing you with the greatest possible comfort.

The women work in the traditional kitchen to prepare local specialties using home-grown produce. The Kasbah overlooks the palm grove and offers a magnificent view of the dozens of houses in the village.

MERZOUGA

AUBERGE DERKAOUA
Erfoud B.P. 64
Tel./Fax: 212 (0) 55 57 71 40
Cell phone: 212 (0) 61 34 36 77
(see page 195)
This is the last oasis before the dunes. The inn, which is nestled among the lush vegetation, was created by a Frenchman who fell in love with the desert, planted hundred of trees, and constructed this series of bungalows. A good place to stop before or after an excursion into the desert.

FEZ

HOTELS

PALAIS JAMAÏ
Bab Guissa
Tel.: 212 (0) 55 63 43 31
Fax: 212 (0) 55 63 50 96
E-mail: resa@palais-jamai.co.ma
(see page 184)
This is one of Morocco's most beautiful hotels, partly because of its incomparable location adjoining the ramparts, and partly because of its past as a luxurious palace: the spirits of the former owner, Grand Vizier Jamaï, and his concubines, are never far away. The panoramic view over Fez, and the paths by the pool through the Andalusian gardens are simply delightful. A memorable and magical stay guaranteed.

JNAN PALACE HÔTEL
Avenue Ahmed-Chaouki
Tel.: 212 (0) 55 65 22 30
Fax: 212 (0) 55 65 19 17
This is another luxury establishment, but in a different spirit. The style is more international and has less local color. Located in the Ville Nouvelle (new town), the hotel has a pool and magnificent garden.

LA MAISON BLEUE
2, place de l'Istiqlal-Batha
30000 Fez
Tel.: 212 (0) 55 74 18 43
Tel./Fax: 212 (0) 55 74 06 86
E-mail: maisonbleue@fesnet.net.ma
Internet: www.maisonbleue.com
(see page 190)
This blue house is located in the medina. Built in 1915, it was the former home of Mohamed El- Abbadi, a professor at the

El-Quaraouine University, and a famous jurist and astrologer. The *dar* was restored and brought back to life by his descendant Mehdi el-Abbadi as a luxury hotel. The spacious rooms and suites are magnificently furnished and the courtyard is lavishly lined in marble and *zelliges*.

RENTAL HOMES

RIAD MAISON BLEUE
33, derb El Mitter Talaa El Kebira
Tel.: 212 (0) 55 74 18 39/55 74 18 73
E-mail: la maisonbleue1@iam.net.ma
Internet: www.maisonbleue.com
(see page 190)
Mehdi el-Abbadi restored this *riad*, which was built in 1880 by another great jurist and man of science, Si Mohamed Bel Arbi el-Alaoui. Located on the ramparts, it is small enough to be rented by a single family or a group of friends. Hotel services can be provided by its sister house, La Maison Bleue. The terrace is ideally situated for enjoying meals against the spectacular backdrop of the Merenid hills. There is a pool in the courtyard.

GUESTHOUSES

DAR EL-GHALIA
Tel.: 212 (0) 55 63 41 67
E-mail: darelghalia@yahoo.com
Internet: www.maisondhotes.co.ma
(see page 170–171)
A distinguished old family offers courteous and discreet hospitality in their magnificent seventeenth-century home situated in the Andalusian quarter of the medina. Here you can experience all the refinement of Fez hospitality in an historical and authentic *dar*, complete with courtyard and suites.

RESTAURANTS

Dar el-Ghalia and La Maison Bleue (*see above*) organize dinners on their stunning courtyards (reservation only). At Dar el-Ghalia, it is the mistress of the house who oversees the kitchen, making sure that her personal recipes are reproduced to perfection. This is a good place to taste the acclaimed cuisine of Fez in an exceptional setting.

PALAIS JAMAÏ
Bab Guissa
Tel.: 212 (0) 55 63 43 31

E-mail: resa@palais-jamai.co.ma
The Moroccan restaurant Al-Fassia, in the old wing, offers a magical setting, with *zelliges* on the floor and tables placed in alcoves, where you can enjoy traditional Moroccan cuisine. A tent is sometimes set up in the extension so that you can dine by candlelight, facing the illuminated medina. For dinner, the Al Jounaïna restaurant offers a high-quality international-style menu. During the day, the Oliveraie offers perfect buffet and barbeque lunches on the terrace overlooking the pool.

HISTORIC MONUMENTS AND MUSEUMS

MEDERSAS
Bou-Inania, Cherratin, Seffarin, Attarin, and Sahrij (Andalusian quarter)
Visiting the many *medersas* in Fez is a marvelous experience, both for the silent beauty that pervades these schools, and for their exquisite examples of plaster, wood, sculpted stone, and *zellige* decoration. They provide a good opportunity to contemplate the secrets and grandeur of Islam, especially as non-Muslims are not permitted to enter most mosques.

DAR BATHA MUSEUM
Place de l'Istiqal
Constructed in the late nineteenth century, this palace is a remarkable example of Moorish-Hispanic architecture. It houses an interesting collection of popular and traditional arts from Fez and its region: carpets, embroidery, weavings, copper objects, *zelliges*, and, above all, superb ceramics, which reflect the perfection achieved by the craftsmen of Fez in the art of pottery. The inner courtyard garden is somewhat overgrown, but remains a pleasant spot of greenery nonetheless.

FABRIC

MECHKOUR MOHAMED
18, derb quartier Labida
Tel.: 212 (0) 55 63 52 30
This is a lovely workshop, with several looms each producing a different type of fabric: cotton, wool, or a cotton and wool blend. The work is beautifully simple and comes in a wide selection of bright colors and lively stripes.

CLOTHES AND ACCESSORIES

TADLAOUI
97, rue Abdelkarim El Khattabi
boulevard Mohamed-V
Tel.: 212 (0) 55 62 23 85
One hundred percent traditional caftans, *djellabas* and *gandouras*, made to order by M. Tadlaoui, who tailors clothes for an upper-class clientele in Fez. He also makes the best-quality versions of the famous garnet-red *tarboosh* with a black pompom, the traditional Moroccan headwear.

BABOUCHES DE LUX
Kissania Kifah
Souk Sebbat no. 316
If you are looking for an unusual pair of *babouches*, this is the place for you. The sophisticated designs feature pointed toes, heels and sumptuous embroidery. They come in all colors—a pair for each caftan, if you like.

CARPETS

DAR MOULAY ABDELKADER JILALI
45, derb Touil
Dar Zarbiya (house of carpets)
30, derb El Hammam Aïn allou
Tel.: 212 (0) 55 63 68 41
Fax: 212 (0) 55 63 31 91
A temple of old and new carpets.

COPPER- AND BRASSWARE

MERRAKCHI
Sbaa Louyat Karaouiene no. 2
Tel.: 212 (0) 63 42 85
A highly reputed craftsman specializing in copper objects.

THE EL IBDAE COOPERATIVE FOR COPPER ARTS
No. 142 lot industriel Benssouda, in the industrial zone of Fez
This is the place to find a huge selection of copper objects, and to watch the craftsmen at work.

ABDERRAHAM BENLAMLIH
75, Talâa Kebira
Tel.: 212 (0) 55 63 54 46
This eminent craftsman also works for the king. His specialty is bronze, with traditional models of chased and dama-

scened drinking cups. He also excels in the production of platters inspired by local architectural decoration, such as a replica of the ceiling of the Fez synagogue.

GUERNANI
35, Talaà Sghira
Tel.: 212 (0) 55 74 02 77
Another craftsman specializing in high-quality, traditional bronzework.

RABAT

HOTELS

LA TOUR HASSAN MÉRIDIEN
26, rue Chellah
B.P.14-Rabat
Tel.: 212 (0) 37 23 90 00
E-mail: thassan@mtds.com
Internet: www.lemeridien-hotels.com
(see page 183)
This upscale, international hotel has managed to retain some of the charm it had as a small hotel during the Protectorate, especially in the old building. It was the headquarters for General Lyautey and Mohammed V, and also Saint-Exupéry's favorite place to stay in the city.

VILLA MANDARINE
19, rue Ouled Bousbaa
Souissi Rabat
Tel.: 212 (0) 37 75 20 77
A beautiful, family-run establishment set in an orange grove. A few of the trees were pulled down to create thirty rooms and six suites, each decorated with refinement. This enchanting spot also has a pool, *hammam*, and sauna for relaxation. You will love the food—extremely fresh products straight from the market, prepared by a talented young chef, Jérôme Meyer.

RESTAURANTS

LA MAISON ARABE
La Tour Hassan Méridien
26, rue Chellah
B.P.14
Tel.: 212 (0) 37 23 90 00
E-mail: thassan@mtds.com
Internet: www.lemeridien-hotels.com
(see page 183)
The restaurant of La Tour Hassan Méridien is in the older section of the hotel, offering

the opportunity of dining in a historic setting while enjoying some of the best food Rabat has to offer.

CAFÉS

LE CAFÉ MAURE
Oudaias Kasbah
(see page 47)
This open-air café facing the Rabat-Salé estuary in the Oudaias Kasbah is a well-known meeting place for locals, who come here to enjoy mint tea and pastries after strolling through the blue- and white-washed streets. A gourmet stop-off

ARTISANAT

ENSEMBLE ARTISANAL
Village of Moroccan arts in Rabat-Salé
Tel.: 212 (0) 37 81 13 54/37 81 13 32
E-mail: vilarmar@atlasnet.net.ma
This enormous crafts center offers a particularly good selection of carpets, basketwork and ceramics. Everything here is authentic and of high quality. The prices are "official" and therefore fairly reasonable, as they are set by the *Direction de l'artisanat*. There is no bargaining in these centers.

TRADITIONAL ARTS AND CRAFTS

AUTOUR DU LIN
3, rue Attayef
Tel.: 212 (0) 37 70 98 12
Leila offers a wide variety of linen fabrics decorated with Moorish patterns, along with magnificent, hand-embroidered tablecloths. This is a good address if you are fond of linen items and Moroccan embroidery.

TERRA MIA
10, rue Bazo
Oudaias Kasbah
Tel.: 212 (0) 37 70 39 99
Tadelakt long ago went beyond its original function as wall decoration for *hammams*. Mounia Berger, the daring designer, now uses this decorative technique on all kinds of objects, and has breathed new life into traditional methods of production. She exhibits her unique and inventive designs in her shop in the lovely blue-and-white Oudaias neighborhood in Rabat. These include platters, dishware, vases and monumental

earthenware jars, with two-tone decors, engraved arabesques, or gold leaf or silver leaf decoration.

JAMIL BENNANI MAÎTRE
Lot 54a, industrial zone
Takkadoum Rabat
This talented cabinetmaker creates all the furniture for the architect Chafiq Kabbaj (see the architect's home, page 120–123). His work is an original combination of Maghreb and Western traditions.

MARRAKECH

HOTELS

LA MAMOUNIA
Avenue Bab-Jdid
Tel.: 212 (0) 44 44 44 09/44 38 86 00
Fax: 212 (0) 44 44 46 60/49 40
E-mail: resa@mamounia.com
Internet: www.mamounia.com
(see page 185)
This hotel's golden age was just before and after the Second World War. It has been expanded and renovated several times, and its legendary garden, with a pool, is still sublime. Rediscover the charm of this legendary establishment in its calm and lush setting.

LES DEUX TOURS
Douar Abiad
Palmeraie de Marrakech
B.P. 513
Tel.: 212 (0) 44 32 95 27/26/25
Fax: 212 (0) 44 32 95 23
E-mail: deuxtour@iam.net.ma
(see page 188)
This village, designed by Charles Bocara and set in the middle of the *Palmeraie* (palm tree grove), consists of *riad* homes built entirely of *pisé*. The full repertory of traditional architecture is showcased with skill: *zelliges*, *tataoui* ceilings, and *tadelakt*. A quiet place, surrounded by lush vegetation, ideal for the perfect break. You can enjoy the pool, beautiful *hammam*, and strolls through the garden.

LA MAISON ARABE
1, derb Assehbe Bab Doukala
Tel.: 212 (0) 44 38 70 10
Fax: 212 (0) 44 28 72 21
E-mail: maisonarabe@cybernet.net.ma
Internet: www.lamaisonarabe.com
The refinement of this establishment

matches that of its owner, Fabrizzio Ruspoli. The luxurious rooms and suites, laid out around the flower-filled courtyard, are decorated with antiques, Syrian and Moroccan furniture, and *tadelakt* on the walls. There is also a pool. Situated at the gates to the city, the hotel provides a shuttle service into town. A cooking school can teach you all the secrets of Moroccan cuisine. Individual or group workshops are available.

LA VILLA DES ORANGERS
6, rue Sidi-Mimoun
Tel.: 212 (0) 44 38 46 38
Fax: 212 (0) 44 38 51 23
E-mail: message@villadesorangers.com
or orangers@relaischateaux.com
This establishment belongs to the exclusive Relais & Châteaux hotel selection. The lovely building is named for its courtyard filled with orange trees—a romantic place for dinner. The spacious rooms are all arranged around the courtyard and a rooftop pool overlooks the city and the Atlas Mountains.

LES JARDINS DE LA MÉDINA
21, rue Derb-Chtouka
Quartier de la Kasbah
Tel.: 212 (0) 44 38 18 51
Fax: 212 (0) 44 38 53 85
E-mail:
lesjardinsdelamedina@caramail.com
or resa@lesjardinsdelamedina.com
Internet: www.lesjardinsdelamedina.com
(see page 189)
This charming place, situated in the heart of the palace neighborhood, was once a palatial *riad*, now converted into a modern, comfortable hotel. The immense garden has a swimming pool and there is an excellent restaurant, run by the brilliant young chef Najiz Hicham.

AMANJENA
B.P. 2405
Main post office, Guéliz
Tel.: 212 (0) 44 40 33 53
Fax: 212 (0) 44 40 34 77
E-mail: amanjenamgmt@cybernet.net.ma
(see page 181)
This is an exceptional place: the monumental architecture, arranged around a huge artificial lake, provides total serenity. The ultimate place to stay, in surroundings that have achieved mythical status. This is unquestionably the best hotel in Marrakech if you are looking for a

luxury experience in the midst of stunning surroundings—a winning combination in keeping with the reputation of the prestigious Aman Resorts hotel chain.

CARAVANSERAI
Ouled Ben Rahmoun
Tel.: 212 (0) 61 24 98 98
Fax: 212 (0) 44 43 71 60
To convert a Berber village into a hotel was the goal of Max Lawrence, Charles Boccara, and his son, Mathieu. They succeeded magnificently: with a combination of Mediterranean and Indian influences, the decoration focuses on color and space. The *hamman*, pool, and gardens (including the one that is a modest copy of the Jardin Majorelle) are all charming.

GUESTHOUSES

RIAD ENIJA
Riad Enija Rahba Lakdima
Derb Mesfioui 9
Marrakech
Tel.: 212 (0) 44 44 09 26 / 44 44 00 14
Fax: 212 (0) 44 44 27 00
E-mail: riadenija@cybernet.net.ma
or riadenija@iam.net.ma
Internet: www.riadenija.com
(see page 167)
This seventeenth-century palace has been tastefully renovated for a unique stay in an unusual setting, which still reflects the original spirit of its owners. A Scandanavian couple receive their guests amid a decor of period *zelliges* and contemporary furniture. The huge original rooms are laid out around the courtyard, where lucky guests can enjoy magical dinners. A stone's throw from the Place Jemaa el-Fna.

RIYAD EL-MEZOUAR
28, derb el-Hammam
Isbtienne
Tel.: 212 (0) 44 38 09 49
Fax: 212 (0) 44 38 09 43
Internet: www.riyad-el-mezouar.com
(see page 168)
Jérôme Vermelin and Michel Durand, interior architect and designer, have restored this palatial eighteenth-century home in the medina in their own highly personal way, incorporating unusual colors (white, willow green, and aubergine) and a collection of Chinese vases. Excellent cuisine.

RIYAD KAISS
Derb Jdid 65
Riyad Zitoun Kedim
Tel.: 212 (0) 44 44 01 41
Fax: 212 (0) 44 38 51 23
The architect-owner of this establishment, Christian Ferré, has transformed this palace into a luxurious guesthouse. The rooms, all decorated in traditional Moroccan style, are placed around the large courtyard, complete with fountains and large trees.

RIYAD 72
72, Arset Awzel
Bab Doukkala
Tel.: 212 (0) 44 38 76029
If you are looking for contemporary design and discretion, this is the address for you.

RENTAL HOMES

MARRAKECH-MEDINA
Reservations and information:
Tel.: 212 (0) 44 44 24 48/42 91 33/44 45 32
Fax: 212 (0) 44 39 10 71
E-mail: rak.medina@cybernet.net.ma
Internet: www.marrakech-medina.com
(see page 158)
This agency specializes in rentals of *dars* and *riads* of different sizes. Some twenty or so homes are now available for rent, all renovated by the architect Quentin Wilbaux and decorated by the designer Valérie Barkowski. The selection ranges from authentic eighteenth-century palaces to estates on the seafront. The most sought-after homes are Dar Qadi (Quentin Wilbaux's own *dar*), Dar Ouali, Dar El Qantara, Dar Kawa (decorated in a highly contemporary style with pure, clean lines), and Dar Dounia. These homes allow you to live in the heart of the medina like a true resident of Marrakech, while enjoying all the conveniences of hotel service.

DAR TAMSNA
In the *Palmeraie*
Tel.: 212 (0) 44 38 52 72
Fax: 212 (0) 44 38 52 71
(see page 163)
These luxurious houses in the *Palmeraie* have been decorated in extremely good taste by Meryanne Loum-Martin. An exceptional place, with fireplaces, huge salons, Art Deco furniture, traditional Moroccan crafts, and other antiques.

VILLA MAHA
Douar Abiad
Tel.: 212 (0) 44 32 95 78
A five-room house and a *caidal* tent in a palm grove garden, with Indian- and Moroccan-style decoration.

LUXURY CAMPING

ATLAS SAHARA TREK
6 bis, rue Houdhoud
Quartier Majorelle
Tel.: 212 (0) 44 31 39 01/03
Fax: 212 (0) 44 31 39 05
E-mail: atlassaharatrek@iam.net.ma
(see pages 196–197)
Bernard Fabry specializes in desert excursions. He can organize luxury camping trips to the most beautiful sites in Morocco, with or without trekking. Each program is custom-designed to suit your individual needs and requests. From mid-September to mid-April head to the desert and dunes toward Mhamid or Merzouga. Late April is a better time to explore the Atlas Mountains, the Aits Bougmes, and other forgotten valleys.

RESTAURANTS

The cuisine in the "great restaurants" of Marrakech is not always consistent. You will be delighted one day, disappointed the next. You can sometimes get better food in smaller, less pretentious places that offer cheaper dishes, and the decor is often charming in these restaurants. Here are three suggestions for great dining in Marrakech. Reservations required.

DAR YACOUT
79, Sidi Ahmed Soussi
Tel.: 212 (0) 44 38 29 29
The highlight of this restaurant is the illuminated terrace overlooking the entire city, as well as the sumptuous decor designed by Bill Willis.

DAR MARJANA
15, derb Sidi Ali Tair
Bab Doukhala
Tel.: 212 (0) 44 38 51 10/44 38 57 73/61 13 70 52
Fax: 212 (0) 44 38 51 52
A highly acclaimed classic. The candlelit passageway hints at the magic of the splendid palace within, where refinement is the watchword, both in terms of the cuisine and the decor.

TOBSIL
22, derb Abdallah ben-Hezzaien
R'mila Bab Ksour
Tel.: 212 (0) 44 44 40 52/44 45 35/44 15 23
Another charming place, situated in a small *dar*. Excellent cuisine.

And here is an equally good alternative to the preceding three restaurants:
LES JARDINS DE LA MÉDINA
21, rue Derb-Chtouka
Quartier de la Kasbah
Marrakech
Tel.: 212 (0) 44 38 18 51
Fax: 212 (0) 44 38 53 85
E-mail: resa@lesjardinsdelamedina.com
or lesjardinsdelamedina@caramail.com
Internet: www.lesjardinsdelamedina.com
(see page 189)
A talented young Moroccan chef is responsible for the delicious cuisine served at this hotel. He uses traditional Moroccan recipes and reinterprets them with brilliant inventiveness. A delightful experience.

A legendary restaurant reopens:
LA MAISON ARABE
1, derb Assehbe Bab Doukala
Tel.: 212 (0) 44 38 70 10
E-mail: maisonarabe@cybernet.net.ma
Internet: www.lamaisonarabe.com
Located within the luxurious setting of this intimate and refined hotel, fashionable during the 1940s, this restaurant offers a selection of the best in Moroccan flavors.

BARS

COMPTOIR DARNA
PARIS-MARRAKECH
Avenue Echouhada
Hivernage
Tel.: 212 (0) 44 43 77 02/44 43 77 10
E-mail: comptoirdarna@iam.net.ma
This is the place to experience Moroccan nightlife in an ambience that combines elements from the Maghreb, Asia, and India. The mixture of decors and cuisine has broken down all barriers, creating a unique magic. Marcel Chiche, who created the original Comptoi in Parisr, has repeated his success here with his partner, designer Jonathan Amar.

TEA ROOM, GALLERY

RYAD TAMSNA
Riad Zitoun Jdid
23, derb Zanka Daika

Tel.: 212 (0) 44 43 85 272
E-mail: dartamsna@cybernet.net.ma
(see page 163)
In this sparkling boutique-*riad*, Meryanne Loum-Martin has imbued everything with her cosmopolitan spirit—including the cuisine. She calls it "fusion food." You can enjoy a brunch, lunch, or organic snack at any time in the courtyard. The refreshing cuisine is based on simple, light recipes, a successful synthesis of Arab and Asian cuisine. Start with an energizing cocktail of fruit or vegetable juices. Main dishes are delicately flavored with herbs and spices. If you are tired of traditional Moroccan restaurants, try this for an inspired alternative.

LA CHÉRIFA
8, derb Charfa Lakbir
(near the Mouassine mosque)
This new literary café in Marrakech was restored by Abdellatif Aït Ben Abdallah, who has created a magnificent place, complete with reading rooms, art exhibitions, library, and cultural events. You can come for a cup of tea, to hear a concert, or browse through the art magazines, among the decor of tall columns, *zelliges*, stucco, and cedar.

SHOPS

RYAD TAMSNA
Riad Zitoun Jdid
23, derb Zanka Daika
Tel.: 212 (0) 44 38 52 72
(see page 163)
Meryanne Loum-Martin places herself squarely in the heart of different cultures, with a fusional approach to decoration and fashion. Her lovely house, converted into a restaurant-gallery-boutique, sells *babouches* made from African fabric; Moroccan trim combined with Asian silk; Laotian hemp adorned with beads from Mali; and Limoge porcelain decorated with Moroccan patterns. This sophisticated blending is the source of her creativity. Essential oils with the scents of the Atlas Mountains are available in her health and beauty section. The gallery, arranged around the courtyard on the upper floor, hosts exhibits by painters or photographers.

COMPTOIR DARNA
PARIS-MARRAKECH
Avenue Echouhada
Hivernage

Tel.: 212 (0) 44 43 77 02/44 43 77 10
Fax: 212 (0) 44 44 77 47
E-mail: comptoirdarna@iam.net.ma
Here is another multifaceted place. The Comptoir has a restaurant and bar, along with a small shop run by Florence Chiche, wife of the manager. She exhibits a selection of unusual and innovative crafts, including leather cushions, tin lamps, bags, scarves, and dishware.

L'ORIENTALISTE
15, rue de la Liberté
Tel.: 212 (0) 44 43 40 74
This interior design shop, in the Guéliz neighborhood, offers a wide choice of Syrian furniture, copper- and brassware, ceramics, and even fine leather Tuareg boxes. You can also find a lovely selection of modern objects and antiques, all in a rich Moroccan style and made by regional craftsmen.

ANTIQUES

MUSTAPHA BLAOUI
Arset Aouzal
Bab Doukala no 144
Tel.: 212 (0) 44 38 52 40
This little-known shop is situated next to all the other antique dealers, and nothing distinguishes it as being anything out of the ordinary. Yet you will find a beautiful selection of antique furniture here. The interior designer Jacqueline Foissac is one of the owner's loyal customers.

CERAMICS

AKKAL
322, quartier industriel Sidi Jhanem
Route de Safi
Tel.: 212 (0) 44 33 59 38
Fax: 212 (0) 44 33 59 41
E-mail: akkal@iam.net.ma
(see page 89)
Charlotte Barkowski has revived traditional pottery with her contemporary approach. She designs her pieces and then has them made by a team of master craftsmen, who work in her huge workshop, located just on the outskirts of Marrakech. Her tableware comes in wonderfully simple shapes and is available in a range of unusual colors such as aubergine, pink, almond green, and cream. She also makes a variety of attractive enameled tagine dishes (lead-free).

CARPETS

BAZAR SUD
117, souk des tapis
Tel.: 212 (0) 44 44 30 04
Fax: 212 (0) 44 44 52 27
A huge selection of high-quality carpets on offer. The owner Moulaï ben-Cheriff is a true carpet connoisseur.

TEXTILES

BOUTIQUE DE L'AMANJENA
B.P. 2405
Main post office, Guéliz
Tel.: 212 (0) 44 40 33 53
Fax: 212 (0) 44 40 34 77
E-mail: amanjenamgmt@cybernet.net.ma
Housed in the legendary Amanjena hotel, this is the place to find Valérie Barkowski's household linen, with its fine embroidery and pompoms. The boutique also carries her elegant Mia Zia clothes alongside magnificent designs by Brigitte Perkins.

FELT
Chez Adellah
53, souk au tapis de selle
Contemporary designs: a range of pouches, shoulder bags, and handbags, all in brightly colored felt.

JENNIFER LLOYD
Atelier SEED
20 quartier Zahia-Majorelle
Tel.: 212 (0) 62 29 78 38
E-mail: lloyd_project@hotmail.com
Jennifer Lloyd, originally from England, designs contemporary handbags which she then has executed by craftsmen in the medina. Her pieces are made of traditional wool felt in ecru or other natural colors. Pillows and blankets also available. She will ship orders.

COPPER
Oueld el-Hachemi Mohamed
38, passage El-Gandouri
Guéliz
Tel.: 212 (0) 61 34 28 63
If you are looking for the increasingly popular, handmade copper sinks, this is the place to go. Passed down from father to son, this antique shop offers sinks in all sizes and in all different types of copper: hammered or smooth, gilded or matt. Other valuable antique objects also available. Located in the Guéliz quarter.

ARGAN OIL

Argania La maison de l'Arganier
95 bis, rue Crimée
75019 Paris, France
Tel.: 33 (0) 1 42 02 50 15
Fax: 33 (0) 1 42 02 50 25
E-mail: info@argania.org
Internet: www.argania.com (USA),
www.argania.org (France).

The virgin oil of the argan tree is on the list of products included in the UNESCO Man and Biosphere program, and is promoted by the world's top chefs. Fatimine Kydjian and Franck Chauveau Bodere founded Argania La Maison de l'Arganier with a production plant in Morocco. They recognize the Berber women's unique expertise and pay them a proper wage for their hard work.

Argan oil is also imported from Morocco by the following:

UNITED STATES AND CANADA

Marco Polo Marketing USA
2321 Kennedy Blvd., Suite 201
North Bergen, NJ 07047
Tel.: (201) 348-5156
Fax: (201) 348-5166
E-mail: mpmfood@yahoo.com.
Imports the Argania brand to the U.S.

Argan3, Aziz Alaoui, Canada
tel.: (514) 482-2079
www.argan3.com
Cosmetic grade argan oil.

GREAT BRITAIN

Wild Wood Groves
P.O. Box 33146
London NW3 7FS
Tel.: 020 8731 7030
www.wildwoodgroves.com
Cosmetic grade argan oil.

MUSEUMS

Aside from the major historical and cultural sites that attract hoards of tourists, there are a few lesser-known palaces and museums that offer another vision of Marrakech's historic past.

PALAIS DE LA BAHIA
Palace quarter
A series of courtyards, patios, and lavishly decorated rooms, created by the best nineteenth-century Moroccan craftsmen for one of the sultan's grand viziers The apartments of his favorite are simply breathtaking.

PALAIS EL-BADI
Palace quarter
Via the Bab-Berrima gate
The ruins of the fabulous palace of Ahmed el-Mansour, which was pillaged by Moulay Ismaïl to decorate his own palace in Meknes, but which still has remnants of its former glory. The palace is used as a venue for the annual Moroccan Folklore Festival.

DAR SI SAÏD
Palace quarter
Derb Si Saïd
This is another great home that was built during the same period as the Bahia, and is worth a visit just to see the house. An added attraction is that it also contains a Moroccan art museum with jewelry, textiles, ceramics, copperware and brassware, carpets, doors, and wood carvings.

MAISON TISKIWIN
Fondation Bernt Flint
8, rue de la Bahia
Dutch professor Bernt Flint exhibits his personal collection of costumes, jewelry, weapons, carpets from the Atlas Mountains, textiles, basketry, Berber doors, and musical instruments in his private home.

GARDENS

JARDIN DE LA MÉNARA
At the end of avenue de la Ménara
(see page 56)
A lovely pavilion stands opposite an immense basin designed by the Almohads in the twelfth century to store water to irrigate the nearby olive groves and orchards. A delightful outing.

JARDIN DE L'AGDAL
Palace quarter
Also from the same period; this is another garden created by the Almohads, but it is four times larger and includes immense orchards sheltered by thick walls. According to medieval texts, the basin was used to teach the sultan's soldiers how to swim.

JARDIN MAJORELLE
Quartier du Guéliz
(see pages 116–117)
Created by the painter Jacques Majorelle, who fell in love with Morocco in the 1920s, this garden was purchased by the French fashion designer Yves Saint Laurent and his partner Pierre Bergé, who have restored it with care. The garden is truly stunning with lush vegetation set off against fences and woodwork painted in a rich "Majorelle" blue. The artist's former studio now houses a museum of Islamic art.

MOROCCAN CALENDAR

RELIGIOUS HOLIDAYS
The dates of religious holidays vary according to the lunar calendar. During Ramadan, the rhythm of daily life changes completely: most of the businesses are closed, and services operate much more slowly. As opposed to the almost total inactivity during the day, everything comes alive at night. The fast is broken as soon as the sun sets, and people get together with family or friends. The end of this period of fasting is celebrated by a three-day holiday, the Aïd es-Seghir. Aïd el-Kébir, seventy days laters, commemorates the sacrifice of the prophet Abraham. Each family kills a sheep and offers a share of it to the poor.

MOUSSEMS
These popular festivals are held to commemorate the memory of a local saint. People come to pay tribute to the tomb of the marabout. Mysticism, Berber traditions, the religious, and the profane are often combined in these events. A large market usually takes place at the same time.

BEN AISSA: May–June. This is one of the largest moussems in Morocco, held at the sanctuary of Sidi Ben Aissa, near Meknes.
GUELMIN: Early June; large dromedary market.
SIDI IFNI: Second week of June.
TAN-TAN: June. Major gathering of the "blue men."
SETTI FATMA: August, in the Ourika Valley.

OUARZAZATE: August, moussem of Sidi Daoud.
ZERHOUN: August, moussem of Moulay Idriss, near Meknes.
MOULAY ABDALLAH: Late August, near El-Jadida; this is one of the largest in the country.
IMILCHIL: September is when the famous marriage moussem takes place, during the pilgrimage to the tomb of the local saint. It is a large event that draws many merchants, while collective Berber wedding ceremonies are held and young girls select their grooms. This event has become quite a tourist attraction in the last ten years or so.
FEZ: Mid-September, moussem of Moulay Idriss II and procession of the guilds.
MOULAY IDRISS: September, national pilgrimage.

LOCAL EVENTS

February: Almond-blossom festival in Tafraoute.
March: Amateur theater festival in Casablanca; Cotton festival in Beni Mellal.
April: Candle festival in Salé.
May: Rose festival in El-Kelaâ M'Gouna in the Dadès Valley.
June: Late May–early June. Folklore festival in Marrakech; Essaouira musical and cultural festival; Cherry festival in Séfrou; Fig festival in Bouhouda (Taounate region); late June–early July. Religious music festival in Fez.
July: Honey festival in Imouzzer (in the Agadir region).
August: International cultural festival in Asilah.
September: Traditional art festival in Fez; Arab theater festival in Rabat; two-week tourist celebration in Marrakech.
October: Festival of dates in Erfoud; Horse festival in Tissa (Fez region).
December: Olive festival in Ghafsaï (Rif); Clementine festival in Berkane.

MOROCCO ABROAD

RESTAURANTS

<u>LONDON</u>

MOMO
25 Heddon Street
London W1B 4BH
Tel.: 020 7434 4040

PASHA
1 Gloucester Road
London SW7 4PP
Tel.: 020 7589 7969

LOS ANGELES

DAR MAGHREB
7651 West Sunset Boulevard
Los Angeles, California 90046
Tel.: (323) 876-7651

NEW YORK

CHEZ ES SAADA
42 East 1st Street
New York, NY 10003
Tel.: (212) 777-5617

ZITOUNE
46 Gansevoort Street
New York, NY 10014
Tel.: (212) 675-5224

LE MOGODOR
101 St. Marks Place
New York, NY 10009
Tel.: (212) 677-2226

SAN FRANCISCO

MAMOUNIA
4411 Balboa St
San Francisco, California
Tel.: (415) 752-6566

SHOPS

GREAT BRITAIN

FEZ
71 Golborne Road
London W10 5NP
Tel.: 020 8964 5573
This is a specialist shop that sells traditional
Moroccan handicrafts and women's
clothing.

GRAHAM & GREEN
4 Elgin Cresent
London W11
Tel.: 020 7727 4594
Lamps, pottery, wooden articles.

MAISON SOUS
104 Uxbridge Road
London W12

Tel.: 020 8932 1211
A Moroccan bakery and patisserie
transported to west London.

LE MAROC
94 Golborne Road
London W10 5PS
Tel.: 020 8968 9783
This supermarket stocks traditional Moroc-
can foodstuffs and sells *halal* meat.

VERANDAH
15B Blenheim Crescent
London W11 2EE
Tel.: 020 7792 9289

UNITED STATES

AGADIR EXOTIC MOROCCAN CLOTHING
117 West 9th Street
Suite 314
Los Angeles, CA 90015
Tel.: (213) 627-8853
The name of the shop says it all.

BROOKE PICKERING MOROCCAN RUGS
1209 Route 213, P.O. Box 37
High Falls, NY 12440
Tel.: (914) 687-8737
Brooke Pickering is the only rug dealer in
the northeastern United States specializing exclusively in Moroccan material. She
travels at least twice a year to Marrakech
and the surrounding areas to select knotted pile rugs, flatwoven rugs, and Berber
weavings such as saddle bags, blankets,
and pillows. By appointment only.

COBWEBS
440 Lafayette Street
New York, NY 10003
Tel.: (212) 505-1558
Receives regular shipments of antique
doors, windows, ceiling beams and panels, as well as vintage chests, ceramics,
rugs, screens, storage vessels and tiles
direct from Morocco.

HAREM DESIGN
12 Moniebogue Lane
Westhampton Beach, NY 11978
Tel.: (631) 898-0020
E-mail: haremdesign@aol.com
A Moroccan interior design and Middle
Eastern special event planning company.
Services and products: interior design and
redecorating, furniture and accessories
import from Morocco, Moroccan and

Middleastern special events, 1001 Nights
home linen collection, design and color
consultation. Their Middleeastern special
events include henna parties, belly dancing workshops, couscous soirées, poetry
reading, and musical perfomances
(event services cover New York City and
Long Island area only).

NOMADS
207 Shelby Street
Santa Fe, NM 87501
Tel.: (408) 609-1289/1 (800) 360 4807
A wide variety of fine Moroccan crafts:
ceramics, hand-painted furniture, lanterns,
old earthenware and newer Fez pottery,
camelbone mirrors and boxes, jewelry, textiles, rugs, etc. Also sells Moroccan olive oil
and salt-cured black olives as well as their
own line of olive-oil based beauty products.

SURROUNDINGS
1708 Sunset Boulevard
Houston, TX 77005
Tel.: (713) 527-9838
Painted furniture, mirrors and pottery.

TIERRA DEL LARGATO
7812 East Acoma, Suite 8
Scottsdale, AZ 85250
Tel.: (480) 609-1289
Ceramics, accessories and painted
tables, imported directly from Morocco.

TILEWALK, INC.
639 South Olive Avenue
West Palm Beach, FL 33401
Tel.: (561) 659-9350
This company imports Moroccan tiles,
lamps, and tables and offers special
ordering and indivudial service to realize
any custom tile design.

MOROCCAN TOURISM OFFICES

Moroccan National Tourist Office
205 Regent Street
London W1R 7DE
United Kingdom
Tel.: 020 7437 0073
Fax: 020 7734 8172

Moroccan National Tourist Office
Place Montréal Trust
1800 Avenue Mc Gill College
Suite 2450
Montréal, QQ H3A-3J6, Canada

Tel.: (514) 842-8111
Fax: (514) 842-5316

Moroccan National Tourist Office
20 East 46th Street, Suite 1201
New York, NY 10017
USA
Tel.: (212) 557-2520
Fax: (212) 949-8148

Moroccan National Tourist Office
P.O. Box 2263
Lake Buena Vista, FL 32830
USA
Tel.: (407) 827-5335
Fax: (407) 827-5129

Moroccan National Tourist Office
11 West Street North
Sydney, NSW 2060
Australia
Tel.: (2) 922-4999
Fax.: (2) 923-1053

INTERNET RESOURCES

MAISON KENZI
www.kenzi.com
email: webmaster@kenzi.com
Tel.: (718) 789-1545 (USA)
This internet site features quality imports
from North Africa for on-line purchase or
phone order, including henna, jewelry,
textiles and slippers. The site also features
an extensive bibliography, music refer-
ences, and useful links on Moroccan arts,
culture and travel.

MAROC DECOR
www.marocdecor.com
This UK-based site offers an extensive
range of Moroccan jewelry, leather
goods, furniture, lanterns, paintings, and
textiles, as well as information on where to
buy *zelliges* in London. Click on "The Flat"
to see photos of a beautifully furnished
appartment available for short-term stays
in Marrakesh.

TOURISM IN MOROCCO
www.tourism-in-morocco.com
This extensive travel and culture site offers
your choice of either English-, French- or
German-language formats. Highlights
include up-to-the-minute temperature
and weather forecasts for major Moroccan destinations.

BIBLIOGRAPHY

GUIDEBOOKS

There are several well-edited guides that give excellent general information and good addresses. Each includes an introduction to the country's history and its artistic heritage and provides descriptive texts, illustrations, maps and practical information. A combination of several guides is bound to meet your needs.

Morocco (5th ed.). Lonely Planet, 2001.

The Rough Guide to Morocco. Rough Guides, 2001.

Escape to Morocco by Simon Russel and Pamela Windo. Fodor, 2000.

Fodor's Morocco. Fodor, 2001.

Knopf Guide Morocco. Knopf Guides, 1994.

Blue Guide Morocco (3rd ed) by Jane Holliday. W.W. Norton & Company, 1998.

ILLUSTRATED BOOKS

BEN JELLOUN, Tahar. *Morocco From the Air.* New York: Vendome Press, 1994.

BONFANTE-WARREN, Alexandra. *Moroccan Style.* New York: Friedman/Fairfax Publishing (Architecture and Design Library), 2000.

BOWLES, Paul. Photographs by Barry Brukoff. *Morocco.* New York: Harry N. Abrams, 1993.

COWARD, Jack and Pierre Schneider. *Matisse in Morocco: The Paintings and Drawings 1912-1913* (exhibition catalog). Washington D.C.: National Gallery of Art, Washington, 1990.

COX, Madison and Pierre Bergé. Photographs by Claire de Virieu. *Majorelle: A Moroccan Oasis.* New York: Vendome Press, 1999.

CROSS, Mary. With an introduction by Paul Bowles. *Morocco: Sahara to the Sea.* New York: Abbeville Press, 1995.

Delacroix in Morocco (exhibition catalog). Paris/New York: Institut du monde arabe/Flammarion, 1994.

DENNIS, Landt and Lisl Dennis. *Living in Morocco* (revised edition). London: Thames and Hudson, 2001.

GENINI, Izza, Jacques Bravo and Xavier Richer. *Splendours of Morocco.* London:

I. B. Tauris & Co. Ltd., 2000.

GIRARD, Xavier. *Matisse: The Wonder of Color.* New York: Harry N. Abrams (Discoveries Series), 1994.

SOLYST, Annette. *Timeless Places: Morocco.* New York: Friedman/Fairfax Publishing, 2000.

TINGAUD, Jean-Marc and Tahar Ben Jelloun. *Medinas: Morroco's Hidden Cities.* New York: Assouline Publishing, 1998.

JEREB, James F. *Arts & Crafts of Morocco.* San Francisco: Chronicle Books, 1996.

PICKERING, Brooke, W. Russell Pickering, and Ralph S. Yohe. *Moroccan Carpets.* Chevy Chase, MD: Near Eastern Art Research Center & Hali Pub., 1994.

FISKE, Patricia L., W. Russell Pickering, and Ralph S. Yohe, eds. *From The Far West: Carpets and Textiles of Morocco.* (exhibition catalog). Washington D.C.: The Textile Museum, Washington, 1980.

ESSAYS, TRAVEL WRITING, LITTERATURE

BOWLES, Paul. *The Sheltering Sky.* New York: New Directions, 1949.

___*Days: Tangier Journal, 1987-1989.* New York: Ecco Press, 1991.

___*The Spider's House.* New York: Random House, 1955.

___*Let it Come Down.* New York: Random House, 1952.

___*Un Thé au Sahara* (in French). Paris: Gallimard, 1952.

___*Their Heads Are Green and Their Hands Are Blue.* New York: Random House, 1963.

BURROUGHS, William. *Letters to Allen Ginsberg 1953-1957* (in English and French). Geneva: Claude Givaudan - Am Here Books, 1978.

___*Naked Lunch.* Paris: Olympia Press, 1959.

CANETTI, Elias. *Voices of Marrakesh: A Record of a Visit.* Marion Boyars Publishers, 1978.

CHRISTIE, Agatha. *Destination Unknown.* London: Collins, 1954.

FERNEA, Elizabeth Warnock. *Street in Marrakech.* Garden City, N.Y.: Doubleday, 1975.

MERNISSI, Fatima. *Dreams of Trespass: Tales of a Harem Girlhood.* Reading, Mass.: Addison-Wesley Pub. Co., 1994.

GREEN, Michelle. *The Dream at the End of the World: Paul Bowles and the Literary Renegades in Tangier.* New York: Harper Collins, 1991.

LOTI, Pierre. *Into Morocco.* Illus. by Benjamin Constant and Aimé Marot. New York: Welch, Fracker Company, 1889. New translation to be published by Columbia University Press (Pierre Loti Library), 2003.

MAALOUF, Amin. *Leon Africanus.* Translated by Peter Sluglett. New York: New Amsterdam Books, 1990.

SAINT-EXUPÉRY, Antoine de. *Southern Mail.* Translated by Stuart Gilbert. New York: H. Smith and R. Haas, 1933.

WHARTON, Edith. *In Morocco.* New York: C. Scribner's Sons, 1920.

MOROCCAN LITERATURE

BEN JELLOUN, Tahar

The Sacred Night. Translated by Alan Sheridan. San Diego: Harcourt Brace Jovanovich, 1989.

The Sand Child. Translated by Alan Sheridan. San Diego: Harcourt Brace Jovanovich, 1987.

Silent Day in Tangier. Translated by David Lobdell. San Diego: Harcourt Brace Jovanovich, 1991.

The Blinding Absence of Light. Translated by Linda Coverdale. New Press, 2002.

With Downcast Eyes. Translated by Joachim Neugroschel. Boston: Little, Brown and Company, 1993.

CHOUKRI, Mohammed

For Bread Alone. Translated by Paul Bowles. London: P. Owen, 1973.

Jean Genet in Tangier. Translated by Paul Bowles and William Bourroughs. New York: Ecco Press, 1974.

CHRAIBI, Driss

Birth at Dawn. Translated by Ann Woollcombe. Washington, D.C.: Three Continents Press, 1990.

The Butts. Translated by Hugh A. Harter.

Washington, D.C. : Three Continents Press, 1983.

Flutes of Death. Translated by Robin Roosevelt. Washington, D.C.: Three Continents Press, 1985.

Mother Spring. Translated by Hugh Harter. Washington, DC : Three Continents Press,1989.

The Simple Past. Translated by Hugh A. Harter. Washington, D.C. : Three Continents Press, 1990.

MRABET, Mohammed

The Boy Who Set the Fire and Other Stories. Translated by Paul Bowles. Los Angeles: Black Sparrow, 1974.

The Beach Café & The Voice. Translated by Paul Bowles. Santa Barbara: Black Sparrow, 1980.

M'hashish. Translated by Paul Bowles. San Francisco: City Lights Books, 1969.

SERDANE, Abdelhak

Les Enfants des rues étroites (in French). Paris: Seuil, 1986.

Messaouda. Translated by Mark Thompson. Manchester; N.Y.: Carcanet, 1986.

COOKING

MORSE, Kitty and Laurie Smith. *Cooking at the Kasbah: Recipes from my Moroccan Kitchen.* San Francisco: Chronicle Books, 1998.

MAZOUZ, Mourad. *The Momo Cookbook: A Gastronomic Journey Through North Africa.* New York: Simon & Schuster, 2000.

BENAYOUN, Aline. *Casablanca Cuisine: French North African Cooking.* Serif Cookery, 2000.

HASSAN, Rebekah. *Moroccan Cooking.* Lorenz Books, 2000.

HAL, Fatema. *The Food of Morocco: Authentic Recipes from the North African Coast.* Periplus Editions, 2002.

HELOU, Anissa. Photography by Jeremy Hopley. *Café Morocco.* Contemporary Books, 1999.

GLOSSARY

AGADAL: Berber word designating a meadow surrounded by a wall on the banks of a *oued* (river). Since the era of the Almohad dynasty, this term has been used to describe royal gardens. This type of design spread to the entire Western Muslim world, resulting in the creation of sumptuous Andalusian gardens.

ALMOHAD (1147–1269): the second Berber dynasty, founded by Ibn Tumart. Under his successors, Marrakech was the capital of an immense empire that ruled over almost all of North Africa and Andalusia.

ALMORAVID (1055–1147): the first Berber dynasty, which originated in the Sahara Desert. It conquered the southern Maghreb and moved northward into Spain. Youssef Ben Tachfine (1061–1107) founded Marrakech.

AMMELN: a Chleuh-speaking Berber tribe in the Anti-Atlas Mountains.

AZULEJOS: decorative painted tiles.

BAB: door or gate.

BARAKA: luck, favorable destiny, divine blessing; it can be granted by saints.

BAROUD: combat.

BEJMAT: small bricks used to make floors.

BLED: countryside. A specific name in the Maghreb designating the countryside; the village as opposed to the city.

BURNOOSE: a large hooded wool mantle or cloak.

CAFTAN: a long woman's garment with buttons down the front, decorated with trim and embroidery.

CAID: during the classical period, this term designated a high-ranking military officer or leader. Today, a *caid* in Morocco is a functionary, who holds power within a district.

CAIDAL TENT: tent reserved for the *caid* and, by extension, for dignitaries. It is recognizable by its conical, light-colored roof and the black geometric patterns arranged in concentric friezes around it.

CALIPH: Al Kalifa in Arabic, or successor of Mohammed, who, in the early years of Islam, headed the community of believers. He held both spiritual and temporal authority, but he delegated military authority to governors.

CANOUN: small stove or barbecue used for cooking

CASBAH: *see* Kasbah.

CHERGUI: hot, dry, southeast wind, also known as the sirocco.

CHERIF (pl. *chorfa*): descendant of the Prophet, a nobleman.

DAR: small house.

DESS: glossy floor surface made using the *tadelakt* technique.

DJEBEL: mountain.

DJELLABA: a flowing cotton or wool garment with hood and wide sleeves, that is pulled on over the head. Worn by both men and women. The sides are often slit.

DOUAR: hamlet, village.

FASSI: a resident of Fez.

FOUTA: striped fabric worn around women's waists as an apron. Specific to the Rif region.

GEBS: carved and painted plaster, also known as stucco.

GLAOUI (the): originating from Telouet in the High Atlas Mountains, he was named pasha in 1908. In 1912, he allied himself with the French, and General Lyautey appointed him administrator of the entire southern part of Morocco. In the 1950s, he criticized Sultan Sidi Mohammed ben Youssef's position in favor of Moroccan independence. He was ultimately overthrown and exiled.

GNAOUAS: A brotherhood of descendants of former slaves from sub-Saharan Africa. They claim to be the spiritual heirs of Bilal; he was a Christian Ethiopian slave freed by the Prophet, who later named Bilal as his muezzin.

GRAND VIZIER: *see* Vizier.

HAIK: thin or thick long veil that women wrap around themselves.

HAITI: fabric, leather, or rush wall covering.

HAMMAM: Turkish-style public or private bathhouse.

JNAN: garden with fruit trees.

KADI: judge, magistrate. His original function was to apply religious law.

KAMMOUN: cumin.

KASBAH: fortress or small castle, usually with four towers, one at each corner.

KISSARIA: market; a covered passage with shops and stalls.

KSAR (pl. *ksour*): fortified village surrounded by an unbroken wall, flanked by corner towers.

KSOUR: plural of *ksar*.

MAALEM: a master craftsman who trains apprentices or supervises a workshop and building sites.

MAKHZEN: The government, the palace, authority.

MARABOUT: a holy man with *baraka*, or highly regarded and charismatic religious leader. By extension, the tomb or shrine of such a holy person, recognizable by its dome or conic roof.

MEDERSA: Koranic school with a central courtyard, rooms around the courtyard, prayer rooms, and lodging for students.

MEDINA: the traditional walled Arab quarter. Today, it is often the old part of the city, as opposed to the newer sections.

MELLAH: Jewish quarter.

MENDIL: striped fabric worn around women's waists as an apron. Specific to the Rif region.

MENZEH: a garden pavilion ranging from the size of a gazebo to the size of a house.

MERENIDS (1269–1465): third Berber dynasty, during which Morocco acquired its current borders. Fez was its capital.

MIDA: round table with a lip, from which couscous used to be eaten.

MIHRAB: the highly ornamented alcove in a mosque that indicates the direction of Mecca, the direction toward which Muslims must pray.

MOUCHARABIEH: openwork wooden louvers placed on windows and balconies; they protect the interior space from view, while allowing light in.

MOUSSEM: major annual and seasonal celebration, and pilgrimage to the tomb of a saint; often held along with a large market and festivities.

MUEZZIN: a religious official in Islam,

responsible for the five daily calls to prayer from atop the mosque minaret.

MUQARNAS: Honeycombed wood or plaster stalactites on the inside of domes or capitals.

OUED: river, stream.

PALMERAIE: in Marrakech, an area of palm trees and olive groves.

PASHA: a title formerly used to describe the governor of a city.

PISÉ: sun-dried earth and clay.

RIAD: an Arab word meaning "garden," and, by extension, a house with an interior garden.

SHEIK: the elder, the wise man, head of a tribal group. A respected figure and sometimes the head of a religious brotherhood.

SOUK: market.

SQALA: bastion or citadel.

SULTAN: title given to Moroccan sovereigns through Mohammed V.

TADELAKT: an ancient wall treatment that originated in Marrakech. Originally, it was made from a type of whitewash available only in this town. *Tadelakt* was first used to cover the walls of *hammams* in Marrakech, as it is highly resistant to humidity. Today, it is used as

a decorative technique throughout the house, but the raw materials and the craftsmanship are still associated with Marrakech. *Tadelakt* is made exclusively from lime, which is transformed into a coating and tinted with natural pigments, the only additional material used. Various flexible trowels and black soap are used to apply the *tadelakt* in a series of thin, smooth layers. The surface is then carefully polished, inch by inch, using a stone, to obtain a final finish. This brings out a natural gloss. The final step with the stone fills the tiny cracks that appear in the *tadelakt* and gives it the characteristic mirrored surface. The final result is a unique, glossy surface, in which constantly shifting reflections appear.

TATAOUI: thin strips of laurel, painted or unpainted, arranged in a tight formation to create a pattern.

VIZIER: title given to a minister serving under a Muslim prince.

ZAOUIA: a sanctuary and center of a religious brotherhood; the patron saint of the brotherhood is buried in the sanctuary.

ZELLIGE: zelliges are made from small pieces of ceramic cut into geometric shapes and placed together to form a composition: ceramic panels placed on the floor or as baseboards.

ZOUAK: the art of painted wood.

INDEX

ACKNOWLEDGEMENTS

Sabine Bouvet and Philippe Saharoff would like to extend their sincere thanks to everyone who so kindly and enthusiastically welcomed them into their homes or provided help in the creation of the book: Yehia Abdelnour, Pierre Bergé and Yves Saint Laurent, Valérie Barkowski and Simon, Charlotte Barkowski, Roland Beauffre, Charles Boccara, Claudio Bravo, Daisy Buckingham, Björn Conerdings, Jean-Marc Colinet, Michel Durand, Habib el Amrani, Bernard Fabry and Martine Cabarez, Atlas Sahara Trek, Jacqueline Foissac, Bert Flint, Christophe Girard, Chafiq Kabbaj, Meryanne Loum-Martin, Joël Martial, Régis Milcent, Elie Mouyal, Jack Oswald, Ombelyne de Richemont, Gilda Schubnel, Christine and Azeddine Sedrati, Sophia Tazi, Jérôme Vermelin, Michel Vu, Laure Welfing, Larbi Yacoubi.

Philippe Saharoff would like to extend special thanks to the architect Elie Mouyal and to Meryanne Loum-Martin for their help in recent years.

Sabine Bouvet would like to thank Antoine Rebillard for his invaluable assistance.

Sabine Bouvet and Philippe Saharoff are also grateful to all those who so generously provided them with accommodation in their hotels or meals in their restaurants: Michel Sautereau and Annie Rigobert, Les Jardins de la Médina in Marrakech; Roger Schwarzberg, Le Mirage in Tangier; Raymond and Dani Lami, Dar Loulema in Essaouira; Dominique Maté and Marie, Baoussala in Essaouira; Michel, Bouchra, and Saïd, Derkaoua in Erfoud; Juan de Dios Romero, Kasbah Ben Moro in Skoura; Farid Lahlou, Hôtel Jnan Palace in Fez; Guy Robert, La Tour Hassan Méridien in Rabat; Hymen and Mourad, La Villa Quieta in Essaouira; Omar Lebbar, Dar El Ghalia in Fez; Mehdi El Abbadi, La Maison Bleue in Fez; Quentin Wilbaux, Béatrice Bailly, and Philippe Poignant of Marrakech-Médina; Robert Bergé, La Mamounia in Mar-rakech; Yves de Boisgency, El Minzah in Tangier: Kasbah Baha Baha in N'Kob; Palais Salam in Taroudant; Palais Jamaï in Fez; Samir Slaoui, Hôtel Transatlantique in Meknès; Alain Kerrien and his sons, Taros in Essaouira; Meryanne Loum-Martin Riyad Tamsna in Marrakech; Najiz Hicham, head chef at Les Jardins de la Médina in Marrakech; Marcel Chiche, Le Comptoir Marrakech-Paris in Marrakech; Madame Viot, Le Cabestan in Casablanca.

The editors would like to thank José Alvarez for his invaluable contribution to the project, as well as Emmanuelle Bons, Mathilde Paris, and Sylvie Ramaut for their help with this book.

They would also like to express their thanks to all the Moroccans or residents of Morocco who opened their doors to their homes, provided recommendations and advice, and shared their best addresses. This book would not have been possible without them.

Translated from the French by **Lisa Davidson**

Copyediting **Penelope Isaac**

Additional research **Ellen Booker, Josh Jordan**

Art direction **Karen Bowen**

Cartography **Édigraphic**

Color separation **Grafotitoli**

Originally published as *L'Art de vivre au Maroc* © Flammarion 2002

English-language edition © Flammarion 2002

ISBN: 2-0801-0878-6
FA 0878-02-VIII
Dépôt légal : 09/2002

Printed in Italy by Canale